80 NOT OUT

MY FAVOURITE CRICKET MEMORIES

80 NOT OUT
MY FAVOURITE CRICKET MEMORIES

DICKIE BIRD
with Keith Lodge

HODDER &
STOUGHTON

First published in Great Britain in 2013 by Hodder & Stoughton

An Hachette UK company

1

A CIP catalogue record for this title is available from the British Library

ISBN 978 1 444 76961 6 Hardback
ISBN 978 1 444 77837 3 Trade Paperback

Printed and bound by CPI Group (UK) Ltd, Croydon, CR0 4YY

Hodder & Stoughton policy is to use papers that are natural, renewable and recyclable products and made from wood grown in sustainable forests. The logging and manufacturing processes are expected to conform to the environmental regulations of the country of origin.

Hodder & Stoughton Ltd
338 Euston Road
London NW1 3BH

www.hodder.co.uk

CONTENTS

Photographic Acknowledgements

The author and publisher would like to thank the following for permission to reproduce photographs:

Paul Barker/PA Images, Barratts/PA Images, Colorsport, Albert Cooper/Mirrorpix, Gareth Copley/Getty Images, Peter Cziborra/ Action Images, Patrick Eagar via Getty Images, Ralph Edwards Productions/TIYL Productions/Fremantlemedia, Mike Egerton/ PA Images, John Giles/PA Images, Julian Herbert/Getty Images, Matthew Impey/Colorsport, Chris Jones/PA Images, Brendan Monks/Mirrorpix, David Munden/Getty Images, Mark Nolan/ Getty Images, Dennis Oulds/Getty Images, PA Archive/PA Images, Rex Features, David Rogers/Getty Images, Hugh Routledge/Rex Features, Sport & General/PA Images, Bob Thomas/Getty Images, Howard Walker/Mirrorpix, Simon Wilkinson/SWpix.

All other photographs are from private collections.

FOREWORD
by Michael Parkinson

IF Dickie Bird is 80, then I've known him for more than 60 of those years. I don't know about him, but it makes me feel very old.

We've both slowed down a bit and when we meet nowadays we walk with measured tread when once we used to race quick singles.

We didn't know what life held for us when we first met at Barnsley Cricket Club in the 1950s, except we shared an ambition to play for Yorkshire. Neither of us, nor Geoffrey Boycott who joined us in our dreams, could have predicted what did happen. Sometimes it's not that dreams come true but that they exceed all expectation.

We met up not too long ago to celebrate 150 years of cricket at Shaw Lane, the home of Barnsley Cricket Club.

H.D. Bird and M. Parkinson – as it used to appear in the scorebooks – reluctantly wore the coloured clothing of the modern game and together we walked out to bat, just as we had done six decades before.

The bowlers lobbed a few dolly drops our way in the vain hope we might make contact. We didn't. For a start, Dickie had left his glasses in the pavilion, and I could barely lift the bat, it was so heavy.

Once upon a time we took on the fastest bowlers the Yorkshire League could offer. Fred Trueman was one.

I wish I could claim it was an overwhelmingly nostalgic trip down memory lane. But it wasn't. It seemed most of the landscape of our youthful ambition had disappeared. The pavilion with its balcony, where we would sit and fantasise our ambitions, had been knocked down and replaced with what looked like a warehouse for bedding plants. The scoreboard – fully automatic, the best in the league – had simply disappeared.

The 'blue remembered hills' had been flattened.

Before I left Barnsley I inspected Dickie's statue in the town centre. Future generations will regard it as simply a tribute to a famous man of cricket. I see it as a reminder of my lifelong engagement with a man of great integrity and unfailing humour who can look back on a long and successful career and be very proud of what he has achieved.

What he can be most proud of is that – unlike the cricket ground of his youth – he hasn't changed nor allowed himself to be demolished and reinvented as someone else. He remains a one-off, an individual, and I treasure our friendship.

For one thing, the fabric of his make-up was so intriguing I found him an inspiring subject to write about. Looking back at the thousands of words I have written about him, I count an article composed twenty years ago as one in which I managed to create an accurate portrait:

To say Dickie Bird loves cricket doesn't get anywhere near describing exactly what he feels for the game. It's a bit like saying Romeo had a slight crush on Juliet, or Abelard had a fancy for Héloïse.

The game consumes his life and defines its horizons. It shapes the very posture of the man.

Like a tree bent and moulded by the prevailing wind, so the curve in his spine, the hunch of his shoulders, the crinkled eyes as he inspects the world, have been sculpted through a lifetime's dedication to cricket.

In years to come, when they ask you what Dickie Bird was like, all you need say is that he dedicated his life and soul to the most wonderful game of them all. If you don't believe me, read on.

Sir Michael Parkinson
February 2013

INTRODUCTION

IT is fifteen years since I retired as a first-class cricket umpire, but I have remained very much involved with the game and hope to be so for many more years to come. It has been the focus of my life ever since my early days with Barnsley Cricket Club.

So much has happened since my last match out there in the middle and I would very much like to share with you some of those adventures – some funny, some frightening – as well as giving you my thoughts on the future of this great game of ours.

At the same time I have, of course, a huge store of memories, and over the past few months I have taken much pleasure in recalling them in the company of former *Barnsley Chronicle* Sports Editor, Keith Lodge, a trusted friend who did such a tremendous job recording my words so faithfully and accurately in my autobiography and its sequel, *White Cap and Bails.*

He has been a great help in compiling the stories and we have spent many happy hours sifting through them prior to the publication of this book to mark my 80th birthday on 19 April 2013.

Inevitably there will be those you have heard before,

especially if you are of a certain age, but I ask for your indulgence in this respect. It is impossible for me to take a wander down memory lane, as I have been asked to do, without making reference to those times which brought so much fun and laughter.

When ex-players and umpires get together we never tire of repeating the oft-told tales and I hope that you will feel the same.

As I have said on previous publication occasions, some of my stories may have been given a little poetic licence along the way, but the essence of them remains, as always, to try to convey to you just how much I enjoyed – and still enjoy – the times spent in the company of so many truly wonderful people in a sport which, for me, is the best in the world.

I do hope that you will find the same enjoyment reading about them.

I am also pleased to tell you that some of the proceeds from the sales of this book will go to the Dickie Bird Foundation, which provides under-privileged youngsters with encouragement and support at a time when they most need it.

Dickie Bird

January 2013

1

THEY THINK IT'S ALL OVER

'WELL, that's it, Dickie lad. Finished. Over and out.'
How well I remember muttering those words to myself after standing at my final Test match – between England and India at Lord's in June 1996. But it wasn't quite over. And I was certainly not out. There were two more seasons in the County Championship to come before my retirement – my last appearance was in the Yorkshire v Warwickshire fixture in 1998 – and a lot more has happened since then.

Now here I am at 80, still involved with cricket, revelling in the present, looking hopefully to the future and being able to look contentedly back to the past with pride and satisfaction.

However, I have to admit that I very nearly didn't make it. There was a time in 2012 when I thought I was going to be caught out on 79.

It was when I had my stroke. It hit me in the early hours one morning – about three o' clock. I felt this almighty pain throughout my whole body, reaching right up to the back of my neck. There's summat wrong wi' me, I thought to myself, being remarkably quick on the uptake.

I could feel myself passing out, drifting into unconsciousness. I don't know how I did it, but I forced myself to keep going through the rest of the night, willing myself to stay awake, although I am sure I must have drifted off now and then, and first thing in the morning I dialled the doctors' surgery in Huddersfield Road, Barnsley.

My speech was slurred and I had difficulty getting the words out. The receptionist, recognising the symptoms, told me quite firmly, in a businesslike yet sympathetic way, 'You don't need a doctor; you need an ambulance. Stay where you are and we'll get one to you straight away.'

She was as good as her word. They were with me very quickly and rushed me the three miles or so to Barnsley Hospital. By this time I was beginning to lose the feeling in my arms and legs, at first down my right side, then down my left. All the strength drained out of me. I didn't know where I was; I was in a complete daze. And by this time I could not talk at all.

When I eventually, and thankfully, recovered I was told that the stroke had been brought about as a result of high blood pressure, which I had been suffering with for some time. It had been diagnosed back when I was in Sheffield Thornbury Hospital with a bladder infection. The people there had written me a letter to take to my doctor, and I was put on tablets, but it seems they had not had the desired effect.

I have to say that the staff at Barnsley Hospital have always been first-class with me, and here again they cared for me extremely well, so much so that I began to make a good recovery. When they discharged me, I was determined to make every effort to ensure that recovery continued. As well as making regular visits to the specialist for a check-up, I launched myself into a rigorous programme of fitness work. Exercise and shower, exercise and shower, exercise and shower. I made myself do it. I'm still a lot weaker than I was before the stroke, but I'm much stronger than I was immediately after it. To look at me now, you wouldn't think I'd suffered one, but appearances, of course, can be deceptive. There are repercussions that are not immediately obvious – or even visible.

I have always been emotional, to say the least, but I'm even more so since my stroke. That's how it can leave you. The specialist warned me about it, and I've talked to a lot of people who have had the same experience. The smallest thing sets me off. I can be just watching television and something completely insignificant will make me well up. Before long, the tears are rolling down my cheeks. People think you're going soft, but you're not; it's caused by the stroke.

Then there are the times when I know what I want to do, but I just can't do it. I used to be a good letter writer, but not now. I know what I want to put, but I can't piece it together. My memory has been affected as well – although some of that might be down to the natural ageing process. It's all so frustrating. It leaves you very depressed at times. That's why I have to keep getting out and doing things. On one visit to the hospital they said I had to rest and take it easy. But if I just sat there in the chair, I'd go bonkers. You've got to keep your mind active.

My voice has come back, but I have to speak slowly. When I try to speak more quickly I can't get the words out. Lots of people who have had strokes tell me that they have been affected in the same way, and I do wonder if speech therapy might have helped.

There are also problems when I swallow. Sometimes food gets stuck fast in my throat and I start to choke. It can be scary. When it happens, sweat pours out of me as I try to get my breath and clear the blockage. It has happened a few times in restaurants and people will say, 'Are you all right, Dickie? Shall we call an ambulance?'

If I can give one piece of advice to people who have suffered strokes, it is this – fight it. I know it's difficult; I know what it's like; but it is the only way. Don't let it get you down. You need willpower to get you through it all. But keep on fighting. Never give up hope. Never. And have faith.

I attend the Methodist Church in Staincross as often as I can and I have no doubt that my faith has helped me through these and other very hard times. Indeed, I am convinced, to this day, that the Good Lord once performed a miracle with me.

There was a time when I was in danger of completely losing my sight. It was as a result of all those years standing in the glaring sun in such places as India, Pakistan, Sri Lanka, the West Indies, Australia and New Zealand – not so much England, I hardly need to add. There were no wrap-around sunglasses in those days, and my eyes became so badly affected that my sight was deteriorating rapidly. I was warned there was a possibility that I might go blind.

Providentially, I was put in touch with one of the top eye specialists, Mr George Turner, at Manchester Royal Eye

Hospital, who gave me hope. After examining me, he told me about a very difficult operation. There was no guarantee it would be successful, but he was willing to go ahead with it if I agreed. I gave him the nod, the operation went ahead – and my sight was saved.

As far as I was concerned, it was a miracle.

The magic of television

It may seem surprising, but in 2010 a television programme called *The Young Ones* did me a power of good – both physically and mentally. It was a restaging of an experiment which tested whether reliving your youth could make you young again. What if you really could turn back the clock? What if you could simply *think* yourself younger? Those two questions formed the heart of the programme, and I was one of six well-known personalities invited to go back to 1975 for a week to see if it could make us feel young again.

The other five were dancer Lionel Blair, that lovely actress Liz Smith, film star Sylvia Syms, newsreader Kenneth Kendall and Fleet Street editor and broadcaster Derek Jameson, who, they tell me, at one time held more power than the Prime Minister!

That year, 1975, was an interesting one for news, culture and sport. Maggie Thatcher was elected as the first female leader of the opposition; the Bay City Rollers were attracting huge crowds; Arthur Ashe became the first black man to win Wimbledon; and, the one that really appealed to me, the first ever

Cricket World Cup final took place at Lord's – with me as one of the umpires.

We were all introduced to Professor Ellen Langer, from Harvard University, who had conducted the original experiment, and Dr Michael Mosley, who remained with us all week, checking how we went on. We had to live as though it was 1975. The only television programmes we could watch, the only radio broadcasts we could listen to, and the only newspapers and magazines we could read, were all from that year.

This caused a problem when me and Derek Jameson, with whom I struck up a great friendship, were particularly keen to hear a certain piece of news from the outside world. So, when everybody had gone to bed, Derek and I slipped out and climbed over the big locked gate on the edge of the grounds. We flagged down this chap in a car, who must have been a bit surprised to see a couple of strange men in dressing gowns and pyjamas. He probably thought we'd escaped from a mental hospital.

Anyway, he wound down the window and asked what we wanted.

'Can you tell us who won the men's singles final at Wimbledon?' we asked.

'Nadal,' he replied.

'Thank you very much,' we said – and climbed back over the gate and off to bed.

Nobody ever found out about our break-out – at least not until now!

The best experience I had that week was being taken to Lord's Cricket Ground to relive the 1975 World Cup final between the West Indies and Australia. I was able to retrace my steps from the umpires' room, through the Long Room, on to the green and then out to the middle, having a chat with the groundsman along the way. It was quite an experience. I really enjoyed that.

Back at the house, I had been delighted on the first day when I walked into my bedroom and saw all the photographs of royalty dotted around the walls. It was almost a replica of the sitting room in my cottage. There was one of me shaking hands with the Queen, another with Lady Diana, yet another with Prince Philip, and so on. There were also photographs of the Yorkshire and Leicestershire teams of that time. It really was a lovely touch, and I felt right at home.

We were all supposed to do our share of the gardening, cleaning and cooking – although I have to say I didn't really pull my weight in the kitchen. Everyone knows I hardly ever cook anything. Thankfully, Derek did my share for me. He was particularly good with the breakfast eggs, boiled or fried. At other times Sylvia Syms helped us out – but don't tell anyone!

Neither of us was much good with the gardening, either. We did a bit of digging, set a few potatoes and then sat down for the rest of the day exchanging stories. Well, you never know with gardening. You've got to be used to doing it. If you are not, it can bring on a heart attack. So Derek and I were taking no chances. A good lad, Derek. We remained good friends and I was really sad when I heard he'd passed away in 2012.

They also brought in a young lady every morning to give us a yoga session, and I found it very beneficial. In fact, I still practise yoga in my bathroom every day in addition to my other exercises. Then I have my shower and I'm ready to face whatever the world might throw at me.

The programme proved a big hit with the viewers, and it did all of us who took part in it a power of good. For example, Liz Smith, a great actress and a beautiful person, went into that house in a wheelchair. She came out at the end of the week walking with the aid of just one stick. That's what it did for her. I could see a complete change in her. It did so much for me as well. I was a new man when I came away from that house. They did an assessment at the end that showed some tremendous improvements.

It was a great programme and I think the BBC should show it again. It was really inspirational for a lot of people. When you consider all the rubbish repeats there are, I can't understand why they don't repeat something really good like *The Young Ones*.

A lot of bleeding nonsense

Despite all my efforts, my blood pressure still goes up and down like a yo-yo, which led to another really scary episode. I got up as usual on the morning of Tuesday, 11 September 2012, went to the bathroom and, whoosh!, blood poured down the back of my throat, out of my nose, out of my mouth. I was in a right mess. Luckily, by this time I had been given an alarm buzzer, and I managed to get to it and press it. The signal was picked up straight away and the paramedics were with me in next to no time.

It was panic stations as far as I was concerned. There was blood all over the place – in the sink, down the side of the bath, on the carpet, even some on the walls. They took me just as I was, in an old pair of jeans and a T-shirt. There was no chance to grab anything else – night things, toothpaste, shaver – nothing.

They got me safely to hospital and I was told they would have to keep me in. They tried to pack my nose, but I continued to lose so much blood it's untrue. In the end, they had to operate to repair a popped blood vessel and I was in for nine days. They again did a very good job on me and, praise the Lord, at the time of writing I've had no bleeding since.

Add to all this the fact that not only had I had a pacemaker fitted some years earlier, but I had also been put on Warfarin, to avoid blood clots. On this occasion I have to be thankful there was no clotting – but on the other hand we couldn't stop the bleeding! And I still have to be very careful because I bleed so easily. But what can you do? As a precaution I have bought myself an electric razor to replace the old cut-throat I have always used, because if I do happen to nick myself . . .

Incidentally, when I went back for a check-up after the blood vessel had popped, the ENT specialist I saw was an Indian chap. As soon as I sat down he said, 'Dickie, delighted to meet you. You're a legend. A legend.'

He then launched into a discussion of some of the great Indian cricketers – Sunil Gavaskar, Kapil Dev, Rahul Dravid, Anil Kumble, Chandrasekhar – and as he mentioned the great leg-spinner, he imitated his action, still sitting there in his swivel chair. Before long he was singing the praises of Sachin Tendulkar. 'I hear there's talk of him retiring,' he said. 'What a player he's been.'

I had to try to change the subject quickly before he thought of anyone else.

'All this is very well, doctor, and I'm really enjoying chatting about these truly great players, but have you any advice for me? What should I do?'

He replied, 'Just make sure you don't knock yourself. We can't have you bleeding again.' And that was it. He got up, shook my hand and said, 'All the best to you, Dickie.'

As I moved towards the door, he called me back and said, 'By the way, could I have your autograph?'

Down to earth with a bump

I've got a new knee as well. About time, too, I suppose. After all, it's sixty-odd years since it was so badly damaged that it cut short my football career. Instead, I focused my attention on cricket, and even then the knee was a problem; not so much when I was an umpire, but certainly as a player. It really restricted me, especially when playing off the back foot. I had four operations on that knee over the years and later it became arthritic, until finally I was advised to have a replacement.

Before performing the operation, the surgeon, Mr London, said to me, 'Can I have a word, Dickie?'

'Aye,' I replied. 'What is it?'

'You've got to sixty-six and I don't know how you've got through all these years playing and umpiring. I've never seen a knee joint like it in all my life. It's a right mess.'

I have no doubt that all my regular exercises helped me to cope with it.

The new knee took a bit of a knock one day last autumn when I was shopping in Barnsley. I tripped up and fell headlong, grazing it quite badly, but thankfully suffering nothing more serious than that. My pride was hurt most. You do feel daft in such circumstances, don't you? Especially when two middle-aged women take an arm each to lift you to your feet, saying as they do so, 'Ey up, it's Dickie Bird! Are you all right, luv; are you sure you're all right?'

To make matters worse, there was my newly bought pork pie rolling down the pavement towards the busy road . . .

2

AS ONE DOOR CLOSES . . .

To my amazement, retirement opened up a new career for me in radio and television. It was quite unbelievable the number of shows I was asked to do after announcing that I was standing down from my umpiring duties, and it simply snowballed from there. I sat down and compiled a list one day, and when I'd racked my brains to remember them all, there were twenty-one different programmes on my sheet of paper – and some of them I appeared in more than once.

For example, I've been on *A Question of Sport* no fewer than six times, including those while I was still umpiring. The most memorable was when I was in Ally McCoist's team along with the great Romanian tennis player Ilie Nastase, who was world number one in 1973–74. Snooker star John Parrott was the opposing captain and his team included Manchester United footballing legend George Best and racehorse trainer Jenny Pitman. They said it was the best edition of *A Question of Sport* they had ever done.

I can see Nastase now, a bewildered expression on his face as he's confronted by the combined babbling of a Yorkshireman and a Scot, turning to host Sue Barker for help because 'I just don't understand you.'

As for Best, he was asked to remember a certain incident

and he said, 'Just a moment, I can't even remember what I did this morning.' Cue an explosion of studio laughter.

Do you remember that other footballer who played for Tottenham Hotspur? An outside-left, as we used to call them in my day. Frenchman he was. David Ginola. I was watching a recording of an earlier show just before I was due to go on for one of my appearances and I saw him present a red rose to Sue Barker.

In typical French style, he went up to Sue and said, 'Sue, you've been my sweetheart for a very long time, so I've brought this lovely red rose especially for you.'

I'll show him, I thought to myself. So before I went for my recording I popped into Barnsley market and bought a rose. I hid it behind my back as I was introduced on television, then I went up to Sue and said, 'Sue, forget about that fellow Ginola and his red rose. I've brought this all the way from Barnsley market for you – the white rose of Yorkshire.'

Then I added, 'It's for your birthday, April 19.'

She was a bit taken aback and said, 'That's very kind of you, Dickie, but how did you know it was my birthday?'

And I replied, 'Because it's the same day as mine!'

Remembering my lines

I also enjoyed appearing in a couple of popular programmes of a very different kind, *Heartbeat* and *Top Gear*.

If you recall, there was a chap on *Heartbeat* who was portrayed as a bit of a simpleton. David, I think they called him in the programme. And he had a vital role in one particular episode involving a cricket match. I was asked to take on the challenging role of umpire and it was a treat to go up there to that glorious countryside just south of Whitby in the heart of the North Yorkshire Moors for the filming.

Brian Close and Raymond Illingworth were also involved, having been asked to form part of the crowd, and typically they kept shouting 'Get on with it, man,' as David tried unsuccessfully to hit the ball over the pavilion for the winning six, as the script demanded. It was at that point that the whole crowd was supposed to cheer in wild excitement. But it seemed we would never get to that stage.

Unfortunately, it was soon evident that dear old David was not a born cricketer. We spent all afternoon filming, and he could hardly hit a ball, never mind send it soaring over the pavilion. Finally, in desperation, I said to the bowler, 'Just send him one down underarm on his leg stump so he can hit it like schoolboys do.' So he did. And wham-bang, straight over the pavilion it went. The crowd went mad – including Illingworth and Closey.

I look back and think that, if it hadn't been for me, we might still have been filming!

I played a similar role in *Top Gear*. I was asked to umpire a staged cricket match on a village green. All of a sudden, in the middle of an over, there was this three-wheel Robin Reliant – a real old banger – charging through the gate, across the boundary edge and on to the square, smack in the middle, where it tore up the pitch, turned over on its side, did another roll and came to a standstill, with smoke billowing all over the place.

As it did so, out stepped Jeremy Clarkson, with his helmet still on, and I spluttered, 'Oh dear. Oh dear, look at the pitch. Do you mind; do you mind, there's a cricket match going on here!'

It was really very funny, as I am sure you will agree if you saw that programme.

Caught out . . . again

I was also the subject of one of the incidents in the Dom Joly show *Trigger Happy TV*. If you remember, Joly filmed people in ludicrous or embarrassing situations in public places and a lot of the humour was provided by the fact that they didn't know they were being set up on television.

I had gone down to London to be on a cookery programme. Why they had invited me, goodness only knows, but I enjoyed it, although I have to admit that I didn't do very well. I really hadn't a clue. I think they eventually regarded me as a lost cause and wrote me off. Anyway, while I was there I was asked by Channel Four to do an interview with Dom Joly at King's Cross station.

When I arrived he was waiting for me with the cameras and we started recording. He made the introduction, saying, 'Dickie Bird, you are without doubt the greatest living Test umpire,' which was all very flattering. Then he asked me a few questions, but he couldn't stop fidgeting and looking at his watch. All of a sudden, he turned on his heel and jumped on to a train!

I didn't know what was happening. I turned to the camera crew and said, 'Where's the bugger gone?'

Desert Island Discs

Another memorable experience was when it was my turn to be the castaway on Radio 4's *Desert Island Discs*. It was broadcast on Sunday, 7 April 1996, after I had made it known that I would be umpiring my last Test at Lord's that summer. I really enjoyed that, chatting to presenter Sue Lawley about my church-going childhood in Barnsley, my anxieties about punctuality, the highlights of my career – and choosing my favourite recordings.

The first was Nat King Cole singing 'When I Fall in Love'. He was a tremendous artist and a great perfectionist. I admired him a lot. I told Sue that the song brought back happy memories of my youth and my love life. Later in the programme, when I made a similar comment on asking to hear Shirley Bassey sing 'Till', Sue wanted to learn more about this 'love life' of mine. After all, everybody knew I was a confirmed bachelor!

I confessed that I had come close to marriage but couldn't go through with it. You see, with all the travelling I did then – and always have done – I was virtually living out of a suitcase, and that wouldn't have been fair on any woman I married. It simply wouldn't have worked. So, as I have said many times, I married cricket instead. And it's been a good partnership.

Do you know, I still get a lump in my throat listening to that recording by Shirley Bassey. What a marvellous singer she is.

Another of my choices, 'Abide with Me', sung by the King's College Choir, brought back childhood memories. My dad was a member of the Young Men's Christian Association and he insisted that I joined as well. I played football for them and they were good times. That early upbringing has stood me in good stead throughout my career, and I have always gone to church, although maybe not as often as I ought.

It's not surprising that, coming from Yorkshire, I have a soft spot for brass bands, particularly when they play some of those rousing quick marches. They sometimes had a band playing at Lord's prior to a Test match and when you walked out on to the pitch to the accompaniment of that kind of music, it added to the thrill of it all. So I also selected Johann Strauss's *Radetzky March* played by the Grenadier Guards. Great stuff!

Everyone knows I am a royalist and I told Sue of the time when the England and Australia teams, and the umpires, were invited to meet the Queen Mother at Clarence House. The latter chided me for not wearing my white cap and I told her, 'Sorry, Ma'am, but I didn't need to have it on today; it was overcast, you see.' She replied, 'Well, I do prefer to see you in the white cap. Then I know it's you.' Having told that story, we then listened to 'Land of Hope and Glory'.

I had to admit to Sue that there was a bit of a mystery surrounding another of my selections. It was listed as Julio Iglesias and Pam Bunning singing that lovely composition 'Feelings' – but I had never heard of Pam Bunning. I've still no idea who she was after all these years. Can anybody help? But it was a good recording.

I also recalled a time when I was relaxing swimming in the sea in Barbados during a trip to the West Indies and I thought I'd bumped into a whale. It was Luciano Pavarotti. That's partly the reason his terrific version of 'Nessun Dorma' was on my list.

That leaves just one artist and one song. My favourite: Barbra Streisand singing 'The Way We Were'. Magic. I remember asking Vic Lewis, a keen cricket follower who was also an agent for some of the most well-known names in show business, who was the best of all the artists he had handled, and he told me, 'There are none to match Nat King Cole and Barbra Streisand.'

In my opinion, Streisand is the best professional artist of them all. I have never met her or heard her sing live, however. That's something I would dearly love to do.

All the castaways are given the Bible anyway, so for my book choice I picked *Wisden*, and as my luxury item I requested a TV set with a satellite dish so that I could still watch all the Test matches!

Game for anything . . . almost

Cash in the Celebrity Attic was a programme that gave me particular pleasure, because it was in aid of my charity, the Dickie Bird Foundation. Gloria Hunniford came to my cottage to do the research, I produced some auctionable items, and off we went to Derby to record the programme. I'm glad to say quite a lot of money was raised. Talking of Gloria Hunniford, she had me on her own show four times.

I also appeared on *Through the Keyhole* three times, and I have three golden keys to prove it. I have to say, though, that they always guessed my identity so quickly that they had to pad out the show with a bit more chat than usual. On one occasion it was the row of white cricket shoes beside the bed that gave it away!

Another time the artist Alan Hydes had been commissioned to do a series of paintings on television showing the gardens of well-known personalities, and it was decided that I should be included. When Alan rang to suss things out, he asked if I had plenty of flowers in my garden and I replied, 'Oh, aye, loads of 'em.'

It wasn't strictly true. It's a pretty big garden with apple trees, plum trees, a few shrubs and an extensive lawn, but I have to admit it's no contender for a Britain in Bloom competition. There is a Yorkshire rose near the doorway but, as far as colour is concerned, that's it. And, of course, the Yorkshire rose is white! So poor old Alan ended up painting the rose – my pride and joy – surrounded by an array of plants obtained from a local garden centre.

At least Alan was pleased with the resulting painting – and I was absolutely delighted with the splash of colour the variety of flowers brought to my garden. More delighted still that it hadn't cost me a penny!

There was one time when I wasn't particularly keen to play ball, however. It was when they wanted to interview me in bed with someone called Lily Savage for *The Big Breakfast* show. They tried to persuade me by telling me that Gary Lineker, Frank Bruno and my mate Ian Botham had had no objection, but I told them in no uncertain terms, 'You're not getting Dickie Bird in there. I'm not going to leap into bed with a fella dressed up in a wig and a nightie and wearing make-up. If you want him – or her – to interview me, it will have to be done with me sitting on a chair, otherwise I'm taking the next train back to Barnsley.'

So that's what they did. Another good decision, I reckon.

It was so very different a few years later when Paul O'Grady, aka Lily Savage, invited me on to his new show. Michael Parkinson, who was celebrating his birthday, was the main guest, and Paul had asked me to make a surprise entry with a special present for my long-time friend. I ended up carrying a crate of wine by taxi to the railway station, on the train to London and then taxi again to the BBC studios. Thankfully, I managed it without breaking a single bottle and the presentation was duly made. Afterwards Sir David Frost invited Parky and myself to a slap-up lunch at a London restaurant, which brought a perfect ending to another very enjoyable day.

Keeping it local

In 1986 it was the centenary of a fund-raising event known as the Barnsley Hospital Sing in the village of Staincross, where I live, and I was delighted to be able to take part, along with the actor Brian Blessed.

On the first day, a parade of decorated floats, bands and groups in fancy dress, extending over a distance of half a mile, wended its way round the village in rather showery weather, but the following day we were blessed with glorious sunshine for the sing itself, which was attended by two thousand people.

It was a wonderful celebration of an event which had been going for so many years, during which time an enormous amount of money had been raised for the hospitals in Barnsley, presenting a perfect example of how ordinary people in places like this all over the country work hard and tirelessly to help those less fortunate than themselves.

Yorkshire Television filmed that weekend – along with interviews, shots of village activities and various organisations – and the following year brought out a half-hour documentary entitled *The Hospital Sing*. It was marvellous. So was the weekend.

Now then, were you aware that a documentary about my career won an award? Harry Gration, of BBC Yorkshire, interviewed me and accompanied me on visits to many places that had played a big part in my career, both as a player and umpire. We went to Barnsley Cricket Club, where it all started, and

Lord's, where my Test career ended, and we shared lots of wonderful memories of all that had happened in between. The resulting programme, *Dickie Bird: A Rare Species*, won the Royal Television Society Sports Documentary of the Year award in 1996.

That was the year that I won the Yorkshireman of the Year Award – an honour that Seb Coe rightly won in 2012. At the time, I could not get to the dinner where the presentation was due to be made, so Lord Harewood invited me to Harewood House to receive it from him personally at a later date. It was marvellous. Just him and me. And he put on a quite wonderful spread.

Sports Personality of the Year

There's one television institution I've been associated with for a very long time. It started for me in 1959, when Yorkshire, having won the County Championship after Surrey had held the trophy for seven years, were voted as the BBC's Team of the Year. We were all invited down to London for their Sports Personality of the Year evening, which was then in its infancy – and I've been invited every year since.

I was back there in London for the 2012 awards, and it was a really special occasion because of the Olympic Games. It was anybody's guess as to who would win the vote for the main prize because there were so many people who deserved it, but it eventually went to cyclist Bradley Wiggins – now 'Sir' Bradley – who won the Tour de France and then the gold medal at the Olympic time trial.

AS ONE DOOR CLOSES . . .

My mate Pete Bristowe took me all the way there and back in his taxi. He's a good lad is Pete, despite the fact that he's a Manchester United supporter, but he can also be a bit forgetful. He had parked his taxi in the enormous underground car park at the ExCel and when we returned after the presentations he could not remember exactly where the car was. As I hadn't taken particular notice either, we were clearly stumped. We spent forty-five minutes wandering around the maze of bays before we eventually found the damn thing.

The individual winner in 1959 was motorcyclist John Surtees, but what I remember most vividly from that occasion was Formula One world champion Jack Brabham actually driving his car into the studio. The vehicle was not quite what you see Lewis Hamilton driving today, but back then it was a very impressive sight.

The cricket memories come flooding back

It always surprises me these days when I am asked to comment on various topics, controversial or otherwise, on radio and television, but I also take pride in the fact that people obviously still value my opinion, and in the autumn of 2012 I was thrilled to be invited by the television production company Twofour to go down to London to talk about three great cricketers – Ian Botham, Viv Richards and Kapil Dev.

Pete Bristowe was on hand again to take me to Wakefield railway station for a first-class trip to the capital city, where I was met on the platform by the production coordinator, and taken to the studios by car. Journalist Hugh McIlvanney was also there, having been a personal friend of Richards's.

I was told that after they had finished with us, the production team were catching the seven o'clock flight that evening to Spain, where they were to interview the players of Real Madrid. After that it was on to the Nou Camp for a session with the Barcelona players. Apparently they were going all round the world to put together a series of programmes called something like *The 80s Greatest*, covering events as diverse as Maradona's notorious 'Hand of God' in football, the space shuttle *Challenger* disaster and the birth of the Internet. I was delighted to be part of it by giving my opinion of three of cricket's greatest.

I told them that when Botham was involved in any match, whether for Somerset or England, the bars and hospitality marquees would empty as soon as he strode out on to the field, such was his appeal. That was the character of the man. He was a match-winner, a Roy of the Rovers, who played the game in a wonderful spirit – having fun but always giving 100 per cent. You don't see his like in the game today. The characters are no longer there. Players don't smile and enjoy themselves as much as they did in that era.

At the same time, Botham had tremendous mental strength and an unshakeable self-belief. I recalled the Headingley Test against the Australians in 1981, one of the most exciting ever. The position at the end of play on Saturday was that Australia, having won the toss, had decided to bat and carded 401 for 9 declared, Botham taking 6 for 95. In reply England had been bowled out for 174, of which Botham had made 50, and they had then been asked to follow on. It seemed there was no way that England could win; so much so that the home team had booked out of their hotel and Botham had invited some of the Australians round for a barbecue; steaks, burgers, chops, the lot.

There was no play on the Sunday in those days, so on Monday morning it was apparently a case of Australia wrapping things up as quickly as possible. Before long, at 135 for 7 it looked a lost cause for England, but then came the incredible turnaround.

'Both' began swinging the bat as only he can and when he was joined by Graham Dilley, he told the tail-ender, 'Give it a bash. Let's have some fun out there.' And, boy, did they give it a bash! Before the Aussies knew what had hit them, the pair had added 117 in 80 minutes, Botham making an unbeaten 149 and Dilley 56. A further 29 from Chris Old helped take England to 356.

That still meant that Australia needed only 130 to win and at 56 for 1 they were back in the box seat, but what people tend to forget about this remarkable match was the magnificent spell of bowling by Bob Willis which clinched a famous victory. He changed to the Kirkstall Lane End, bowled quick and straight and took 8 wickets for 43 runs, the best analysis of his career, and Australia were all out for 111. When people recall that game, Willis's contribution is often overshadowed by that of Botham and Dilley, but he played a massive part.

Australia v England 3rd Test

Headingley, Leeds, 16–21 July 1981

Australia 1st innings

		Runs	Mins	Balls	4s	6s
J Dyson	b Dilley	102	294	234	14	0
GM Wood	lbw b Botham	34	71	55	4	0
TM Chappell	c Taylor b Willey	27	161	135	2	0
KJ Hughes*	c & b Botham	89	270	208	8	0
RJ Bright	b Dilley	7	48	36	1	0
GN Yallop	c Taylor b Botham	58	208	167	5	0
AR Border	lbw b Botham	8	35	20	1	0
RW Marsh†	b Botham	28	65	50	5	0
GF Lawson	c Taylor b Botham	13	45	35	2	0
DK Lillee	not out	3	8	6	0	0
TM Alderman	not out	0	0	0	0	0
Extras	(b 4, lb 13, w 3, nb 12)	32				
Total	**(9 wickets dec; 155.2 overs)**	**401**				

Fall of wickets: 1–55 (Wood), 2–149 (Chappell), 3–196 (Dyson), 4–220 (Bright), 5–332 (Hughes), 6–354 (Border), 7–357 (Yallop), 8–396 (Lawson), 9–401 (Marsh).

Bowling: RGD Willis 30–8–72–0; CM Old 43–14–91–0; GR Dilley 27–4–78–2; IT Botham 39.2–11–95–6; P Willey 13–2–31–1; G Boycott 3–2–2–0.

England 1st innings

		Runs	Mins	Balls	4s	6s
GA Gooch	lbw b Alderman	2	17	7	0	0
G Boycott	b Lawson	12	89	58	0	0
JM Brearley*	c Marsh b Alderman	10	64	53	0	0
DI Gower	c Marsh b Lawson	24	58	50	3	0
MW Gatting	lbw b Lillee	15	58	29	2	0
P Willey	b Lawson	8	29	22	0	0
IT Botham	c Marsh b Lillee	50	80	54	8	0
RW Taylor†	c Marsh b Lillee	5	36	23	1	0
GR Dilley	c & b Lillee	13	30	17	2	0
CM Old	c Border b Alderman	0	4	4	0	0
RGD Willis	not out	1	5	4	0	0
Extras	(b 6, lb 11, w 6, nb 11)	34				
Total	**(all out; 50.5 overs)**	**174**				

Fall of wickets: 1–12 (Gooch), 2–40 (Brearley), 3–42 (Boycott), 4–84 (Gower), 5–87 (Gatting), 6–112 (Willey), 7–148 (Taylor), 8–166 (Botham), 9–167 (Old), 10–174 (Dilley).

Bowling: DK Lillee 18.5–7–49–4; TM Alderman 19–4–59–3; GF Lawson 13–3–32–3.

England 2nd innings (following on)		Runs	Mins	Balls	4s	6s
GA Gooch	c Alderman b Lillee	0	2	3	0	0
G Boycott	lbw b Alderman	46	215	141	1	0
JM Brearley*	c Alderman b Lillee	14	33	29	3	0
DI Gower	c Border b Alderman	9	36	22	1	0
MW Gatting	lbw b Alderman	1	10	10	0	0
P Willey	c Dyson b Lillee	33	84	56	6	0
IT Botham	not out	149	219	148	27	1
RW Taylor†	c Bright b Alderman	1	9	9	0	0
GR Dilley	b Alderman	56	80	75	9	0
CM Old	b Lawson	29	54	31	6	0
RGD Willis	c Border b Alderman	2	31	9	0	0
Extras	(b 5, lb 3, w 3, nb 5)	16				
Total	**(all out; 87.3 overs)**	**356**				

Fall of wickets: 1–0 (Gooch), 2–18 (Brearley), 3–37 (Gower), 4–41 (Gatting), 5–105 (Willey), 6–133 (Boycott), 7–135 (Taylor), 8–252 (Dilley), 9–319 (Old), 10–356 (Willis).

Bowling: DK Lillee 25–6–94–3; TM Alderman 35.3–6–135–6; GF Lawson 23–4–96–1; RJ Bright 4–0–15–0.

Australia 2nd innings (target: 130 runs)		Runs	Mins	Balls	4s	6s
J Dyson	c Taylor b Willis	34	119	83	3	0
GM Wood	c Taylor b Botham	10	9	10	2	0
TM Chappell	c Taylor b Willis	8	68	56	0	0
KJ Hughes*	c Botham b Willis	0	14	9	0	0
GN Yallop	c Gatting b Willis	0	2	3	0	0
AR Border	b Old	0	13	8	0	0
RW Marsh†	c Dilley b Willis	4	18	9	0	0
RJ Bright	b Willis	19	49	32	2	0
GF Lawson	c Taylor b Willis	1	2	2	0	0
DK Lillee	c Gatting b Willis	17	22	15	3	0
TM Alderman	not out	0	6	5	0	0
Extras	(lb 3, w 1, nb 14)	18				
Total	**(all out; 36.1 overs)**	**111**				

Fall of wickets: 1–13 (Wood), 2–56 (Chappell), 3–58 (Hughes), 4–58 (Yallop), 5–65 (Border), 6–68 (Dyson), 7–74 (Marsh), 8–75 (Lawson), 9–110 (Lillee), 10–111 (Bright).

Bowling: IT Botham 7–3–14–1; GR Dilley 2–0–11–0; RGD Willis 15.1–3–43–8; CM Old 9–1–21–1; P Willey 3–1–4–0.

Umpires: DGL Evans and BJ Meyer

England won by 18 runs

I didn't umpire that match, but I was on duty for the next one at Edgbaston, which was just as remarkable. Australia were 87 for 3 in their second innings, needing only 151 to win. It was just a matter of time. Or so everyone thought. England captain Mike Brearley, who was fielding by me at square leg, asked, 'What do you think, Dickie?'

I said, 'I think you've had it, skipper. If I were you I'd put yourself on, bowl a few long-hops and get it over with, then we can all go home.'

He smiled and said, 'Thanks for the suggestion, Dickie, but I'm going to put the Gorilla on at the City End for a final attack.'

I can see Botham now, eagerly peeling off his sweater as Brearley said to him, 'Come on, give me 100 per cent.'

Now, Botham respected Brearley as captain. He would have jumped over the pavilion for him. So he said, 'For you skipper, make that 200 per cent.'

And he went on to take five wickets for one run to win the Test, a victory which also clinched the series, the last Test at The Oval ending in a draw.

Is it any wonder that the series has gone down in history as 'Botham's Ashes'?

That is all the more amazing when you consider what had gone before. If you remember, Botham had been made captain for the series, but in the first two matches he hardly got a run or a wicket, so the selectors took the captaincy off him. I was always pleased that he had been given that opportunity to captain England, because I do not think there is any greater honour in sport, but it was clearly not working out for him.

Then, in the build-up to the next Test at Old Trafford, the new captain, Brearley, went up to him and said, 'I'm sorry, Ian, but we're going to leave you out of this Test match.'

Botham told him, 'You must be joking! Look, you play me at Old Trafford and I'll not only win that game for you, I'll win the series for you as well.'

Brearley replied, 'That's just what I wanted to hear. You're playing.'

That was a mark of the great captain Brearley was. He had Botham sussed. He knew what his reaction would be to being told he was being left out of the side. It was great psychology.

Those were my memories of Botham as recounted in that interview. I was also asked if he was the greatest all-rounder I ever saw. You will, no doubt, know the answer to that one. I have always maintained that Garfield Sobers was the best. But Botham has his place in company with the other greats such as Imran Khan, Kapil Dev, Richard Hadlee and Michael Procter.

The most important thing for Ian was the team. He wasn't bothered about figures, averages and all that. So long as the team won, he was happy. Now he is one of the cricket analysts on television, and he is doing a good job there as well. He always has something worthwhile to say. People listen to him because of what he himself achieved; he has earned the right to express his opinions.

The next great cricketer I was asked to talk about was Viv Richards. I first saw him on the international scene in the 1975 World Cup final, which was the best game of cricket I have ever umpired.

West Indies batted first and made 291 for 8 from their 60 overs and at that stage everybody was writing the Aussies off. Yet they failed by only 17 runs, and had it not been for three run-outs, I am convinced they would have pulled off an astonishing win.

First to go was Alan Turner, and the Chappell brothers, Greg and Ian, followed. A young Richards was the player responsible. Fielding in the cover point and mid-wicket areas, he swooped three times, pouncing and throwing in one graceful movement, to leave the batsmen stranded. It was fielding of the very highest order and it had a big bearing on the eventual outcome. In fact, I'd say that Richards's brilliant fielding was the match-winner.

As a batsman, Viv was a butcher. His footwork was exceptional; he was a great timer of the ball; he picked the line and length quicker than anybody else; and he simply tore attacks apart. He was so full of confidence as well. Indeed, there was a cockiness about him when he went out to bat. He would swagger to the crease, chewing his gum, twirling his bat and relishing every minute of it. He was brave, too. He never wore a helmet, preferring the West Indian cap, in which he took great pride.

Like Botham, he was an exciting match-winner who thrived on the big occasion. There was always a buzz when he strode out to bat. I was umpiring when he scored double centuries at Trent Bridge and The Oval and he was right up there with the greatest of all batsmen. If I was picking a World XI, he would be my number three.

*   *   *

Then we came to Kapil Dev, who was a fine all-round crick-eter; I've seen him turn Tests inside out with both bat and ball. Opening the attack, he bowled with pace and swung the ball late, and when you do that you will get even the top bats-men out.

He was also captain of the India side which won the World Cup at Lord's in 1983, and it was his inspirational leadership that secured victory against the odds.

India batted first and made only 183 on a perfect batting pitch. It seemed a formality for the West Indies run machine to overhaul that modest target, but in the interval Kapil Dev got his team together and told them, 'I can see by your body language that you're down; I can see by the expression on your faces that you're down. But we're not out of this yet. I want you all to put a smile on your faces; I want you to run out there; I want you to show them that they've still got a fight on their hands. I tell you, we're going to win this game.'

It was quite Churchillian – and it worked. He inspired his players to a memorable victory. It all went to prove what a good captain can do.

The big red book

Sharing my thoughts in that television interview brought the memories flooding back. It seemed like only yesterday. It was difficult to believe that, in fact, we had been talking about people and events of thirty and forty years ago. And it's strange, too, to think how far back you have to go to discover when I was the subject of *This is Your Life*. With hindsight, they ought to rename it *This is Half Your Life*.

People often ask me if the celebrities who appeared in that popular programme really were surprised when they were confronted with that famous red book. Well, I don't know about the others, but it was certainly a surprise for me.

I was lured to the Leeds studios by Don Mosey, the well-known cricket commentator, asking if I would go on a show to tell some of my cricketing stories. When I arrived they said they weren't quite ready for me, so I warned them, 'Well, you'd better get a move on; I've got to get up to Durham for a County Championship match.'

After what seemed an eternity they said we could go ahead and I began to chat to Don in front of what I thought was a studio audience, not realising it was made up of television workers and backroom staff.

Don was a good interviewer, so I began to relax and enjoy myself until he asked, 'Tell me, Dickie, what's the most awkward situation you have encountered in your career?' Now, I had been given notice of the kind of questions that Don was going to ask – and this was not one of them. Off the cuff I couldn't think of anything.

'Well?' Don persisted.

I began to waffle, playing for time until I could come up with something. 'Er, awkward moment? Let me see. The most awkward moment? Er, well, that's a bit er . . .'

It was then that Michael Aspel walked on. 'Oh, hello, Michael,' I said. 'What are you doing here? Are you on the show with me as well?' With that he produced the aforementioned book and replied, 'Not exactly; you are on the show with me. Dickie Bird, this is your life.' Don's question was finally answered. *That* was the most awkward situation of my career.

I was so taken aback that they had to take me into a dressing room to calm me down. Then I was led into a bigger studio, where there were loads of people I knew. Sir Garfield Sobers had flown from the other side of the world! And there were filmed tributes from Dennis Lillee in Australia; Ian Botham, Viv Richards, Graham Gooch, Allan Border, David Gower, Imran Khan, Michael Parkinson, Brian Johnston and John Major.

Former Yorkshire players Geoff Boycott, Ray Illingworth, Brian Close and Freddie Trueman were also in the studio, with John Hampshire representing the umpires. Alf Broadhead, the man who took me under his wing when I went for a trial at Barnsley Cricket Club, was brought on in a wheelchair, and that was a very emotional moment for me. When 'Chunky' Charlton, my old pit manager at Monk Bretton colliery, also walked on, I blurted out, 'Mr Charlton – I thought you were dead.'

3

LAYING THE FOUNDATION

Having been born into a miner's family in the heart of the Yorkshire coalfield and grown up in the war years, I have experienced what it is like to struggle to find the money to buy all the equipment needed to take up sport – in my case football and cricket. And, as the years have gone by, I have come to appreciate more and more what my dad did for me in that respect.

Money was very tight, and it took my dad all his time to put food on the table, never mind anything else. But he saved and saved, no doubt doing without things himself, in order to buy me my first pair of football boots and my first cricket bat. Without my dad's sheer perseverance and sacrifices, I would never have got into cricket; never have had the opportunity to achieve what I did as an umpire. Makes you think, doesn't it?

Even then, there were times when I had to make do with second-hand stuff. I once played in a schoolboy football final at Barnsley's Oakwell ground in a pair of borrowed boots. By half-time I had so many blisters I could hardly walk, let alone run.

Reflecting on this in my retirement days, I came to the decision that I would do all I could to help those parents who were struggling in the harsh economic times of today to make sure that their children could take part in sport. Sport had given me so much that I wanted to put something back. I was determined to do something to help get kids off the streets, drag them away from their computers and television sets, and get them taking part in some kind of sport, which is not only great for keeping fit and healthy, but also develops character and, in some cases, the ability to work as part of a team.

Eventually I hit on the idea of forming an organisation which would be able to make grants to under-privileged kids from poorer families, and therefore give them a leg-up at a time when they most need support and encouragement. The Dickie Bird Foundation was set up in 2004.

It was hard at first. I had to put in a lot of my own money to get it off the ground, and there were some difficulties in the early years, but a big change in the board of trustees in the autumn of 2007 proved the turning point. In came Ted Cowley, a retired financial accountant from Leeds; Steve Mowbray, a Wakefield-born PE teacher; local umpire Keith Dibb; and Wendy James, who works at Bradford City Football Club. New operating structures were put in place, along with tighter operating controls, fully endorsed by the Charity Commission, and now we are going from strength to strength. Dave Callaghan also does a lot of work for the foundation, organising various functions to raise money. For example, when Yorkshire play at Scarborough he very often arranges quizzes between the White Rose players and those from the opposing county. His efforts behind the scenes with such promotions as these are invaluable.

Many people think that because it's the Dickie Bird Foundation it's all to do with cricket, but that is not so. We consider grants for all recognised sports. We have helped boys and girls to follow their dream in horse racing, ice skating, golf, athletics and table tennis, among others – as well as cricket and football.

For example, there is a ten-year-old called Josh Cutts, from Cundy Cross in Barnsley. I went to present his grant to him at Barnsley YMCA and as I watched him give a table tennis demonstration with his brother, who is also a good player, I could not believe the talent that young kid had. He was practising with the Yorkshire team and had travelled to China to learn from the best players in the world.

Sadly, I have seen so many talented youngsters, in many different sports, fall by the wayside – very often because of a lack of hard work and dedication – so I told Josh, 'You've got everything, young man. Don't throw it away. It's entirely up to you. If you say you are going to succeed, you will. You must have that mental strength; you must believe in yourself. It is essential.'

I will watch his progress very carefully and with great interest, because it has been a privilege to have been in a situation where I have been able to give him some help in fulfilling his dream of reaching the very top of his chosen sport. His mother was over the moon after seeing Josh receive his grant and I had a lovely letter of thanks. It does give me a warm glow of satisfaction when that happens.

One of our main goals is to increase the number of grants we offer every year, while still sticking to strict guidelines which, hopefully, ensure that the grants are distributed in a fair and proper manner. For example, we give grants only to individuals under 18 years of age. We did have one application from a team of over-50s footballers. We had to turn that down on two counts – they were too old and it was a team rather than one person. We have also had enquiries from the National Playing Fields Association, but again we had to say no. Our aim is to offer help specifically to young individuals, and we are determined not to be swayed from that.

Applications can be made online and we have to rely on the honesty of the parents when they are asking for a grant on behalf of their children. They have to be vetted by our board of trustees and one of the things those applying for the grant have to do is declare how much money is going into the home. Wendy James is our grants officer and this lovely lady does a tremendous job in making sure that the grants go to the young people who need them most.

We are also indebted to the many clubs, groups and organisations who raise money on our behalf, enabling us to continue with what we believe to be a very worthwhile cause. We then make sure that the money goes out in the form of a grant as soon as it comes in. It's the only way to run a successful charity. The scheme operates nationwide, from the tip of Scotland in the north, to Cornwall in the south, and the grants are mainly to help with the cost of clothing and equipment, although we do also make small contributions towards travel expenses within the UK.

My ambition in all this is to give young people throughout the country an equal opportunity in the sport of their choice, irrespective of their background and upbringing. Watching the London Olympics in 2012, it struck me how many youngsters, particularly in rowing and cycling, but also in athletics – the marvellous Jessica Ennis, for example – had sacrificed so much to achieve their dream of an Olympic medal. And I thought how wonderful it would be if, at some future Olympics, we could point to a medallist who had, at an important early stage, been given priceless assistance by the Dickie Bird Foundation.

That alone gives us the incentive to carry on and do all we can for the sporting kids of today. A grant could be a godsend. It could result in Olympic gold. Who knows?

The early Bird

The foundation played a part in the award of my OBE in 2012, to go with the MBE I received in 1986. The citation was 'for services to cricket and charity'. As well as the foundation, I also help several other charities as patron.

I could hardly believe it when I received a letter from the Prime Minister saying that they 'had it in mind' for me to receive the award. And then I had an anxious wait until it was verified.

Receiving the OBE was the pinnacle of my career. I felt very, very proud, but also very humble. It was a double delight for me because I am a royalist through and through. Without a shadow of a doubt, I reckon we've got it absolutely right with the royal family as head of state – figureheads if you like – and a democratically elected government. None of this republican nonsense for me. The Queen, the Duke of Edinburgh, Prince Charles and Princess Anne have, for years, been out practically every other day on some official duty, and they all work extremely hard. Now, of course, we've also got Wills, Kate and Prince Harry! Harry might be a bit of a lad at times, but his heart is in the right place.

I think the Diamond Jubilee celebrations in 2012 showed just how highly thought of the royal family is by the vast majority of the British people.

I have met the Queen on no fewer than twenty-seven occasions, one of them being at Buckingham Palace in November 1990. I was sitting at home one day when the phone rang. When I picked it up a voice at the other end of the line said, 'This is the Master of the Household ringing from Buckingham Palace. I have been commanded by Her Majesty the Queen to see if you are available, Mr Bird, to have lunch with her on Tuesday, November the twentieth.'

I thought at first it was somebody taking the mickey, but I replied, 'If I really have been invited to have lunch with the Queen at Buckingham Palace, I'll walk from Barnsley to be there.'

For those who know me it will come as no great surprise when I tell you I was up with that other bird, the lark, when the big day dawned. I travelled down from Barnsley and arrived at King's Cross at twenty past eight in the morning. Even taking it steady, I was outside the Palace at twenty past nine – and my appointment wasn't until one o'clock!

An on-duty policeman saw me wandering about and he enquired, 'What are you doing here, Dickie? There's not much cricket in the middle of November.'

'No, officer,' I replied. 'I've been invited to lunch with the Queen.'

I wasn't sure whether or not he believed me, so I showed him the invitation.

'Hmm,' he said. 'Well, I'm afraid you're going to have a long time to wait. We've got the Changing of the Guard first. Can't stop that.' He smiled and added, 'Not even for Dickie Bird.'

So it was off to a coffee shop for me. I'm not sure how much coffee I got through in the next four hours . . .

But it turned out to be another great day. To sit in the lounge of Buckingham Palace after a magnificent lunch and talk to the Queen over a few drinks was something very, very special for me. It was one of the best days of my life.

Then there was the time, in my retirement, when I received an invitation from the Queen to attend Buckingham Palace for a reception for sports personalities arranged by the Central Council for Physical Recreation. Unfortunately I was paying a visit to New Zealand at the time. But how could I refuse, even if it meant a twenty-nine-hour flight?

When I was introduced to Her Majesty in the White Room she said to me, 'You've done very well to come all the way from New Zealand to be here.'

I replied, 'Thank you, Ma'am. I was actually outside the palace gates four hours ago. I was determined not to be late.'

I was very tired at the end of the day. But, boy, had it been worth it. I wouldn't have missed it for the world – even though it meant travelling halfway round it.

As for the Duke of Edinburgh, I think he's a great bloke. He has his critics, and occasionally he does make some extremely provocative statements, but he's just like a good Yorkshireman. He says what he thinks.

Did you know that I once substituted for him? It was at the Cricket World Cup dinner in London. All the teams, managers, coaches and officials had been invited and the Duke was the main speaker. It was a really big do. However, a protest march had been planned in London for the same day and so, in the interests of safety, the Duke's appearance was cancelled. The teams were also told to stay away.

The dinner itself went ahead because at such short notice it was impossible to let everyone know what was happening. In fact, I was already on my way, having set off early by train. It was only when my cab was stopped halfway to the Guildhall that I realised something was wrong. We were told that we could go no further because the roads were blocked off.

In a way I was glad about that, because I'd already totted up a £50 taxi fare and the meter was still ticking. I asked the cabbie for directions and set off to walk. I managed to skirt round the trouble spots and eventually arrived at the Guildhall looking rather dishevelled. I had my dinner jacket on – including dickie bow, naturally – and, this being in the middle of summer, sweat was pouring off me after the two-mile hike.

It was then that I was told that the teams, officials, dignitaries and the Duke of Edinburgh would not be attending because of the trouble on the streets, but the dinner was still going ahead. Then came the bombshell. They asked if I would stand in for His Royal Highness as guest speaker. I was stunned. I didn't know what to say. But I couldn't let all those people down, could I? It was a case of 'After the Lord Mayor's Show', because the Lord Mayor spoke first and I followed. Happily it was not a dust-cart performance, and the speech went down well.

Shortly afterwards I met His Royal Highness when I presented the Duke of Edinburgh Awards at St James's Palace, and he thanked me personally for deputising for him. 'They tell me you did a tremendous job,' he said.

These are all wonderful memories for me, but the best day of all – until 2012, that is – came that amazing June day in 1986 when I was awarded the MBE in the Queen's Birthday Honours List. Immediately afterwards I was on duty at a County Championship match between Lancashire and Worcestershire and when I walked out with fellow umpire John Jameson at the start of play the crowd stood up and cheered me all the way to the middle. That was something, I can tell you. The tears flowed; the hanky was out again. I still get emotional now just thinking about it. There was I, a Yorkshireman, at the headquarters of Lancashire cricket, being given a standing ovation. Unbelievable!

For me that said it all. It was the game of cricket acknowledging an award which I regarded as an honour, not just for me, not just for the umpires, but for the sport of cricket in general. It was also an honour for my home town of Barnsley and the county of Yorkshire.

Needless to say, I was a little early on the day of the presentation. There was I, in my top hat and tails, feeling a bit like Fred Astaire, and fully aware that everyone was staring at me. Fortunately I had my sister Marjorie and my niece Rachel with me, and my nerves were eased as we chatted to sightseers and tourists until the time came for me to go inside.

I was, of course, very emotional. I just can't help it. It's in my nature. No matter how much I try to keep back the tears, I can't. Those great Olympic medallists of London 2012 will know what I mean! Just ask Chris Hoy – and he's a Sir!

But, you know, the Queen has this wonderful knack of putting everyone at their ease, and we were soon chatting away like old friends as she handed me my medal. I remember her telling me, 'I'm coming to the Test match on Friday, so I'll see you there. You will give me time to sit down and have my cup of tea, won't you?'

'Yes, of course, Ma'am,' I replied. Well, what else could I say?

Then she added mischievously, 'Oh, and by the way, I don't want you bringing them off for bad light.' Now, what did she mean by that?

We both had a little chuckle, and as I made my way from the presentation I could not help reflecting on what a wonderful, caring, down-to-earth person the Queen is. And her little cameo with Daniel 'James Bond' Craig in the opening ceremony at the London Olympics proved that she is a really good sport as well. It just about stole the show, didn't it?

Memories of those royal occasions came flooding back to me in 2012 when I returned to Buckingham Palace to receive my OBE from Prince Charles, who shared a joke with me during the awards ceremony and put me completely at ease – just like his mother.

Incidentally, during the photo-shoot with the press afterwards, some beefeaters suddenly came out of the Palace and asked if they could have their pictures taken with me. I said, 'Certainly.' Well, you can't say no to a beefeater, can you? They'd have had me locked up in the Tower of London before you could say 'that's out'.

'You should have smashed it in, Dickie!'

Just after I had received my OBE I was invited to a football match at Sheffield United's Bramall Lane and I was surprised and delighted when the chairman, Kevin McCabe, and his wife, Kathy, presented me with a United shirt that had 'Dickie Bird OBE' and a large number one printed on the back, plus a Blades tie and a card signed by all the players.

My links with Bramall Lane go back a long way. It was the first home of Yorkshire County Cricket Club and Championship matches were played there until the mid-1970s. It was sad when the owners decided to convert the site into a purely football arena. It is now the oldest major stadium in the world still hosting professional football.

In my days as a young player just making my way, I used to practise in the old shed where the football car park is now situated. There was no heating, and it was always bitterly cold in winter. The pitch we practised on was concrete, and I can still feel my hands jarring. I went back there later on with Yorkshire Seconds, and I always enjoyed playing in matches at Bramall Lane. I loved umpiring there as well.

There used to be a big clock on the pavilion and players would have bets on who could hit it. Memory plays strange tricks, but I seem to remember the great Australian Keith Miller winning his bet one day.

By the way, I've never taken that Sheffield United shirt to Barnsley's ground, Oakwell. I'd get lynched if I did. But Barnsley themselves also did me proud in recognition of my OBE. They introduced me to the crowd at the big derby game with Leeds United and when I paraded round the perimeter track I got a tremendous reception from both sets of fans. The Leeds supporters were all chanting, 'Yorkshire, Yorkshire, Yorkshire.' Then I got a ball and dribbled it from one end of the field to the other and the crowd went berserk.

I got right into the penalty area and, looking back, I should have fired it into the net, but I didn't. At my age I was a bit stiff after the length-of-the-field dash towards the goal at the Ponty End where all the Barnsley fans were congregated and I didn't want to pull a muscle shooting! But I should have had a go. Everybody said to me afterwards, 'You should have smashed it in, Dickie.'

The Leeds supporters have something of a bad reputation, not helped last October when a fan ran on to the pitch and assaulted Sheffield Wednesday goalkeeper Chris Kirkland, which was unforgivable. But that day at Oakwell they were marvellous with me – a Barnsley season ticket-holder – so much so that I wrote to their chief executive congratulating them on their behaviour. He put the letter in the next match-day magazine.

In fact, I could not have had a better reception from both sets of supporters – and to put the icing on the cake, Barnsley won the game.

Hobnobbing with the great and the good

I have had invitations to receptions and lunches from three prime ministers. In 1981 I was at Downing Street for a reception put on by Lady Thatcher, mainly for show-business people, including Eric Morecambe and Ernie Wise, Terry Wogan and Ronnie Barker.

Ten years later I received an invitation from John Major to attend a buffet luncheon at Chequers. Having stayed overnight at a small hotel nearby, I was on his doorstep at nine o'clock next morning.

There were guards at the top of the drive leading to the house and you had to show your pass so that they could let you through. They looked at me, looked at the pass, and then said, 'You're very early, Dickie; we'd better ring the Prime Minister and see what he has to say.' So they did. Apparently he told them that he had only just got out of bed, but then added, 'Tell Dickie to come down and he can have breakfast with me.' So I had breakfast as well as lunch, and I was treated to a tour of the building.

There was a similar scenario when I was invited to Chequers by Tony Blair. When I turned up, the Blairs were still at church, and I ended up bouncing little Leo, as he was then, on my lap until they returned. It was Tony Blair who also treated me to a visit to 10 Downing Street and showed me all round that historic building. He even took me into the Cabinet Room and let me sit in the PM's chair.

I settled into the seat and said, 'Right then, let's get on with the meeting.'

He told me, 'This is where all the big decisions are made, Dickie.'

'Not all,' I said. 'Quite a few are made in the middle of a cricket field.'

I have remained friends with both John Major and Tony Blair. In fact, the former has been a terrific help in organising events to raise funds for my foundation and I'll always be immensely grateful to him for that. Politics don't enter into it. This is a cricket thing.

Cricket also enabled me to meet one of the greatest men of my generation, Nelson Mandela. South Africa were playing a Test match at the Wanderers Club in Johannesburg and I was one of the fortunate people invited to be presented to the president in the executive suite. It was a huge honour and privilege to shake hands and exchange a few words with the man who had endured so much in order to bring an end to Apartheid in that wonderful country, having served twenty-seven years in prison on Robben Island. I was struck, not only by the twinkle in his eyes and his obvious zest for life, but also by his great humility. It was an unforgettable experience.

Through this wonderful game I've been able to mix with royalty, top politicians, great leaders and some of the richest men in the world, including cricket-loving Paul Getty, and have forged lasting friendships with them. Not bad for a coal-miner's son from Barnsley. I also have many friends among the less famous and less well off, and again I have cricket to thank for bringing us together.

Take, for example, Roger, a road-sweeper in Scarborough. It all started five years ago when I was enjoying a coffee in one of the seafront cafés and this young man, a Council employee cleaning the area around The Spa, came up to me and said, 'Hey, sorry to trouble you, but are you Dickie Bird?'

'As a matter of fact, I am,' I replied.

'Marvellous,' he said. 'I'm a big admirer of yours. Would you sign my cap for me?'

So I signed his cap. I was glad to do so. He kept that seafront at Scarborough spotless, which is no mean feat when you con-sider all the fish-and-chip and other fast-food outlets in the area, not to mention the ice-cream and sweet stalls and the like. He did a great job.

I see the lad every time I go to Scarborough. In fact, he now comes and sits with me and has a coffee, and maybe a sand-wich or some other snack. Then, in the summer of 2012, he was laid off because of Council cut-backs. As time went by I could see the difference. The seafront was nowhere near as clean and tidy as it was when Roger was in action. He was gutted to lose his job, and I felt really sorry for him. Here's someone who's worked hard and well – and his living has been snatched away from him. I know there's no money about, and cuts are necessary, but it's not fair, is it?

He's really taken to me, just as much as I've taken to him. It's another friendship forged through cricket. And I'm glad to say he's still wearing his cap.

Remembering Don Wilson

My closest friend amongst my playing colleagues was Don Wilson, and I was devastated when I could not go to his memorial service in 2012 because I was in hospital. Don loved his cricket and enjoyed every single moment of his career. He was a very good slow left-arm bowler who reminded me of Bishan Bedi in many ways. He was not a great spinner of the ball, but he had superb variation of flight. He was also a brilliant fielder in the midwicket and cover-point areas. He was a lot like me in that he was so very proud just to be part of that Yorkshire squad.

I well remember the first day he came to the county nets. He never laid bat on ball for twenty minutes.

Arthur Mitchell, the great Yorkshire coach who had himself played for the county and also for England, came over to me and asked, 'What does this lad do for a living, Birdy?'

'He's a joiner from Settle, Mr Mitchell,' I told him.

'A joiner is 'e? Then tell 'im from me, the next time 'e comes, 'e'd better bring an 'ammer, some nails an' a few planks o' wood to board that end up. 'E needs summat ter protect 'is stumps, 'cos that bat's neether use nor ornament.'

It is true that Don was not exactly the best batsman in the world, but he was a good enough bowler to go on and play for England. He was head coach at Lord's for a time and later did a wonderful job as coach at Ampleforth College.

He once told me that when he was at Lord's he saw me out in the middle one winter's morning doing a bit of training. Apparently he called all the young lads over and said to them, 'Look, there's my old pal Dickie Bird. He's going to be a Test umpire. He practises his art at every opportunity and I'm asking you all to do the same. Practice, practice, practice. It's the only way. What's good enough for him is good enough for you.'

Then I started to go through my signals, and Don said to the youngsters. 'Now, take a good look at this, lads, because I don't think you'll see anything quite like it again.'

Don and I used to travel together when we played for Yorkshire and I spent many happy times staying with him and his parents in Settle.

When Yorkshire sacked Johnny Wardle, Don and I were playing for the second team at Scarborough. A telegram came through from the Yorkshire secretary, Mr Nash, asking for Don and myself to report to Middlesbrough the next day for the start of the County Championship match against Essex. Don was drafted into the side in Wardle's place. It was his first-team debut and he took five wickets. The rest, as they say, is history. He became a regular in the side and also played for England.

Me? I was twelfth man – again!

At the last match of the 2012 season Yorkshire's statistician told me that Don and I hold the ninth-wicket partnership for any county against Glamorgan. It was when I hit my highest score of 181 not out at Bradford, and Don stuck with me to the end. Not a lot of people knew that. Including me!

I always remember one particular incident with Don when we decided to while away an hour or two in Scarborough's Peasholm Park. There's a lake there and Don persuaded me to hire a rowing boat, despite the fact that I'm a poor sailor. It was flat calm, as you might expect, but when we reached the middle of the lake I said to Don, 'I don't feel so good.' Don retorted, 'Well, we're not going back yet; we've only been in the boat two minutes.' I said, 'Well, I'm off, otherwise I'm going to be sick.' So I stepped out of the boat into the water – it wasn't deep – and walked back to dry land. It was Don who had paid for the boat, so it was no skin off my nose.

Bearing this in mind, just imagine my thoughts when I was asked to go as a speaker on a cruise ship which was due to sail through the notorious Bay of Biscay. I was frightened to death. But I remembered the advice of West Indies fast bowler Malcolm Marshall which had always stood me in good stead. He told me that whenever I went abroad – India, Pakistan, Sri Lanka – I should always take with me a small bottle of Angostura bitters. It's what they put in pink gin and you can get it from any supermarket. Malcolm told me to put it in any drinks I might have – tea, coffee, whatever – and it would settle the stomach. I would have no problem. It has worked wonders for me, and it did the trick again.

Also on the ship's speaking team were jockey Bob Champion, boxer Frank Bruno, football's Jack Charlton and snooker player Willie Thorne, who now commentates on the sport. I discovered that Bob was an even worse sailor than me, which is saying something. In fact, he refused point-blank to sail through the Bay of Biscay. He insisted, 'I'm not going and that's that. I'll fly to Madeira and pick the ship up there.' So that is what he did.

When we were due to make the return trip we managed to convince him that the Bay of Biscay was a doddle really; nothing to worry about at all. Unfortunately there was a bit of a swell, to put it mildly, and Bob was far from champion. He never left his cabin. The first we saw of him was when he was being carried off the ship, face as white as my cap, on a stretcher.

That apart, it was a marvellous trip and I felt really proud of myself. Through the Bay of Biscay, not once, but twice. Peasholm Park would hold no terrors for me from now on!

4

BEST-SELLING AUTHOR

AFTER retiring from the game all those years ago I wrote my autobiography, which sold three-quarters of a million copies. I was stunned. I never dreamed it would go like that. It was simply amazing that a book by an umpire should become one of the best-selling cricket books of all time!

I still can't explain it, although it was obviously published at the right time, with my name still fresh in everyone's minds. Part of the reason for its success, I suppose, is that I always talk to everybody, young and old alike. I never refuse a request for an autograph. And I did a lot of signing sessions!

Wherever I go, people even now come up to me and tell me how much they enjoyed that book. And that's really nice. It shows tremendous respect. And that's all I have ever sought from officials, players and the general public. Respect means everything to me.

Writing the book really was a labour of love: looking back at all the wonderful times I had enjoyed from my schooldays as a miner's son, through my youth in Barnsley, my early days as a cricketer, then my career as an umpire. I also revelled in recalling some of the funny stories – and there were bound to be a lot of those in the days of such characters as Allan Lamb and Ian Botham.

Having gone from thread to needle in that lifelong account, I had no thoughts about writing another, but early in 1998 Hodder and Stoughton's consultant editor Roddy Bloomfield suggested over lunch one day that I ought to write a book focusing primarily on my experiences around the County Championship grounds. The outcome was *White Cap and Bails*. Compiling it was hard work, but it was also a great pleasure taking another wander down memory lane, county by county, recalling so many humorous occasions, some of which had been only hazy recollections until my memory was given a timely jog. I laughed and cried as I relived all the incidents on those grounds, because they had been like second homes to me during my long career as player and umpire.

Dickie Bird's Britain

That, surely, was that, I thought, as far as my literary career was concerned. But Roddy had other ideas. He obviously didn't want me sitting there with nothing to do in my retirement and fading away from sheer boredom, because in 2001 he rang to suggest that I write yet another book. I was even more taken aback. There really was nothing left for me to say, I told him. But he was insistent. He said that the Bird supporters wanted more, and he told me that he had come up with an idea for a travel book with a difference.

Now, it is quite true that, after journeying the length and breadth of Britain to fulfil cricket appointments, I had often talked about the marvellous places and fascinating people I had been lucky enough to encounter. I have always been very proud to be British, so he suggested that I write about this great country of ours as I see it, and take a photographer with me on my travels.

The more I thought about the idea, the more I liked it. I could see that here was a chance to write about people I regard very highly; I could include chapters on some of the great houses and gardens of England, and on some of the great British institutions, including bank holidays, bed-and-breakfast establishments, traditional food such as fish and chips, the weather, and our marvellous sporting heritage.

That appealed to me, because I get fed up with people knocking Britain. I have travelled all over the world and every country has something to offer, but British is best as far as I am concerned. Of course we have our problems – you have only to pick up your newspaper or watch the television news to realise that – and we need to sort those problems out, but at the same time I believe we should revel in the achievements and history of this country. We should have a sense of pride.

Wheels were consequently set in motion and for nine months I had a marvellous time driving from Devon in the south of England to Tyneside in the north, from the valleys of Wales to the Highlands of Scotland. Derry Brabbs was the photographer who accompanied me and he did an absolutely brilliant job with his eye-catching full-colour photographs. The book that resulted from all this was *Dickie Bird's Britain*.

I would have liked to include Ireland, but my knowledge and experience of that wonderful country was far too limited to do it justice. I had paid just two visits. One was while I was playing with Yorkshire, when I remember scoring 61 in Belfast. The other was with Leicestershire and it proved a bit of a disaster. The ferry crossing from Liverpool was so rough that I was violently seasick and I spent the whole four days of that trip in my hotel room feeling very much under the weather and dreading the return journey.

However, as far as the rest of the British Isles was concerned, I revisited places I knew and discovered others where I had never been. In the process I renewed old friendships and formed new ones.

Cliff Morgan, the born storyteller

I was delighted to be able to meet some outstanding figures in sports other than cricket – people such as Cliff Morgan, one of the most famous of all Welsh rugby players. I had dinner with him at the Queen's Club in London and it was a joy and a privilege to sit there and listen to this born storyteller speak so passionately about the country of his birth.

What he said reminded me so much of my own background in the coal-mining villages of South Yorkshire. Cliff's father, like mine, had been a miner. He used to take home £3 a week if he was lucky. But they always had plenty to eat. Cliff's mother had learned from her mother how to make wonderful meals that cost very little. For example, she bought cheap cuts of neck of lamb for a broth, which would last two days. She also made beautiful apple tart, using apples from an orchard across the road. Back in Barnsley we had something similar called Eve's pudding, which was made with sponge rather than pastry.

I licked my lips when Cliff went through a typical week's menu in the Morgan household, and I couldn't help but marvel at the resourcefulness and imagination of those mining families, both in Wales and the Barnsley area. I had to smile when he said that you could always tell the day of the week from the food his mother put on the table. I knew so many families like that.

Monday, said Cliff, was always cold meat left from the Sunday lunch, sometimes made into rissoles. The meat was cooked on the Saturday night, so as not to interfere with attendance at chapel on Sunday morning. On Tuesdays a chap with a horse and cart sold fish at the door, so that night there was hake and chips. Wednesday and Thursday it was the lamb broth, and so it went on. There were never any surprises. Same menu, same day, week in, week out.

Cliff recalled that although they never had much money his mother always managed to place some in the envelope at the chapel. It was the first thing she put to one side when his father took home his pay. It was not until after his mother died that he discovered that for seventeen years, while he was living in London, she had put half a crown into an envelope every week in his name, to keep his membership of the chapel.

As kids, Cliff and his mates were greatly influenced by their parents, by the chapel and by the village as a whole. They could trust the schoolteacher, the headmaster, the doctor, the village bobby. They used to touch their caps to them as a mark of respect. Life centred round the chapel. They went three times on a Sunday – morning service, Sunday school in the afternoon and then evening service, followed by choir practice.

Again it all sounded very much like my days as a young boy in Barnsley. And, although times were hard, they were good times, happy times. Money can't buy memories like that. Sadly those wonderful days appear to have gone. It's so different today. Cliff told me that the door of his house was never locked. His mother would go out and leave the insurance book – and the money – on the living-room table; the insurance man would walk in, enter the amount, take the money and leave the book. Nothing was ever stolen.

Like most mothers in Wales – and in Yorkshire – Mrs Morgan shopped for almost everything at the Co-op. The system was that every so often you bought a certain number of Co-op cheques, say a pound's worth, and then used them to pay for your bills for as long as they lasted. The cheques, therefore, were very precious. Yet Cliff's mother would leave them on the front doorstep with the empty bottles to pay for the milk without a second thought.

Having been brought up in a church-going family, I was very interested to hear Cliff say that the essential difference between his days as a young lad in Trebanog and today was that back then the chapels were full. The influence of the chapels was enormous. He said there was always a feeling of belonging. There were sermons, he recalled, that took you to heaven, if only for five minutes.

I smiled. Maybe occasionally I hear sermons like that at my local Methodist Church today, but there are also times when I struggle to understand what on earth – or even in heaven – the preachers are talking about.

Having said that, does Cliff have a point? Are so many youngsters going off the rails because they no longer have that church background, which taught them right from wrong and what it means to care for other people?

I loved the story Cliff told of the time when he made his debut for the Welsh rugby team. On the day of the match he boarded the bus as usual – no flash car or taxi in those days – and heard two men talking about the international against Scotland.

One of them said, ''Ow the 'ell will Morgan cope with their big fellows? He's only a titch. He's too small. I know. I see 'im regular. Bet you 'e's no more than ten stone wet through.'

His companion replied, 'Don't talk daft. He's more than that, mun. Saw 'im at a do last week. Got great big shoulders, he has. I reckon he's eleven stone if he's an ounce.'

And so it went on until one of them turned to Cliff. 'You're standing there saying nothing. What do you think Morgan weighs?'

'Twelve stone,' he replied decisively.

'Rubbish.'

'I tell you he is,' Cliff maintained.

The chap turned to the other folk on the bus and barked, 'Would you credit it. It's always the same. Them who knows bugger-all about it always argue the toss.'

What a trip – I loved every moment of it

Later in the year I paid a visit to Wales, to Llanelli to be precise, where I met up with another great Welsh rugby player of the past, Phil Bennett, and visited the Stradey Park Stadium, where Llanelli used to play their rugby. My guide for the next two days was the Llanelli club's match announcer and chaplain, Reverend Eldon Phillips, a small, balding vicar who was delightful company.

Eldon also did rugby and cricket commentaries for his local radio station and was press officer for the diocese of Swansea and Brecon. What I particularly liked about him was his sense of humour. He was also prepared to laugh at himself. For example, he was once rambling on in one of his sermons and lost track of time until he heard a little lad in the front pew turn to his mother and say, 'Mam, is it still Sunday?'

Not a lot of people know this, but I once had the privilege of playing football for Barnsley's Northern Intermediate League side in a fixture at St James's Park, the home of Newcastle United, so it was tremendous to be able to go back there while writing the book, to meet Sir Bobby Robson, then still going strong at the age of 69 – the same age as me at the time – as the boss of a side challenging for the Premiership title.

He had this wonderful footballing philosophy. 'One goal more. You score one goal more than the other side and you win.' It was put into practice the day I spent such an enjoyable time in his company. I stayed on for the match against Bolton. Newcastle twice fought back from behind to win 3–2.

Sir Bobby, who was also a very keen follower of cricket, came out with some classic quotes in his time and, sure enough, there was one in the post-match press conference that day. Summing up Newcastle's title chances, he said, 'You can't start counting your chickens before they are hatched, otherwise they won't lay the egg.'

I was very sad when I heard that he had become a victim of cancer in 2009. He was a wonderful man.

Sir Steve Redgrave was another top sportsman on my itinerary and I caught up with the record-breaking Olympic rower at Henley, where he described in graphic detail the moment he realised he had won his fifth gold medal. 'I was gasping for breath, my lungs were screaming for oxygen, my arms and legs were aching like mad and I was hurting all over. But at the same time I was thinking, that's it, five gold medals. Nobody can take that away from me now. That's it for life. That's never going to go away. The pain will.'

I also paid a visit to York racecourse, where I have spent many happy hours. I love going to the races. You meet people from all walks of life, there is a wonderful atmosphere and the hospitality is always first-class. However, I never have a bet. I don't believe in gambling. I have seen it ruin too many good people and I have always been determined it would not happen to me.

The nearest I came was one day at York when I bumped into Ian Botham. He told me he had a horse running and tried to persuade me to have a flutter on it. I said, 'Come on, Both, you know I'm not a betting man, and I'm not going to start now.' However, in the end I reluctantly gave in. I went up to this bookie and told him I wanted to bet 50p on Botham's horse. But he wouldn't accept the bet. He said 50p wasn't enough. So the only time I actually tried to bet I was turned down.

It was a similar story on another York occasion when I was in the company of Sir Michael Stoute, who trained the Queen's racehorses. I met him in the parade ring and he gave me the name of a horse which was, he said, a near cert to win the next race. I told him the same as I had told Botham. I didn't gamble. He said, 'Just a little flutter, Dickie. I can assure you that you're on to a good thing.' But I resisted. Needless to say, the horse romped home – and six weeks later it won the Derby.

Mind you, even if I had made that bet, a 50p stake wouldn't have won me much, would it?

The invitation to join Sir Michael Stoute on that day had come a little while before, when we both played in a charity match at Windsor Castle in aid of the Injured Jockeys Association, of which Her Majesty the Queen is Patron. She is, of course, a very keen horsewoman and she has a remarkable knowledge of racehorses.

This was another of those occasions when I was honoured to have lunch with her. There were just three of us at our table, the Queen, myself and champion jockey Lester Piggott, so that was quite something.

My round-Britain journey continued with a bank holiday weekend in Scarborough; a fling at the Highland Games; a discussion on poultry rearing with the Duchess of Devonshire at Chatsworth House; being amazed by the exhibits at the North of England Horticultural Society's annual show at Harrogate; some food for thought as I devoured some delicious dishes, including the Barnsley chop; a nostalgic trip to Hambledon, the cradle of cricket; tea at the Ritz; dinner at Simpson's in the Strand; learning more of the work of Christians in Sport; exploring Yorkshire and Scotland; visiting castles; reliving my time in Devon; and meetings with lovely down-to-earth Yorkshire folk such as Macmillan nurses, fish-and-chip shop and corner-café proprietors, pigeon flyers and lots, lots more.

What a way to spend a chunk of your retirement. I loved every moment of it.

And now Roddy's got me at it again!

5

THE SANDS OF TIME

I N 2007 I was asked to come out of retirement to umpire a
beach-cricket tournament in Australia. I wasn't too sure
about it, but former Aussie captain Allan Border sold it to
me. When I asked him what it was all about, he went into a
detailed explanation which really grabbed my interest. 'I've
always played beach cricket,' he told me. 'It's great, Dickie,
you'd love it. As an Aussie, it's part of growing up and then it
becomes something you do with your own kids. It's probably the most relaxed way to play cricket – you've got the
boardies on, sand in your toes and the added bonus of being
able to land in the water when you go for a spectacular
diving catch.'

But it was when I learned who was taking part that I was
really hooked on the idea. The three teams included my old
mates Dennis Lillee and Jeff Thomson from Australia; Viv
Richards, Desmond Haynes and Courtney Walsh from the
West Indies; and our own Graham Gooch, Allan Lamb and
fellow Yorkshireman Darren 'Dazzler' Gough.

The opportunity to be reunited with players like that was
too good to refuse. And it turned out to be a simply amazing
experience. We attracted gates of between 10,000 and 12,000
for each of the matches, played on three of Australia's most

beautiful beaches, Coolangatta in Queensland, Maroubra in Sydney and, one which held a great deal of personal appeal to me, Scarborough, in Western Australia.

They were all transformed into fantastic stadiums, and spectators queued for hours to be first in line to catch a glimpse of their cricketing heroes. The tournament lasted three weeks and it all came down to a last-ball finale to decide the winners. That it was England who clinched the crown was the icing on a delicious cake, as far as I was concerned.

After the final in Sydney, Border summed it up by saying, 'We all like to play well and as a team we like to win. So it is never good watching the English boys take home the trophy.' Then he added, 'After all, they don't even have nice, sandy beaches in England.'

How dare he! Has he never been to Yorkshire's fabulous east-coast trio of Scarborough – this is the original one we are talking about! – Filey and Bridlington? At least they have stretches of good, firm sand; not like those in Australia, where it is soft and makes life very difficult for batsmen, bowlers, fielders – and umpires.

Another problem was the ball. It was more like the ones they bash about at Wimbledon than the hard one I'm used to, and you just couldn't tell if it had come off the bat when the players appealed for a catch. There was hardly any sound. Most odd. Despite all this, however, it was a very enjoyable experience, although we had to be careful not to get caught by the incoming tide. I also faced the constant threat of being thrown into the sea by Lamby and co., but thankfully I managed to avoid that. There are too many sharks about in that part of the world for my liking.

And that reminds me . . .

Part of the delight of those three weeks was spending time reminiscing about the old days. For example, Lillee and Thommo reminded me of another incident in that first World Cup final, between Australia and the West Indies at Lord's in 1975. Dennis came to the crease as the last man to partner Thommo with Australia's reply standing at 233 for 9 and still 59 short of victory. I can see Dennis even now taking guard, winking at me, and saying, 'Don't worry, Dickie, we'll get these.'

I said, 'Dream on, Dennis; you've no chance.' And, honestly I couldn't see the Aussies doing it, not in a million years. But gradually the gap was closed and we all began to wonder if a cricketing miracle was about to unfold.

Even the West Indians, who had been so much in control, were beginning to have doubts. Then, however, Thommo failed to connect cleanly with one hefty swing of the bat too many and the ball fell into the welcoming hands of Roy Fredericks. The crowd went mad. To coin a famous phrase from the world of football, they thought it was all over. But it wasn't. As thousands of people swarmed on to the pitch, and my white cap, three sweaters and a spare ball were yanked from my grasp, I realised that Thomson and Lillee were still running between the wickets, dodging the hordes as they did so. What they and the rest of us on the field had heard, but the crowd obviously had not, was that my colleague Tommy Spencer had shouted 'No-ball.'

And there was Lillee, muttering to Thomson as the two passed each other for the umpteenth time, 'Keep going, keep going, we'll soon have it won at this rate.'

When Lillee reached my end I asked him, 'How many is that you've run?'

'It's you who should be keeping count,' he grumbled. 'But I make it about seventeen.'

'In that case, I shouldn't bother running any more. The best I can give you is four.'

You see, after catching the ball Fredericks had hurled it at the stumps attempting a run-out, but it missed and disappeared into the middle of the onrushing tidal wave of excited fans. According to the Laws of Cricket, therefore, we had to award four runs and call the ball 'dead'.

Ironically, it was a run-out that finally ended this last-wicket resistance and the West Indies eventually won by 17 runs.

What memories!

As for Viv Richards, we looked back at the three World Cup finals we had shared together – but also another occasion that sticks in my mind. It came later in his career, when he was part of the West Indies touring team captained by Clive Lloyd.

Viv found himself facing an up-and-coming fast bowler from Wales who was determined to make the Test selectors sit

Australia v West Indies Prudential World Cup final
Lord's, London, 21 June 1975

West Indies innings (60 overs maximum)		Runs	Mins	Balls	4s	6s
RC Fredericks	hit wicket b Lillee	7	14	13	0	0
CG Greenidge	c Marsh b Thomson	13	80	61	1	0
AI Kallicharran	c Marsh b Gilmour	12	26	18	2	0
RB Kanhai	b Gilmour	55	156	105	8	0
CH Lloyd*	c Marsh b Gilmour	102	108	85	12	2
IVA Richards	b Gilmour	5	12	11	1	0
KD Boyce	c GS Chappell b Thomson	34	43	37	3	0
BD Julien	not out	26	54	37	1	0
DL Murray†	c & b Gilmour	14	11	10	1	1
VA Holder	not out	6	1	2	1	0
Extras	(lb 6, nb 11)	17				
Total	**(8 wickets; 60 overs)**	**291**				

Fall of wickets: 1–12 (Fredericks), 2–27 (Kallicharran), 3–50 (Greenidge), 4–199 (Lloyd), 5–206 (Kanhai), 6–209 (Richards), 7–261 (Boyce), 8–285 (Murray).

Bowling: DK Lillee 12–1–55–1; GJ Gilmour 12–2–48–5; JR Thomson 12–1–44–2; MHN Walker 12–1–71–0; GS Chappell 7–0–33–0; KD Walters 5–0–23–0.

Australia innings (target: 292 runs from 60 overs)		Runs	Mins	Balls	4s	6s
A Turner	run out (Richards)	40	85	54	4	0
RB McCosker	c Kallicharran b Boyce	7	29	24	1	0
IM Chappell*	run out (Richards/Lloyd)	62	125	93	6	0
GS Chappell	run out (Richards)	15	24	23	2	0
KD Walters	b Lloyd	35	52	51	5	0
RW Marsh†	b Boyce	11	34	24	0	0
R Edwards	c Fredericks b Boyce	28	51	37	2	0
GJ Gilmour	c Kanhai b Boyce	14	16	11	2	0
MHN Walker	run out (Holder)	7	10	9	1	0
JR Thomson	run out (Murray)	21	32	21	2	0
DK Lillee	not out	16	29	19	1	0
Extras	(b 2, lb 9, nb 7)	18				
Total	**(all out; 58.4 overs)**	**274**				

Fall of wickets: 1–25 (McCosker), 2–81 (Turner), 3–115 (GS Chappell), 4–162 (IM Chappell), 5–170 (Walters), 6–195 (Marsh), 7–221 (Gilmour), 8–231 (Edwards), 9–233 (Walker), 10–274 (Thomson).

Bowling: BD Julien 12–0–58–0; AME Roberts 11–1–45–0; KD Boyce 12–0–50–4; VA Holder 11.4–1–65–0; CH Lloyd 12–1–38–1.

Umpires: HD Bird and TW Spencer

West Indies won by 17 runs

up and take notice by claiming the scalp of this master batsman. The first ball, inevitably, was a bouncer. And a good one, too. Viv casually swayed out of the way to avoid being hit. The next ball was a perfect outswinger. This time Viv got a nick and was almost caught at slip.

The cocky young Welshman glared down the pitch at Richards and taunted him, 'Look yer, boyo, don't you know what a cricket ball looks like? It's red and round and weighs five and a half ounces.'

Viv said nothing. He just stared back at the bowler, twirled his bat in that familiar fashion of his, looked round the field and settled down to face the next ball. It was just a fraction over-pitched. Viv was on to it in a flash. The ball soared over the boundary and right out of the ground, landing with an almighty splash in the river which runs alongside.

Viv sauntered down the pitch and addressed the upstart bowler, who was still gazing in astonishment to where the ball had vanished in the far distance. 'Look you, boyo,' he said, with a certain amount of irony. 'You know what it's like – red, round, and weighs five and a half ounces. So bloody well go and find it.'

I also teased Des Haynes by asking him if he was still friends with West Indies colleague Malcolm Marshall. The friendship, you see, had been stretched to the limits one day when they were in opposing teams in their native Barbados. Haynes hit his pal arrogantly for four and Marshall didn't take too kindly to that kind of treatment. The next ball split Hayes's protective box!

It turned out they *were* still on speaking terms – although Desmond's voice seemed to be a little more high-pitched than I recalled.

Then it was Mark Waugh's turn. He reminded me, not for the first time, I might add, of the day I gave him out on a run-out appeal in a Test between England and Australia at Headingley, forgetting to consult the third umpire, as I should have done. 'It's a good job you got it right,' he said, 'otherwise all hell would have been let loose.'

And so it went on. It was just great to share a few memories over a drink or two with these terrific players of the past. As far as we were concerned, those really were the good old days.

I was also touched by the pen portrait which appeared alongside a photograph of me in a book brought out to commemorate the beach-cricket tournament. This is what it said:

Equally admired and respected by the fans and the players, Harold 'Dickie' Bird, with his white cap, twitching shoulders and forearm stretch, umpired his first Test between England and New Zealand in 1973. His legacy to the game is top-quality umpiring – calm, consistent and impartial, despite his obvious love of all things England.

Coming from the Aussies, that really was something!

'They go barmy here for that white cap!'

All this brings back memories of another trip to Australia many years earlier – 1977, in fact. It had all started when I was umpiring a Test match between England and Australia at Trent Bridge – the game in which Derek Randall was run out by Geoff Boycott – and at tea-time on the Monday I was having a cup of tea and a scone in the umpires' room when an attendant came in with a message to ring a number in Sydney. He also mentioned that I could reverse the charges, which came as quite a relief.

I thought at first it was someone taking the mickey, but when the attendant assured me that it was genuine I said, 'Doesn't this fellow in Sydney, whoever he is, know that I'm in the middle of a Test match?'

I collared Rodney Marsh at the close of play and asked his advice as to the best time to make the call and he told me nine o' clock in the evening, our time. So, at nine on the dot I rang the number in Sydney. There was a lengthy pause before a grumpy-sounding voice asked, 'Hello, who is this? You've just got me out of bed.' Tentatively I asked what time it was out there and he replied, 'Six in the morning.' I never did find out whether Marshy had done it deliberately or had simply made a miscalculation.

After I had made my apologies and revealed who I was, the man at the other end of the line became much more friendly. He told me that his name was Bill Currie, managing director of Berry Currie Advertising, and he wanted me to do a television advert for Volkswagen cars. He also asked if I could go out there immediately.

I told him, 'Well, not exactly immediately. You see, England still need 172 to win this Test. And they wouldn't be best pleased if I left right now.'

When he said they were willing to pay me £1,000, a sum which was just about half of what I earned from a whole season as umpire in those days, I agreed to go as soon as the Test finished, providing Lord's would agree. In any case, I had to be back for the Gillette Cup semi-final, which was scheduled just eleven days after the Test.

He said, 'That's great. And don't forget the white cap. They go barmy here for that white cap.'

Incidentally, I later learned that he had wanted someone associated with cricket, but not particularly a player, more of a 'father figure' – and the Australian players had suggested me. Me! A father figure? I wasn't even married!

Anyway, I rang Donald Carr at Lord's and explained the situation to him. I half expected him to say, 'No way,' but his response was, 'We'll give you permission to go, Dickie, but we can't take you off the semi-final. If you can get to Australia and back, you can do the advert.'

So off I went. After an exhausting 24-hour flight I was chauffeur-driven to a hotel for a wash and brush-up, then it was straight to the television studio. I did the commercial that day, dressing up in my umpire's outfit and reading a script about VW cars. Remarkably, it was screened the next night on Channel 9.

Next day there was a message asking if I could go to the studios to see Dennis Lillee, who was commentating on the live feed from the Headingley Test back home in England. Now, Dennis has always been a mate of mine, so how could I possibly refuse? I was dog-tired, but I went. And it was exciting, as well as a little strange, out there in an Australian television studio, commenting on Geoff Boycott batting at Headingley, while at the same time sitting alongside a man who could have made so much difference to the series.

At the time, you see, Lillee was not playing because he had signed up for the financially rewarding Kerry Packer series, which he thought would be a success. I had turned down an offer, stressing my ties to English cricket, and I couldn't believe the number of letters which poured through my letter box, all congratulating me on rejecting Packer and staying loyal to the established game in this country.

One was from an old lady in Sheffield, which read:

Dear Mr Bird,

This is from an old lady of nearly eighty-nine years of age. I want to tell you how you bucked me up when I heard you on the telly and read about you in the papers. Congratulations and good luck to you, wherever you are. I must tell you how refreshing it was to hear about what I call a real Englishman. They are few and far between these days. That Tony Greig wants to go back to South Africa where he belongs. As you will guess, I am a true cricket fan. I used to visit Bramall Lane when they played cricket there and have seen most of the greats of the game. I just love it and even at my advanced years I never miss cricket on the telly. Thank you for being so loyal to England and to the game.

Yours sincerely,

Mrs H Forbes

P.S. This is the first fan letter I have ever written.

That letter touched me deeply. Money can't buy sentiments like that.

Mind you, from the tone in which she mentioned Tony Greig, she was obviously unaware that I had once saved his career.

I have checked to find out the exact moment and it came after the last ball before tea on the Monday of the 1974 Test between England and Pakistan at The Oval, when Sarfraz Nawaz bowled a beamer at Greig. It was very fast and very straight. Greig, who was extremely tall if you recall, somehow managed to duck out of the way, but he was absolutely furious. To my horror, he started to stride down the pitch towards Sarfraz and threatened, 'I'm going to wrap this bat round your head.' To which Sarfraz responded, hands on hips, 'I'm waiting.'

I whipped off the bails and stepped between them, at the same time declaring, 'That's tea, gentlemen,' and urging both of them to calm down. Thankfully, that defused the situation. By the time we resumed after the break tempers had cooled.

Afterwards Greig admitted to me, 'You know, Dickie, you saved my career then. The way I felt I really would have hit him over the head with my bat.' He's right. If he had done that, he would never even have played for England again, let alone captained them.

As it was, Greig, along with Kerry Packer, went on to become responsible for a cricketing revolution which changed the face of the game for ever. Greig felt very strongly about a fair day's pay for a fair day's work in days when cricketers were paid comparative peanuts and were often treated with little respect, and in 1977 he became the main recruitment agent in the Packer-led innovation of World Series Cricket in Australia. I turned Packer down because of my principles, choosing instead to stand by the established game which had given me so much, but there is no doubt that without Packer and Greig the game would not be where it is today.

It was, therefore, so very sad early in 2013 to hear that Tony, who had throat cancer, had died of a heart attack. That sadness doubled shortly afterwards with the news of the death of that excellent commentator and journalist Christopher Martin-Jenkins. Both men did so much for cricket in their different ways and in such a short space of time we lost two giants of the game.

But I digress. By the time I got back to England after that hectic trip Down Under, I have to admit I was not in the best shape to stand at a semi-final. Thankfully that Gillette Cup encounter was an easy match to umpire – there was even a rain interruption to allow me a bit of rest – and it was just as well, because my tired eyes were rolling and the Old Father

Time weather vane was dancing around on top of the stand, despite the fact there wasn't a breath of wind. I don't know quite how I got through it all without mishap, but I did.

My furry friends

There is a permanent reminder of that trip to Oz sitting in a chair in my cottage – a cuddly koala bear, which was presented to me by the advertising people. It has the company of several other bears that I've been given, some by charities for whom I've done some work, and others by cricketing organisations, including the *Cricketer* magazine on my retirement.

Perched on the back of the chair is 'Lucky Bird', a pelican presented to me by St Luke's, a Sheffield cancer charity, while across the room, sprawled out on another chair, is a tiger. When young kids come in to visit they are a bit frightened at first. Some ask, 'Is it real?' However, when they realise that it's just an oversized cuddly toy, they start pulling its ears and stroking it.

People often ask me if it was presented to me when I umpired in India. I have to confess it was not. I won it in a raffle!

Well, I tried to warn him

There was another trip to Sydney, much less stressful, which had repercussions back home in dear old Blighty.

Jack Simmons, who later became chairman of Lancashire County Cricket Club, was at that time an off-spin bowler, who had the nickname 'Flat Jack' because he bowled them flat. We were going to Australia to do a spot of coaching and on the flight out he said, 'Tell me something, Dickie – why do you never give me lbws?'

'Good question,' I said. 'The reason, Jack, is this: you bowl very wide of the return crease. In order to stand any chance of getting an lbw you need to get closer to the wicket. Tell you what I'll do; I'll work with you in the nets, coaching you to bowl wicket to wicket, but you must also remember to run off at the end of your delivery.'

So that's what we did, all winter long. At the end of it he had it all perfectly coordinated, and I told him, 'You've got a good shout for lbws now, Jack. Let's see what happens when the season starts.'

Would you believe it, when I was handed my fixtures, I saw that the first match was Lancashire at Old Trafford. On the opening day Jack pulled into the car park at the same time and he met me with a broad grin on his face. 'I've remembered all that coaching, Dickie. I'm ready for that first lbw shout. Hope you are.' I smiled back and wished him good luck.

Lancashire lost the toss and were asked to field and eventually Jack was called on with his off-spinners. I forget who the batsman was, but the ball hit him on the pad flush in front of the stumps and Jack was leaping in the air with an almighty appeal.

I said, 'Not out.'

Jack was stunned. 'How do you mean, not out? You said I'd got it perfect. It must be out.'

'Sorry, Jack,' I said, shaking my head. 'Close to the wicket, yes; wicket to wicket, fine – but you forgot to run off. You were smack in front of me, blocking my view. I couldn't see the ball hitting the pad. So I had no choice other than to give not out.'

He's still telling the story to this day. So am I, for that matter.

Like quite a few cricketers, Jack was also a more than decent footballer. He showed a lot of promise playing for his hometown club, Great Harwood. He was always telling me that he was a fearless, bustling centre-forward, typical of the old school, with a natural ability to put the ball in the back of the net. In fact, Everton were once interested in signing him, but nothing came of it, and possibly the fact that he broke his leg three times in ten months persuaded Jack that his future was with cricket rather than football. Lancashire, I know, will be eternally thankful for that, because his influence at times of crisis made the difference between victory and defeat on many occasions.

Spreading the word

One country I have visited that you might not associate with cricket is Holland, but there is actually a lot of interest in the game out there. I once went to Amsterdam to give a talk to some Dutch umpires and I was taken to a restaurant where there were pictures on the walls of such stars as Liz Taylor, Richard Burton and Shirley Bassey, as well as that great Dutch footballer Johan Cruyff.

The owner must have seen me looking at the photographs and he said to me, 'I would like to have a big picture of Mr Dickie Bird.'

I said, 'I'll do my best to get one for you, but where are you going to put it? The walls seem full already.'

He replied, 'I am going to take Cruyff down and put you up there in his place.'

I said, 'What? You can't do that! He's one of the best footballers the world has ever seen.'

But he insisted, 'You are more important just now than him. We are promoting cricket and you are the best in your business. He comes down; you go up!'

He also presented me with some gin in a special container. It's years since, but I've still got it. I haven't touched it. You see, I don't really drink. I was warned by my father, 'If you want to be a successful sportsman, steer clear of women in nightclubs, keep off cigs, and don't drink.' I took that advice to heart. I never smoked and I drink only in moderation, usually red wine, which my doctor assures me is good for the circulation. So, I've been left with so many bottles that people have given me, and it seems such a waste. Why don't they present me with a box of chocolates? They'd soon go, I can tell you.

Mad dogs and Englishmen

Over the years, I've umpired a number of internationals in Sharjah, in the United Arab Emirates, but one visit there was almost the death of me – before I even got there. Everyone knows what a worrier I am, and on this occasion I was at panic stations. For several hours.

As is my custom, I arrived early in London for an evening flight. To while away the afternoon I popped into a café for a cup of tea, with all my luggage in tow. Time, I thought, to double-check that everything was in order. As I did so, it suddenly dawned on me that I'd left my passport at home. What was I to do? I contacted one or two people I thought could give me advice and they said the only thing they could suggest was to go to British Airways and explain the situation to them.

Usain Bolt would have struggled to get there quicker than me. But the people told me, 'You're booked on the evening flight, so if you can't produce a passport by then, you can't go. Simple as that.' Perhaps they could see how panic-stricken I was, because they added, as an afterthought, 'You could try the Passport Office, see what they can do, but you've not got much time.'

So, sweat pouring off me, I raced across London to the Passport Office. To my dismay, the queue was a mile long. In desperation I pushed my way to the front – you can, therefore, imagine some of the abuse that was thrown at me – and told the girl at the counter who I was, where I was going, what the problem was, and could I see the person in charge immediately, otherwise I was destined to miss my flight.

They were still playing hell in the queue behind me, but thankfully the head man appeared almost straight away and, even better, he was a very keen cricket fanatic. He said, 'Well, Dickie, if you can get a photograph of yourself pronto we'll process a passport for you.'

Luckily there was a tube station close at hand and it had one of those little booths where you can take your own picture. You could say it was a photo-finish. I hurried back to the Passport Office, still hauling my luggage around with me, and I was absolutely shattered. It felt like a ton weight by this time. I can't remember what the photographs looked like – I dread to think – but they must have been okay because I was given a replacement passport and I arrived at the airport in the nick of time.

So I ended up with two British passports!

It was an Arab businessman, Abdul Rahman Bukhatir, who pioneered cricket in the Arabian Gulf and the Asia Cup was his brainchild. He financed a magnificent stadium in Sharjah, the grass pitch alone costing £2 million.

I was asked to umpire the inaugural event in 1984, and from then on David Shepherd always went with me. I'll never forget that first time because Bukhatir asked me to take out some stumps. I contacted Duncan Fearnley, who provided all our stumps for the Test matches, and he let me have a full set. I was very relieved when I finally got there, I can tell you. Those stumps took some carrying in addition to my usual luggage.

You know how rain and bad light were always the bane of my umpiring life? No such problems in Sharjah. But it is the only place I have umpired where a sandstorm has stopped play. There was one match where I had to advise the players that I was taking them off the field as we could not see a thing because of all the sand that was being whipped up by a strong wind. Former Yorkshire and England all-rounder Richard

Hutton was playing in that game and I remember him shouting, as we all fled for the shelter of the pavilion, 'I can hear you, Bird, but I can't see you.'

People ask me how I coped with the heat out there. I tell them that you get used to it. In any case, it wasn't much different from the heat I experienced in other places, such as India, Pakistan, Sri Lanka, South Africa, the West Indies and Australia.

I liked India. It's not to everyone's taste, I know, but for me it is a wonderful country, full of mystique. There is surely no finer sight in the world than the Taj Mahal by moonlight. It has to be moonlight to get the full effect.

I have been back to Bombay in more recent times to do an advert for Coca-Cola. They dressed me up as a judge. I sat there, brought my gavel crashing down on to the table – and out flew a bottle of the popular drink. Not a great deal to it, really. Other than that, I had time to do a bit of sightseeing and I really enjoyed that trip very much. I've also been back to New Zealand, and if there is any place that compares with England it is New Zealand. But that's mainly because it is so similar in terms of climate.

All the countries I've mentioned have their own special appeal and I have had only good experiences wherever I've been. People ask me if I've ever fancied a visit to America, and I have to say no. After all, they don't really play cricket there, do they? I have stopped off at Los Angeles and San Francisco when I've been travelling to other parts of the world, but that's it.

Above left: A very young cricketer, pictured during my memorable years with Yorkshire.

Above right: Now wearing the Leicestershire sweater – a move I was to regret.

Right: Two of my greatest friends in cricket, Jack Birkenshaw and Don Wilson. Jack also played with me at Leicestershire as well as Yorkshire.

Bomb scare? What bomb scare? I am surrounded by excited spectators who had run on to the pitch during the dramatic interruption to the England v West Indies Test at Lord's in August 1973.

I watch full of admiration as West Indian captain Clive Lloyd strokes his way to a magnificent century in the World Cup final against Australia at Lord's in 1975 – the best one-day game I ever umpired.

Right: Viv Richards, who would bat at No 3 in my World XI selection, points out some spectator movement in front of the sightscreen during the 1976 Test at Trent Bridge.

Below: One electronic gadget of which I do approve – umpiring colleague Barrie Meyer and photographer Patrick Eagar (*centre*) join me in a demonstration of the light meter, which we introduced for the first time in the England v New Zealand Test at Lord's in 1978.

No need for me to raise the finger. Ian Botham clean-bowls Terry Alderman for a duck to clinch a remarkable victory in the fourth Test against the Australians at Edgbaston in 1981 – one of the most exciting Tests I have umpired.

For me the perfect bowling action from the best pace bowler I have ever had the pleasure of umpiring, as Dennis Lillee reaches delivery stride in the Centenary Test between England and Australia in 1980, with Geoff Boycott at the non-striker's end.

Celebration time for one of the game's biggest characters, Ian Botham, after his match-winning role in England's victory over Australia at Edgbaston in 1981. Congratulating him are one of the best captains, Mike Brearley, and one of England's most prolific opening batsmen, my ex-Barnsley colleague Geoff Boycott.

It is the World Cup clash between England and Pakistan at Old Trafford in 1983 and another opportunity for me to see at close hand the wonderful technique of Abdul Qadir, who I regard as the best spin bowler of my era.

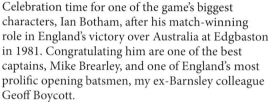

South African Barry Richards, the best batsman I have seen, in elegant action for Hampshire against Middlesex in 1968.

It's the way I tell 'em! Her Majesty the Queen is obviously amused by something I said at the England v New Zealand Test at Lord's in June 1986 – and Richard Hadlee appears to think it was absolutely hilarious! England captain Mike Gatting is to my left.

Diana, Princess of Wales, gets a rare glimpse of an umpire's thermal underwear on a chilly occasion at Bristol, where Gloucestershire were entertaining Somerset in 1989.

In Sharjah Stadium, United Arab Emirates, with long-time colleague David Shepherd and John Holder in 1993.

There's the problem! I point an accusing finger towards the hospitality suite at Old Trafford as the sun's reflection from the windows brings play to a halt during the fourth Test between England and the West Indies in 1995.

Courtney Walsh is obviously impressed by my hokey-cokey demonstration while signalling a leg bye in that same game.

The crying game! Time for an emotional tear or two as the members stand to applaud me on my way down the steps at Lord's on the first day of my final Test, in June 1996, when India were England's opponents.

It's now too late; my globe-trotting has come to an end. I've been all over the world and loved every minute, but now, at the age of 80, I've got to the stage where it's all a bit too much for me. I don't want the hassle of airports.

There's no place like home

These days I like to book myself in at the Crown at Scarborough and take it easy. I go there every Christmas and stay right into the New Year. There is a health club at the hotel that I can use for my general exercises, plus a sauna and a swimming pool. I also wrap myself up warm and go walking right at the edge of the sea, round both the bays, north and south, and it's really beautiful, especially on a cold, crisp, sunny morning.

If I'm feeling peckish I can have a lovely meal at Angelo's Italian restaurant – Tuscany, in St Nicholas Street – although I have to confess I usually opt for fresh mussels, lobster or a fish dish rather than anything continental. Plus, of course, a nice glass of red wine.

In the summer I never miss the Scarborough Cricket Festival. I've always said that Lord's is the finest ground in the world, but of the out grounds Scarborough takes some beating, and you see some great cricket there as well.

It provides a wonderful setting for cricket, with the cliffs overlooking the glorious North Bay nearby, although they are not visible to spectators. It was here that Bill Bowes, one of the best bowlers Yorkshire and England have ever had, was so humorously misquoted when covering a match for the

Yorkshire Evening Post after he had retired from playing. He was faced with the usual problem of telephoning his reports from the ground to the sports desk back in Leeds, and during one Festival Week he sent the following piece of copy: 'After a quiet spell, Parfitt went down the wicket to Illingworth and edged him over the slips and into the deep for three.'

Unfortunately, the young lady on copy-taking duty that day had no interest whatsoever in cricket, and was therefore in an east-coast fog when it came to the terminology of the game. She was, however, fairly well acquainted with the seaside resort itself. So, struggling to overcome the additional problems posed by a bad line, she typed out, 'After a quiet spell, Parfitt went down the wicket to Illingworth and edged him over the cliffs and into the deepest parts of the sea.'

One of the most amazing feats at Scarborough is to hit the ball over the towering buildings at the Trafalgar Square End, and only two batsmen in the history of county cricket have managed it. One was a chap called Charles 'Buns' Thornton, the father figure of the festival itself. I am told that after Thornton had cleared the buildings in 1886 word got round that his big hit had landed in Trafalgar Square, and a lady of his acquaintance asked, 'Were you playing at Lord's or The Oval?'

The other fellow to hit such a massive six was Cec Pepper. He achieved the feat in the first festival after the Second World War, striking Eric Hollies, the Warwickshire leg-spinner, way over the roof-tops. He did so after being challenged to attempt it by Arthur Wood, the bouncy Yorkshire wicketkeeper, largely because he never turned his back on a reasonable bet.

I have to admit that sometimes, if you go to Scarborough for a county match at the beginning of May, it does blow bitterly cold off the North Sea and thermals are advised, but give me the east coast of Yorkshire – Scarborough, Ravenscar, Whitby, Robin Hood's Bay, Filey, Bridlington – any day. You can also move inland to find some of the most beautiful scenery and villages you could wish to see in the Yorkshire Dales and on the North Yorkshire Moors. You simply can't beat that part of the world. I would like it a bit warmer, but then we'd lose that glorious greenery. You can never have everything. So I'm satisfied, happy and thankful for what we've got in God's own county.

6

HOME-TOWN BOY

More than sixty years ago three young cricketers from mining families in the South Yorkshire coalfield sat on the balcony of their local club wondering what life had in store for them.

Today, not only have all three reached the top of their different professions, but one of them is a knight of the realm, one has an OBE and the other has both the MBE and the OBE.

It sounds like a wonderfully inspiring work of fiction. Not so. It is fact. I know, because I am one of the three. The other two are Sir Michael Parkinson and Geoffrey Boycott.

I can picture us now, there on the balcony of the marvellous old pavilion at Barnsley's Shaw Lane ground, gazing out over the cricket field through the hazy sunshine to the town beyond and Parky saying, 'I wonder what the future holds for us?'

In 2012 the three of us were back together at Shaw Lane for the first time since those playing days as Barnsley Cricket Club celebrated its 150th anniversary. We had previously returned separately and in pairs, but never as a threesome, so it was really special for us, and we reminisced, naturally, about our own balcony scene. And we reflected, with a great deal of pride, on what we had achieved. Boycott, a cricketing run machine who played with distinction for both county and country; Parkinson, respected journalist, TV presenter and chat-show host; and Dickie Bird, county cricketer with Yorkshire and Leicester, and Test and World Cup umpire.

It's an amazing triple rags-to-riches story. You really couldn't make it up, could you? If you did, they probably wouldn't believe you.

Parky and I have remained very, very close friends, and he has done so much for me, helping in so many ways. I've lots to be thankful to him for. He has come up to Yorkshire many a time to do some promotion for my foundation and he has never charged a ha'penny. I still ring him if I want help or advice and he rings me. That's what friends do, isn't it? I keep telling him he's no spring chicken – but then neither am I. Two old codgers together, that's us.

People sometimes wonder why I never appeared on Parky's television show. It was said that he had interviewed everybody worthwhile except for two people, Frank Sinatra and Dickie Bird. I don't know what made him miss out on Frank, but with me I think it was because we are such close friends. It just wouldn't have seemed right, somehow. It would, however, have been an honour, because I thought he was the best chat-show host of them all.

A Barnsley fan – through thick and thin

When it comes to football, I make sure to give Parky a bit of stick now and again because I still support my home-town club, while he can be seen regularly at the Madejski Stadium cheering on Reading, who won promotion back to the Premiership last year.

One of the best days of my life was when I sat with Michael, complete with red scarf draped round his shoulders, in the old wooden West Stand at Oakwell on Saturday, 26 April 1997, and watched Barnsley beat Bradford City 2–0 to clinch promotion to the Premier League for the first time in their 110-year history.

We sat there side by side, Parky and I, two Barnsley lads, tears in our eyes, and proud as punch. I had a real lump in my throat at the end of that game, as fans swarmed all over the pitch and the players came back out to receive the applause. Everyone joined in singing 'You'll Never Walk Alone', on loan from Anfield, as well as the chorus that had been composed by the fans themselves, 'It's Just Like Watching Brazil'.

I was really pleased for all those fans, especially the 2,000 or so who had followed the team all over the country, even when they were bottom of the old Fourth Division and struggling to stay in the Football League. I dearly hoped that there were still a few of them present on that memorable day when top-flight football came to town. There had been great games, great players, great moments, but nothing to match that afternoon.

I have to say, though, that, for me, Barnsley's best player is from a different era. I go back to the days when I used to go to Oakwell with my dad, sit on his shoulders so that I could see better, and thrill at the performances of a Scottish winger called Johnny Kelly, who was pure magic. Kelly loved nothing better than to take on a full-back, beat him, then turn and beat him again. It was a joy to watch. His ability on the ball was absolutely marvellous. What an entertainer!

Then there was a pocket-sized centre-forward called Cec McCormack, who used to down a few pints in the White Hart pub in Peel Square before a match and then go out and score a hatful of goals – five in one game. In fact, he still holds the club record for the number of goals scored in a season. An exceptional player. A big Irish lad, Eddie McMorran, also springs to mind.

Barnsley were in the Premiership for only one season, but it made me really chuffed to be a fan of this grand club. It was a really special time. I'd like to see us back up there, although I'm not sure I'll live long enough to see that.

I do believe that Mike feels the same. You see, I'm sure that he still supports Barnsley deep down, but he has to watch Reading because he lives nearby and is a big mate of the chairman.

While playing in the Premiership is the pinnacle of the club's achievements, Barnsley have also won the FA Cup – but that was way before even my time. It came in 1912, the same year that saw the sinking of the apparently unsinkable *Titanic*. Mind you, I thought we were going to win it again in 2008 when we beat Premiership giants Liverpool and Chelsea on the way to the semi-finals.

I had kept telling people that if Liverpool manager Rafael Benitez decided that it would be an easy afternoon for his side and consequently rested some of his star players, it would be a massive mistake and Barnsley would win at Anfield. Well,

Benitez did muck about with the team. Among the players he left out was their inspirational captain, Steven Gerrard, and, as I had predicted, Barnsley pulled off the shock of the day.

Then, after beating Chelsea 1–0 at Oakwell, it was on to the new Wembley for a semi-final clash with Cardiff City. In the first half our big centre-forward, Kayode Odejayi, who had headed a brilliant winner against Chelsea, was put through with only the goalkeeper to beat. He had the goal at his mercy; it seemed harder to miss than score. But miss he did, and Cardiff eventually won their way through to the final, where they were beaten by Portsmouth. I am convinced to this day that had Odejayi scored, we would have gone on to win not only that game but the final as well, and so claim the famous old trophy for the second time in the club's history.

Through the years I have received invitations from many of the top clubs, including Manchester United, to attend their games, but I much prefer to go to Oakwell. I love going down there on match days, chatting with the supporters and meeting so many old friends, who have also been going there for donkey's years. That's what it's all about, as far as I am concerned – supporting the team of the place where you were born and bred. I have no time for people who support teams from miles away simply because they are successful. I do sometimes wonder, for example, how many Manchester United fans actually come from Manchester.

Things have not been going too well at Oakwell in recent years, but the fans around me in the West Stand are still very passionate in their support. They still play merry hell with the referee. They go berserk if a decision is given against the Reds. They see only one side of any incident. Rose-tinted glasses spring to mind. If a foul is given against us it's always the wrong decision, even if someone in a red shirt has kicked one of the opposing team's players into the second row of the stand. And it's never a penalty, is it? Not when it's awarded against us. My fellow West-Standers also go mad when we score, jumping up and down and shouting and cheering and clapping.

As for me, I just keep quiet. I can't afford to get too excited. It might send my blood pressure soaring – or bring on another stroke. So I just sit there, suffering mostly, but occasionally smiling in quiet satisfaction. You've got to remember that I have spent much of my life as a totally impartial umpire.

The seat next to me used to be occupied by a grand old man called Frank Moore, who was in his nineties and had supported the team all his life. Sadly he is no longer with us, but I remember him, frail as he was, travelling on one of the coaches at the age of 95 when the Reds played in the Championship play-off final against Ipswich Town at the old Wembley Stadium. He wouldn't have missed it for the world.

It's not quite the same these days, I have to admit. I can't connect with the players like I used to do. I can go back into history and so many names spring to mind of players who lived in and around the town and were therefore part of the community. You could nip into Woolworth's in the town centre and have a cup of coffee with them. Happy days.

Some of them even worked down one of the many pits that were dotted around the area. I remember a player called

Johnny Logan, who lived near me at Smithies. He used to do a shift down the pit early Saturday morning and then play for the Reds in the afternoon. You could see him coming home in his muck and I would say to him, 'All the best this afternoon, Mr Logan,' and he would go out and play a blinder after six days spent in the bowels of the earth, hewing coal. And there were others like him, such as Frank Bokas and Duncan Sharp.

Duncan was a very shy person off the field, but a lion on it. No one dared mess with him. He was a centre-half of the old school, all right. But the best centre-half I've seen play for Barnsley was George Spruce, an elegant footballer in the Bobby Moore mould – an excellent reader of the game who always seemed to have so much time to display his defensive skills.

The names roll off the tongue: outside-right Gavin Smith, inside-right Jimmy Baxter, Irish international wing-half Danny Blanchflower, still learning his trade at Oakwell but even then a great talent. He wasn't one for coaching. He used to tell Bob Shotton, the trainer, that he would work out his own ideas how to play and he would plot moves on the training ground with his inside-forward partner Steve Griffiths.

Gordon Pallister was probably the best left-back the club has had, although he was given a bit of a run-around by the legendary Stanley Matthews in an FA Cup tie at Oakwell in the 1948–49 season. After my retirement, I was speaking at a dinner with Stan Mortensen, the other half of that famous combination which was so successful for Blackpool, and we both recalled the occasion. Mortensen described how Pallister kept backing away from Matthews until he was almost in with the crowd on the Spion Kop, and was helpless to prevent the great man putting in a cross, which Mortensen converted for what turned out to be the only goal of the game.

After we had shared the memory, Mortensen confided to me, 'Do you know, Dickie, I mis-hit my shot. It went in off my pad.' But did he care? Not bloomin' likely. It doesn't matter how it ends up in the back of the net, you see.

I was once told that Stanley Matthews had become friendly with a well-known Barnsley butcher called Albert Hirst, who was famous for his pork pies. Apparently, whenever he was playing for Blackpool in a game within striking distance of Barnsley, Stanley would pop in for one of the pies. He couldn't resist them. I recently bumped into Albert's son when I was doing a presentation at Barnsley YMCA and he confirmed that it was absolutely true. Would you credit it – fitness fanatic Matthews gorging on a Barnsley pork pie!

My memory is sadly not what it once was, but do you know I can go through the England team of those days without pausing for breath: Frank Swift in goal; Laurie Scott and George Hardwick full-backs; Frank Soo right-half, centre-half Neil Franklin, left-half Joe Mercer; outside-right Stanley Matthews, inside-left Wilf Mannion, centre-forward Tommy Lawton, inside-right Raich Carter, outside-left Tom Finney.

I can remember all these names from the past; I can tick off players from more than sixty years ago, but ask me to name a few of the current Barnsley side and I'm struggling. Part of the problem is that the team is constantly changing. Loan players come and go; even the more permanent signings don't seem to stick around too long; and there is no one of outstanding skill or personality.

On top of all this, the players no longer mingle freely with the supporters during the rest of the week. Very few actually live in the area, and even then you would not be likely to bump into them in Woolworth's – even if that establishment still existed.

Yet I still get a real lift, feel great pride, in watching my team do well, and the affinity is so strong that I stick with them in the bad times. There have been quite a few of those, but when you come through them together it brings a warm glow of satisfaction and well-being. I couldn't experience that with any other club, no matter how mighty and successful.

Even when I was umpiring Test matches all over the world I was on edge on the Saturday until I found out how Barnsley had got on back home.

Home is where the heart is

On retirement I could have gone and lived a life of comparative luxury in a country retreat, a London apartment, or even abroad. But I stayed in Barnsley, as I have always done.

Some people may find that strange. I suppose most of them think of Barnsley as a typical mining town – dirty and dowdy, surrounded by slag heaps and populated by families made up of a flat-capped father, a mother with curlers in her hair and a cigarette in her mouth, umpteen kids and pet whippets. Maybe in my young days that was not too far from the truth. But not any more. The slag heaps have been covered with grass and trees, lakes have been reclaimed and cultivated, and within easy reach there is some of the loveliest scenery. For example, I can look out of my cottage window and see the Pennines in the near distance. You could hardly ask for a better view.

I have travelled all around the world, but I have always looked forward to coming back. It feels marvellous to walk up my pathway, unlock the door, throw my gear into the kitchen, put the kettle on and slump in my favourite armchair with a nice cup of strong Yorkshire tea. I look around me at all the familiar, comfortable things, and I think, thankfully, There, I'm home.

As for the people, well, what can I say? They are the salt of the earth, honest and straight as a die. They will never say anything behind your back. If they have any criticism, it is to your face – and I've had some of that, I can tell you.

A former editor of the local newspaper once said that people in the town didn't just call a spade a spade, they called it a bloody shovel. And that sums them up perfectly. But if you are in trouble, there is always a helping hand. The pits may all have gone – and there is no doubt that the running-down of the mining industry caused a lot of anger and resentment, not to mention severe unemployment and family problems – yet the people have not changed. They are still as warm-hearted as ever and I have a lot of time for them.

When I go into the village or nip into town, people greet me with 'Good old Dickie', or 'Look out, here's Dickie with his bags of shopping', or 'Ey up, Dickie, how's things?' It's just great to be among friends like that, to feel wanted. This is a good little town. I enjoy the company of its people. I enjoy meeting up with them and chatting – arguing at times – about cricket, football, or whatever takes their fancy.

Just one small example of what I mean. The story involves a local Methodist minister, Derek Hinchliffe, Barnsley-born and a great follower and supporter of cricket. This particular Sunday morning I had been watching a Test match on the telly before going to Staincross Methodist Church. Derek was taking the service and the time came for us to receive Holy Communion. When I went up and he stood in front of me to give me the bread and wine, I whispered to him, 'I think you'd better say a prayer for Pakistan, Derek.'

He paused, looked at me and then, thinking no doubt that there had been some catastrophe out there that he hadn't heard about, whispered back, 'Why's that, then, Dickie?'

'Because,' I informed him, 'they're seventy-six for six.'

One of his sons told the story at Derek's funeral last year.

I have never moved away from Barnsley, and I never will. This is where I was born. This is where I have lived my life. And this is where, like Derek, I will rest when I die.

A fine figure of a man

When that day comes there will be something for people to remember me by – my statue, which was erected on 30 June 2009, very near the spot where I was born.

I am pleased to say that the six-foot bronze statue was created by a Barnsley man, Graham Ibbeson, and he did a great job. I had to sit for him, of course, finger poised in the appropriate position. Those sittings took place at Barnsley College and I was amazed how Graham built up the work, first with wires, then putting wax on, taking it off and starting all over again. It is quite a long and complicated process. But the end result is magnificent. He really does have a special gift.

I had been very impressed with other statues he had done, particularly the dual one of Laurel and Hardy at Ulverston, Cumbria, which is Stan Laurel's home town. He is also responsible for the famous figure of Eric Morecambe, which was unveiled by Her Majesty the Queen. That stands in the seaside town from which he took his name.

It was an unforgettable day when Prince Charles came to see my statue in Barnsley early in 2012. He thought it was a very good likeness of me – although he wasn't too sure about the 'that's out' finger. He seemed to think it was the wrong way round. Not so. But maybe it is at slightly the wrong angle, as other people have pointed out. The plinth could be higher, too. As it stands, it can result in rather unsavoury items, which I am loath to describe in detail, being draped over the Bird digit! Students from the college just across the road are the chief suspects.

It seems that people come from all over the world to see my statue. When the Australians were at Headingley a couple of years ago a busload of their supporters wanted to know how to get to Barnsley so that they could take a look, and there have been people on a visit from India who have made a special trip to the town for that same purpose.

They have even come from Lancashire! They get up trips to come to Barnsley market, which is renowned in the north of England, and these days a little detour to see the Dickie Bird statue is always on the itinerary. It really does make me feel so proud. I mean to say, not many people can boast that they have a statue of themselves in their home town – at least not while they are alive. They usually erect a statue in someone's memory when they are dead!

Incidentally, the statue was nothing to do with Barnsley Council, as many people seem to think. Money for its erection came from business people from Leeds, Leicester and Shef-field, as well as Barnsley. What the Council did was give permission for it to be sited on that particular spot. And I am grateful to them for that.

I have also been given the Freedom of the Borough of Barns-ley. It is an honour that means more to me than people realise. To be recognised in that way by your home town is something very special. I can hardly believe it. It's really amazing. A tre-mendous honour.

A lot of people have asked me what having the Freedom of the Borough entails. What does it entitle you to do? I tell them, and I'm telling you, it means that I could go to a sheep farmer, get a herd of sheep, walk them up the main street in Barnsley to the grass in front of the Town Hall and let them graze there. Honestly. I haven't tried it yet, although one or two have suggested that I should. I am also expected to be at civic receptions and visits of royalty – and I can inspect the local jail. I haven't done that, either.

It's been an honour

Other awards to have come my way include honorary life memberships of Yorkshire CCC, Leicestershire CCC, Cambridge University CC, the MCC and Barnsley FC; and honorary doctorates at Sheffield Hallam, Leeds and Huddersfield universities.

It was a terrible day when I was due to receive my doctorate at Sheffield. Heavy snow was posing all kinds of problems on the roads. I managed to make it as far as Worsbrough Bridge, just south of Barnsley, but could go no further, so treacherous were the conditions. I tried to phone to explain my plight but I couldn't get through. The people at the university even sent out a search party, but that got stuck at the Sheffield end. I don't know whether or not they sent out a search party to look for the search party, but the ceremony was eventually switched from morning to afternoon and some people did manage to get there. Unfortunately it was 'snow' use to me – I had to go at a later date.

My most recent award came last October when I was made the first honorary life member of the ECB Association of Cricket Officials and I was doubly delighted to receive the award from my old friend Sir Michael Parkinson.

I travelled down to Lord's for the presentation, which was made at the organisation's national conference at Lord's. The citation said it was for an outstanding contribution to officiating over many years. It was very kind of them to make me a life member and I was thrilled to accept. There were three hundred or so club umpires and scorers present and I was near to tears when they gave me a lengthy standing ovation.

To complete a perfect day, to raise money for my foundation, they auctioned a signed picture of me walking down the steps at Lord's for my final Test match.

Talking of awards, not many people are aware that I was once the recipient of the man-of-the-match award in a final at Lord's. It was in 1984 when Clive Radley and Paul Downton put on a fifth-wicket stand which swung the match Middlesex's way, John Emburey scoring the winning run off the last ball in a thrilling finish to clinch the NatWest Trophy.

At the end of the game I went up to receive my umpire's medal and looked at it proudly. But then it struck me that there was something rather odd about it. My name wasn't on it. But Clive Radley's was. Meanwhile Radders, with whom I had built up a very close friendship through the years, was going bananas in the dressing room, having realised that he had my umpire's medal instead of his man-of-the-match award.

We did a swap, of course, but it still does not alter the fact that I remain the only umpire to have been presented with a man-of-the-match award at a Lord's final.

7

HOW IT ALL STARTED

Lord's has always been like a second home to me as an umpire. But what about my first? Where and when did it all start?

Well, do you know, I haven't a clue as to what happened in the first five or six years of my life. I can't remember anything at all. It's a complete blank. What is it with memory?

My first recollection is being taken to the Sunday school at the Elim Pentecostal Church in Barnsley. Unfortunately, it is no longer there. It has been knocked down, in common with many other churches of that time. Most of those that remain have been turned into carpet warehouses or car showrooms. And I find that really sad.

Sunday was also the day we visited my mother's sister. I remember having sandwiches for tea before going to the evening service. I always ended up being chased down Summer Lane by Auntie Sarah because never a week went by without me getting up to some sort of mischief, and she gave me a right rollicking when she caught me, I can tell you!

I was one of three children. I had two sisters, Sylvia and Marjorie. Sylvia grew up to be one of the most Christian people I've ever known. Not a drop of the demon drink went to her lips nor a cigarette to her mouth and she travelled all over the county as a lay preacher. I have nothing but warm memories of a wonderful woman.

Even now I can't stop the tears coming to my eyes when I think of her, because she died suddenly from a brain haemorrhage at the age of 41. You have moments of great triumph in life. And times of great tragedy. This was one of the latter. My mother felt it most of all. She could not come to terms with the fact that she was still alive and her daughter had been taken from her at such a young age, especially when she had served God with so much distinction.

Mother always said that the Good Lord must have called her home for a purpose, but it was still hard on her. It came as such a big shock and she never really recovered, bless her. It's difficult to believe, but Sylvia would have been in her seventies now. And I still miss her.

She would have been so proud of her son, Graham, who has done very well for himself after gaining an honours degree in mathematics at Bristol University.

Thankfully Marjorie is still with us – she's been a great help to me through the years – and then there's her daughter, Rachel. But that's all the family I have. And while there have been times in my life when I've found it a lonely existence living as a bachelor, I find it even more so at the age of 80, with no one to share my lovely White Rose Cottage and that magnificent view. Yet there is comfort, in that the cottage provides a link with the religion of my childhood days. The great preacher John Wesley stayed there during one of his visits to Staincross and actually slept in the bedroom I now occupy.

Songs of Praise

My Christian faith has played a big part in my life from my earliest days. Now I go to the Methodist church in Staincross as often as I can. Two churches in the village joined together twelve years ago and there was great excitement when the new church building was opened by a former president of the Methodist Conference, the Reverend Inderjit Bhogal. The members had performed miracles to raise £650,000 in five years and it was a great example of what faith – and prayer – can do.

Before that I attended the old Barnsley Road Methodist Church, where I was featured on the BBC television programme *Songs of Praise*. My great friend Keith Lodge is a local preacher who was also sports editor of the *Barnsley Chronicle*, and covered the whole of my career. He sat alongside me with his wife, Pat, as we sang 'Rejoice, the Lord is King'. Then Marjorie and I looked back over our early life. My sister reminded me that I was always the apple of my dad's eye, and I recalled going to Sunday school and singing choruses such as 'What a Friend We Have in Jesus', clapping along to the rhythm. It was a delight to listen to Huddersfield Choral Society's youth choir singing that same chorus in the North Gawber Colliery pit yard in the centre of the village, with the winding gear as a backdrop.

Two guests were members of Christians in Sport: former England pace bowler Devon Malcolm and the Reverend

Andrew Wingfield Digby, or 'Wiggers-Diggers' as I always knew him. He was a director of the movement, and lived out his faith in cricket.

I remember Andrew playing against Leicestershire in 1975, when he edged one to wicketkeeper Roger Tolchard, who took a good catch.

'Shit!' spluttered Andrew.

'I beg your pardon,' said Roger. 'It is true, isn't it, that you're going to be a vicar?'

'Yes,' replied Andrew.

'Well then, you can't use language like that.'

'You should have heard what I used to say,' retorted Andrew.

Andrew went on to become chaplain of the England team, but just after Ray Illingworth had been appointed team manager, Andrew took a call on his mobile from a journalist asking if he had anything to say about being sacked. Andrew told him he didn't know what he was talking about. Then on the Monday morning of the first Test at Trent Bridge, Garry Richardson rang from Radio Four. 'Could you give us a comment on why you've been sacked by Ray Illingworth?' Obviously he couldn't because he still had no idea what was going on.

On the way to his office he was caught up in some traffic and a chap in an adjacent car wound down his window and asked, 'Hey, are you Andrew Wingfield Digby?' Andrew, thinking he had found fame at last, admitted that he was the very same. The guy exclaimed, 'Thought so. Your picture's in the *Sun* next to a headline which says, "Knickers to the Vicar."'

It turned out that some members of the press had added two and two together and made five, but the matter was eventually sorted to the mutual satisfaction of all concerned.

Andrew was brought up in the church but did not become a true Christian until he worked with the Reverend David Sheppard at a family centre in Canning Town in the time between leaving school and going to college. Sheppard is the England cricketer who went on to become the Bishop of Liverpool, and it was a great privilege for me to go and talk to him on *Songs of Praise*.

I asked him if there was anything he had been able to take from cricket that had helped him in the church, and he told me, 'Two things, Dickie. Firstly, you need great powers of concentration in order to build an innings and make a lot of runs; you have to shut everything else out. I believe that ability has helped me in my church work. Secondly, cricket is very much a team game, and I have found that experience very valuable, as I have had to enter into a lot of partnerships in my work and life as a bishop.'

When David Sheppard was playing for England, a certain Freddie Trueman was not too impressed with his slip-catching prowess, and after seeing another chance put down he strolled over and muttered, 'I did think, Reverend, that when you, of all people, put yer 'ands together, you'd mek it stick.'

On the television programme, that Sheppard interview was followed by choristers from Liverpool Cathedral singing 'O Jesus, I Have Promised', and two choristers from Worcester Cathedral were also featured when I paid a nostalgic visit back there. I always used to go to the cathedral when I played and umpired at Worcestershire's New Road ground, which is one of the most picturesque in the world, with a wonderful view looking through the trees to the cathedral and the River Severn.

A gospel group called Black Voices sang 'Light at the End of the Tunnel', the congregation at Barnsley Road belted out 'I Know that My Redeemer Lives', a young boy soprano sang 'When I Needed a Neighbour', and the programme closed with the famous Grimethorpe Colliery Band playing one of my favourite hymns, 'The Day Thou Gavest, Lord, is Ended.'

It was a joy for me to appear in that programme. It was one way of expressing my thanks to the Good Lord for the wonderful career that he had given me.

As well as here in England, I always made a point during my travels abroad of seeking out a place of worship. I remember on one particular occasion I went to a Methodist church in Barbados and sat right at the back. I thought I hadn't been noticed, but then the preacher stood up.

'Brothers and sisters,' he said, 'we have a great surprise for you today.'

An expectant 'ooooh' echoed round the church.

'Yes, brothers and sisters, we have in our midst Mr Dickie Bird, the Test umpire from England.'

The church erupted and the congregation stood and clapped and cheered excitedly. After the service I couldn't get away. Everyone wanted to talk to me and shake my hand. It was a great feeling. There I was, thousands of miles away from home, yet among so many friends. That is what belonging to a church family does for you, and I do honestly believe that my faith has helped me through many dark times in my life.

Back to the beginning

But I'm jumping ahead of myself, aren't I? It's that memory thing again. Recollect one thing and it sets off a chain reaction. Before you know it you've leaped halfway across the world.

So, where to start? At the beginning might be the very best place, I suppose.

I was born on 19 April 1933 in a two-up-two-down terraced house in Church Lane, in the centre of Barnsley. We had no bathroom. We had a tub that we used to take down from the back of the door and fill with water in front of the fire – and an outside toilet. A little later we really went up in the world. We moved to a house on the New Lodge Estate at Smithies, on the outskirts of Barnsley, which had an extra bedroom and a 'proper' bathroom.

I was christened Harold Dennis Bird, but from a very early age I was known as Dickie. I didn't like it at first – it sounded like a bit of a mickey-take – but I soon accepted it, and now that's how I am known all around the round.

The war years are just a blur to me. The only thing about them I can remember is hiding under the desks at school whenever the siren sounded. But Barnsley escaped relatively unscathed by the bombing; it was Sheffield which was slated, and that probably explains why that dreadful time passed me by. Plus the fact, of course, that my dad was commissioned to work down the pit rather than being called up to fight.

But a miner's life was very hard. My father worked down the pit from the age of 13 and retired at 65. He had dust in the lungs and lived only five more years after that. He died in 1969. He never did see too much of life or the outside world. He never went abroad and most of his working life was stuck below the ground. Sometimes the seam would be just eighteen inches high. When he crawled through, his trousers sometimes got caught and he'd carry on without them.

In those days miners had no automatic tools or conveyor belts to take away the coal. They had to hack it out with picks and throw it into tubs, which they then had to push to the bottom of the shaft – sometimes more than a mile away.

Yet no matter how tired he was on coming home from the pit after the day shift, Dad used to spend hours playing football and cricket with me. He played football himself for Barnsley YMCA, who won the Yorkshire YMCA Trophy, and I've still got his medal.

Happy schooldays

Times were hard, as you can imagine, but my parents always made sure there was sufficient food on the table for all of us. I am sure they sacrificed a lot to make that possible. And my schooldays, I have to say, were some of the happiest days of my life. Not that I was particularly bright academically, but I lived and breathed football and cricket, and there was plenty of scope for both sports at the two schools I attended, although at Burton Road Primary there were no facilities to speak of. We didn't have a cricket pitch. Not even a football pitch. All our games were played in the playground with a tennis ball or a sponge ball.

That was when I first came across Tommy 'Tucker' Taylor, who went on to play football for Barnsley, Manchester United and England. Every day in winter we used to play football on a rough piece of ground until it was dark and in the summer we would play cricket. There were stones and broken glass and the home-made ball flew off at alarming angles, but it was our Headingley, and we spent many happy hours there. It was certainly ideal practice for later years when I had to face up to the likes of Frank Tyson and Brian Statham.

I also played football in the same school team as Tommy at Raley Secondary School, me at inside-right and Tommy at centre-forward. It was there that his talent really started to blossom, and I'll never forget the day he was left out by the master in charge, Arthur 'Pop' Hudson, because he didn't have a proper pair of football boots. He turned up in clogs. Nevertheless, Pop did so much for both of us over the years, training with us, coaching us and encouraging us.

Tommy came from a tragic family. His father, a coal-miner like mine, went blind, and his mother died of cancer. Then, of course, as you will all know, Tommy himself was killed in the Manchester United air crash at Munich in 1958.

The school had no cricket pitch, all our games being played on the flattest part of the football field. Needless to say, it wasn't a particularly good strip on which to bat!

I do think, though, that it taught us how to deal with difficult conditions and to become mentally strong. It was a really good grounding and Raley produced some fine sportsmen over the years. Sadly the school is no longer there. And, to our shame, many of the school playing fields, not only in Barnsley but countrywide, are no longer there, either.

During the dinner-time period at Raley, Pop and another of the teachers, Harold Rushforth, gave us batting practice on the asphalt playground. They put pennies instead of bails on top of the stumps and if we knocked them off we were allowed to keep them. What an incentive to bowl straight!

Rushy was also in charge of the Barnsley boys' team. I was in and out of that side, because he said I was too small. How daft was that? But that was the way of schoolboy football in those days. If you were a big strapping lad and loved to get stuck in, then you were virtually assured of a place in the side. The little 'uns were always overlooked, no matter how much talent they had.

I mentioned Tom Finney a little earlier. Did you know that he was never recognised at schoolboy representative level because they said he was too small?

Tommy Taylor was tall, strong and well-built, so he was a shoo-in for the Barnsley boys' team. But he had the class to go with the physique. He was lightning fast, good on the ball and quite brilliant in the air. I used to chip the ball to him and he would leap to head it. I can just picture him now. Even in those days, he had a remarkable ability to hang in the air until the ball reached him and then – bang! – it would fly like a rocket into the back of the net. Or it would have done if we'd had a net! What a talent. Incredible. He was, without doubt, the best header of a ball I have ever seen – and that includes Tommy Lawton, who readers of my age will remember with equal reverence.

Ken Taylor, who played cricket with me at Yorkshire and was Huddersfield Town's centre-half for years, played against Tommy when my old mate was with Manchester United, and he said he was the best centre-forward he had ever come up against.

And yet, do you know what Harold Rushforth did? He played Tommy at left-back in the town team. I couldn't believe it. Neither could my dad. You know what fathers are like. He and Tommy's dad, Charlie, were not only workmates, they were also pals, and they used to have a pint together at the Royal Arms. I remember him shouting out, 'Tha's no idea, Rushy! Tha knows nowt at all abart football.'

Maybe that was a bit harsh. But Tommy, as we all expected, went on to make a name for himself at centre-forward, not full-back. He signed first of all for Barnsley, then moved to Manchester United and played nineteen times for his country, scoring sixteen goals. That was an amazing ratio, especially for his age. It was a big loss to football when he died so tragically and so young. He was very, very special. I can't help wondering what he might have achieved had he gone on to have a full career in the game – or what he would have been worth, had he been around today.

I feel privileged to have grown up with Tommy, and I take some pride in the fact that I helped in his early development in some small way.

A few years ago I was extremely honoured to be asked to unveil a plaque to Tommy on the house where he had stayed in digs as a young Manchester United player. I was invited to perform the ceremony because I had been his friend at school. At the same time Sir Bobby Charlton unveiled a plaque to Duncan Edwards, another of the Busby Babes who had been killed at Munich, at a house just around the corner.

Bobby had a lump in his throat when he performed the ceremony, because he was such a close friend of Duncan's. If you remember, Bobby at first said that he would never play again after surviving Munich. He couldn't face it after losing so many of his team-mates. Thankfully, he did play again and was one of England's greatest ever. But he never really got over Munich. It has haunted him for the rest of his life. He told me that Edwards was the finest footballer he had ever seen and, again, we can only speculate as to how great he could have been.

When cricket and football clash

I mentioned Ken Taylor just now and he is one of that select number who have played both cricket and football at the top level. It is well-nigh impossible to combine the two sports in this day and age and it has never been easy, as was demonstrated one day when I was playing for Yorkshire, just before the start of the soccer season.

Ken and I were padded up, ready to go out and open the innings, when who should storm into the dressing room but

Bill Shankly, who was manager of Huddersfield Town at the time.

He yelled at Ken, 'What do you think you're doing?'

To which Ken replied, 'I'm just about to go out and bat for Yorkshire.'

'Oh, no, you're not! Get those pads off. You should be back training with us.'

Just at that moment Yorkshire captain Brian Sellers popped his head round the door. 'What the hell's going on?' he blasted.

Cue heated argument between two people who were very rarely known to leave the last word to anyone, but in the end it was Shanks who gave way and Ken duly went out to bat.

Sellers was a real disciplinarian and there is a story told of Arthur Booth, a spin bowler who took 100 wickets in a season just after the war and finished top of the English bowling averages, yet remarkably played only that one season for Yorkshire, although he later served the county as a very good coach.

Arthur was stood talking to the crowd, hands in his pockets, while fielding on the edge of the boundary at Headingley, when one wag said to him, 'Better look out, Arthur, he's watching thee, tha knows.'

'Who's watching me?' asked Arthur.

'Sellers, who else?' came the reply.

Arthur felt in his pocket, brought out a handkerchief and started blowing his nose. He then put it back in his pocket. At the end of the over, as he walked round the boundary edge, Sellers came up to him and said, 'It's a good job you had a handkerchief in your pocket, Arthur.'

Never missed a trick, didn't Mr Sellers.

As for Shankly, he was the one, remember, who brought an insignificant-looking lad called Denis Law down from Scotland. He was a young, skinny kid who wore glasses. I dread to think what Rushy would have thought of him. But Shanks had obviously seen that something special that all the greats have, even at an early age, and, as we all know, Denis went on to become a legend in the game. Different in style and build he may have been, but he was up there with Tommy as one of the best strikers it has been my privilege to have seen.

Leaving schooldays behind

My happy schooldays came to an end when I left Raley and went to work at Monk Bretton Colliery. At the same time I signed amateur forms for Barnsley Football Club, whose manager was Angus Seed. But my football career was short-lived. There was this Saturday when I should have been playing for Barnsley's Northern Intermediate League side against Hull, but the match was called off because the ground was unfit and Jock Steele, who coached us young lads and went on to become a manager himself, told me I could go and play for Barnsley YMCA instead, along with another amateur, Arthur Kaye, who later played for Blackpool and the England B team.

It was a day I'll never forget. The match was against Dodworth on their ground and I injured my knee so badly that I never played football again. I was devastated at the time, because at the age of 15 I had my eye on playing both football and cricket at a professional level. It wasn't to be, unfortunately, and I might have been lost to cricket as well, had it not been for the intervention of a chap called Alf Broadhead, a slow left-arm bowler at Barnsley Cricket Club, who worked on the railways.

I had gone to Barnsley's Shaw Lane ground carrying my boots, shirt and trousers in a carrier bag, and asked for a trial. I was told to go away. I was just about to leave, rather sadly as you can imagine, when I heard this voice shout, 'Hey, son, what's your name? Come and bowl to me in the nets.'

It was Alf. He continued to give me tremendous encouragement and I owe him a lot. He helped me develop into a county cricketer.

Not many people are aware of this, but I thought of myself chiefly as a pace bowler at that time, although I could also bat a bit – a 'nudger' and a 'pusher', as someone once said.

Before long I had been persuaded to concentrate on my batting. And that's how it all started.

8

TEENAGE TRIALS

I shudder when I think back to the time, in my teens, when I used to attend the winter nets at Headingley.

I had to get up at four thirty in the morning to go to work at Monk Bretton Colliery. When I'd finished my shift I'd have a bath, get changed, grab a bite to eat, get my cricket gear together, pack my bag and then off I'd go to take the bus from Barnsley to the centre of Leeds. From there I caught a tram to Headingley. I know the memory can play tricks but, as I recall, if it wasn't lashing it down with rain or blowing a gale, it was snowing like mad and bitterly cold.

It wasn't much warmer in the indoor nets, either. There was no heating and we practised on old wooden boards. It was heaven to get back in the dressing room, where there was a fire to thaw out numbed fingers and thumbs. Even now, I can picture the coach, Maurice Leyland, wrapped up in an overcoat, cap on head, warming his hands in front of that fire.

Afterwards it was back on the tram to Leeds, then the bus home. By the time I flopped into bed it would be about eleven thirty. I'd snatch five hours' sleep if I was lucky, before clambering bleary-eyed out of bed for work next morning.

I did that two nights a week every January and February until I finally signed for Yorkshire.

Those were the days, eh?

I have to admit that there were times when I wondered if it was all worthwhile. But I said to myself, Come on, Dickie lad, don't let all this be for nothing. Now I can look back with great satisfaction and think, It wasn't, was it?

Working for Chunky

I might not have been able to take advantage of that winter coaching, however, had it not been for Mr Charlton, the manager of the Monk Bretton pit.

Now, I must make it clear that I have never ventured down a coal mine. I went to the colliery on leaving school at the age of 15 because there were few other jobs in Barnsley. It was usually the mines or nothing. If a father worked down the pit, then so did his son. But they were not going to get me underground – no matter how much they paid me. So I got a job as a fitter on the pit top, which was a double bonus, because being employed by the National Coal Board saved me from having to do National Service.

Edward Charlton, known to all and sundry as 'Chunky', was the one I had to ask for time off to go to Yorkshire CCC for a trial when I was recommended to them by Barnsley.

The response was typical Chunky. 'No, and if tha teks it, tha's sacked!' But, being the astute fellow that he was, he struck a deal with me. I could have the day off, he said, if I agreed to play for Monk Bretton in the pit knock-out competition.

Now, the rules stated that only one professional was allowed in the team, and there were two of us, me – I played for Barnsley – and Harry Beechey, who played for Rockingham, so technically we would be breaking the rules if we both took part. Everybody warned Chunky about the possible repercussions if he decided to go ahead with the two of us – we could be thrown out of the competition – but he didn't take a blind bit of notice. He was the pit manager and he didn't think anybody would dare challenge him.

We duly won through to the final and played Grimethorpe. Harry took six wickets and we came out on top. Chunky, proud as punch, strode up with a huge smile on his face to receive the trophy. As he raised it in triumph, a member of the tournament committee butted in.

'Sorry, Mr Charlton,' he said, almost apologetically, 'but there's been an objection.'

You could have heard a pin drop. Then Chunky snarled, 'You what?'

'It seems, Mr Charlton, that Grimethorpe have lodged an objection to Monk Bretton playing Beechey as well as Dickie Bird, and I have to tell you that the committee has upheld the objection. The trophy will therefore be handed to Grimethorpe.'

At this there were loud cheers from the Grimethorpe contingent, but Chunky was having none of it. It just so happened that four members of the committee worked at his pit and he turned to them and ranted, pointing to them one by one, 'You, you, you and you – don't bother coming in to work tomorrow. You're all sacked!'

Eventually everything was sorted out, with Chunky getting his own way as usual. He didn't stand for any nonsense, didn't our Mr Charlton. I remember one day at the colliery he came to the fitting shop, demanding to see one of the workers, Jack Schofield. I said I didn't know where he was. He had, in fact, locked himself in the office because he was scared to death of Mr Charlton and had heard that he was on the warpath. Chunky tried the door and when he couldn't open it, he grabbed hold of a big hammer and smashed it down. There was no hiding from him. And I didn't hang around to see what happened to Jack!

Persistence pays off

Anyway, thanks to Chunky, I was finally given leave to go to Headingley for my Yorkshire trial and, as you can imagine, I was a bag of nerves, although it helped that Michael Parkinson was also having a trial.

The coach, Arthur Mitchell, came up to me and asked, 'Is this bloke wi' thee?'

'Yes, Mr Mitchell.'

'Mm, does 'e fancy 'imself as a batsman?'

'He does, Mr Mitchell. He's an opener.'

'Is 'e now?' he said, thoughtfully stroking his chin. 'And tell me, as 'e got a job?'

'Oh, aye, he's a journalist, Mr Mitchell.'

'A journalist, eh? Well, 'aving just seen 'is efforts as a crick-eter, would you mind passin' on a bit of advice from me? Tell 'im to stick to journalism.'

Then it was my turn to get padded up.

Mitchell, who was a really dry character, turned to me and queried, 'Reight then, and where are you from, son?'

I stuck out my chest proudly. 'Barnsley,' I answered.

'Oh, no, not another one! Not a batsman as well, are you, by any chance?'

'As a matter of fact, I am, Mr Mitchell.'

'Then put pads on, and them three likely lads theer will send thee a few balls down. Let's see what tha's made on.'

I looked at 'them three' – and trembled. They were Freddie Trueman, at that stage a highly-thought-of 18-year-old who was already making quite a name for himself; Bob Appleyard, a marvellous off-cutter; and Johnny Wardle, a slow left-arm bowler at the peak of the powers which earned him a place in the England team. To add to my discomfort, I was to face them on a rain-affected strip.

Wardle bowled the first ball. It was a Chinaman, which turned and lifted. My tentative forward prod was nowhere near it. Then came Appleyard with one that went straight through the gate. Finally Trueman roared in and I played my shot nearly a fortnight after the ball had sped past me.

I was in the net for fifteen minutes and I can't recall making contact with a single delivery. At the end of the session Mitchell strolled over to me and said, 'If tha's going to play like that, it's not worth thy while coming here again.'

I thought that was the end of my Yorkshire prospects and I almost didn't go back. But Dad had other ideas. 'Tek no notice. Thee go back, son, and show that old so-and-so.'

And I did. Surprisingly Mitchell and I got on like a house on fire after that. He appreciated the character, determination and stubbornness that I had shown. It was what he had been hoping for. It was a method he had of sorting the men from the boys.

'I didn't drop it on purpose'

Mention of Wardle leads me to a story told about him during a match between Yorkshire and Surrey at Bradford. Johnny was bowling to that supremely graceful batsman Peter May, and he brought Mike Cowan to midwicket as he prepared to bowl his renowned Chinaman. It worked a treat. May went for the drive and hit the ball straight at Cowan – who dropped it! Wardle's language was dreadful.

Cowan apologised profusely. 'I'm ever so sorry, Johnny,' he said. 'I didn't drop it on purpose.'

'Bugger off to the boundary,' snapped Wardle. 'I'll put someone who can catch at midwicket.'

Next ball was another Chinaman. May struck it in the air. It soared to the heavens and then started to drop to where Cowan had been stationed on the boundary edge. Wardle watched from the middle, arms crossed.

'He'd better catch the bugger this time,' he was heard to mutter.

Cowan positioned himself perfectly for the catch, but, possibly fearful of what Wardle might say if he missed it, he allowed nerves to get the better of him. The ball bounced off his chest and fell to the ground. Wardle was furious.

At the end of the over Cowan went up to him and said, 'Oh, Johnny, I'm ever so sorry.'

Wardle looked at him pityingly and replied, 'Don't worry, lad, it were my fault for putting thee theer.'

'Keep on running, Dickie; the pavilion's that way!'

At the time I had my Yorkshire trial I was a £4-a-week professional at Barnsley and I opened the club's Yorkshire League batting with Parky many times. In fact, there was one Yorkshire League game where we put on 200 for the first wicket. He made 100 and I was 92 not out. It was form like that which earned us the invitation to attend the Yorkshire nets. Parky was a pretty useful left-hand batsman with a big ambition, like me, to open the batting for Yorkshire, and, do you know, I reckon that if he had been playing now, he would have been good enough to play for the county, but not then, because they had such a strong side.

I really enjoyed those days at Barnsley's Shaw Lane ground, when you could always rely on the wags in the crowd – there were plenty of them around – to liven up proceedings. There was one match when the pitch needed patting down at frequent intervals and on one occasion I gave it a right whack with the bat. As I did so I heard this chap shout out, 'Here, don't bash it too hard, Birdy; there's men working under there.' He was right. A seam from Dodworth Colliery ran right under the ground.

Also in the Barnsley team was yet another miner's son, a schoolboy from the mining village of Fitzwilliam by the name of Geoffrey Boycott, who batted at six when he first arrived but gradually worked his way up the order.

I remember all too clearly being 49 not out against Sheffield United at Shaw Lane and turning the off-spinner neatly through a gap on the leg side towards the midwicket boundary. In those days they always went round with the hat to take up a collection for half-centuries, as well as centuries, and as there was a fairly large crowd I was looking forward to picking up a bob or two.

I set off for the easy single, calling 'Come one' as a matter of course. The aforementioned Boycott was at the other end – and he remained stubbornly anchored to his crease. As I reached him he said cheerfully, 'Keep on running, Dickie; the pavilion's that way.'

Geoff, of course, became infamous for such incidents, as was illustrated at one cricket function much later on when that great batsman Colin Cowdrey turned up wearing a new tie which showed the three lions of England with a number 75 underneath. Someone asked what the 75 meant and he explained, 'Oh, that's the number of batsmen Geoff Boycott has run out in Test cricket.'

At the same event another England batsman, Peter Parfitt, was spotted with a similar tie, except that his carried the number 5. 'In case you're wondering,' he said, 'that represents the number of people Geoff Boycott *hasn't* run out in Test cricket.'

There was also the time when Geoff refused to open the innings for Barnsley's Yorkshire League side. Hubert Padgett usually opened with me but was unavailable for a game at Hull and so our captain, Norman Umbers, asked Geoff to take his place.

He retorted, 'No way! I'm not opening. I'll bat at number three. Let someone else go in and knock the shine off the ball, then I'll go in and finish it off.'

In the end wicketkeeper Eddie Legard, who went on to play for Warwickshire, volunteered to open.

So we went out there, Eddie and me, with Hull having made 186 in their opening knock – and we knocked the runs off without losing a wicket!

As we walked in triumph from the field into the dressing room, expecting to be congratulated on our match-winning partnership, we were met by the sight of a furious Boycott flinging his bat across the room and shouting, 'Why didn't one of you get out and give me a chance to bat?'

Well, he did have his chance, didn't he? I reckon it was an open-and-shut case.

I eventually signed as a professional with Yorkshire in 1952, at the age of 19, for £12.50 a week.

9

WELCOME TO MY WORLD

Time flies. I often get into conversation with people and they think I've only just retired. It was fifteen years ago, for goodness' sake. But I know how they feel, because it seems like only yesterday that I was umpiring my first World Cup final – and that is thirty-eight years ago. Can you believe it?

It was the first time a World Cup final had been staged, and I was thrilled to have been chosen to stand as one of the umpires. It also turned out to be the best of the three finals at which I officiated. It was an absolutely magnificent game, with one of the best individual one-day innings I have ever seen, fine bowling, superb fielding, a memorable fight-back and a dramatic finale. What more could you wish for?

Not a lot, you might say. But there was an additional feature in the build-up to the 1975 tournament which was a great thrill for me. All the teams and umpires were invited to attend a buffet lunch at Buckingham Palace, where we met the Queen, Prince Philip, Prince Charles, Prince Andrew, Prince Edward, Princess Anne and the Queen Mother.

As the final itself approached, I went weak at the knees just thinking about it and, guess what, there were tears in my eyes as I walked out to the middle at Lord's. I kept thinking to myself, 'You've done it, Dickie, you've done it. The World Cup final. And *you* are umpiring it.'

It was captain Clive Lloyd, of course, who produced one of the greatest knocks in the history of one-day cricket, scoring 102 in only 85 balls after the West Indies had been reduced to 50 for 3 by that formidable Australian pace attack of Dennis Lillee and Jeff Thomson.

The West Indies had earlier suffered a stroke of bad luck with the dismissal of opener Roy Fredericks, who was basking in a warm glow of satisfaction after belting a spectacular six off Lillee's bowling when it was revealed that he had knocked off a bail in making the shot, and that, quite literally, put them on the back foot, so much so that Rohan Kanhai said to me, 'This looks bad, Dickie. It will be very hard to win from here.'

I agreed with him. But then Lloyd ambled to the wicket and took the bowling by the scruff of the neck. By the time he departed, caught down the leg side off the persistent Gary Gilmour, the West Indies were back in cruise control, eventually setting the Aussies a victory target of 292 in their 60 overs.

That meant that Australia had to score at a rate of five an over if they were to win, and nobody gave them a snowball in a hot oven's chance against the relentless battery of West Indian quick bowlers. Yet, had it not been for the brilliant fielding of Viv Richards, they might well have recorded one of the most remarkable results of all time, although it has to be said that he was helped by some suicidal running between the wickets.

'Have you heard of Mr Dickie Bird?'

My fee for that match was £100 and I also received a large silver medal presented by Prince Philip, who, knowing of my habit of arriving for events on the early side, said to me, 'So, what time did you turn up this morning?'

'Eight o' clock, sir,' I told him.

'My goodness,' he said. 'You've had a long day. You must be very tired.' He checked his watch. 'Just look at the time; it's past nine o' clock. I'll be in trouble when I get home, I can tell you!'

Prince Philip also remarked on the absence of my white cap. 'Are you all right, Dickie?' he asked. 'I notice they stole your white cap.'

'Yes sir,' I replied. 'That's another one gone. It's a good job I always keep plenty of spares.'

Now, there was a sequel to this. The following year I was due to stand at a County Championship match between Middlesex and Surrey at Lord's and, having travelled down from Yorkshire by train, I took a bus to my hotel. This big West Indian bus conductor came to take my fare and I couldn't believe my eyes. He was wearing a white cap that looked remarkably like one of mine.

So I said to him, 'Excuse me, young man, but where did you get that white cap?'

His eyes lit up and he became very excited. 'This cap?' he said. 'Man, have you heard of Mr Dickie Bird, the great Test match umpire? This is one of his famous white caps, and I am so proud to have it. Do you know,' he confided, 'I took it off his very head in the 1975 World Cup final when we beat those Australians in a wonderful game at Lord's. Hundreds of us ran on to the field, and I managed to get hold of Dickie Bird's cap. I have worn it ever since.'

Obviously he hadn't recognised me; goodness knows why. And I didn't let on.

There were two letters in particular that I received a couple of days after the match that I treasure to this day. The first was from the defeated Australian team and it was signed by their tour manager, Fred Bennett. It said, 'On behalf of Ian [Chappell], myself, and the team, I would like to say how much we appreciated your efforts in the World Cup final at Lord's last Saturday.'

The other was from former England captain Colin Cowdrey, who wrote, 'Many congratulations on your superb handling of the World Cup final. It contributed much to the success of everything, and it is nice to be able to say that England has the best umpires in the world.'

When I look back now, these are the kind of things that stand out in the memory and, honestly, if I had never umpired again I could always say that I'd done the big one – the first World Cup final, one of the greatest matches ever played.

When Clive Lloyd dropped Geoff Boycott . . .

I thought that 1975 final would be the pinnacle of my career. I had always said that there was nothing to beat the atmosphere at a Test match, but the final of a World Cup is extra special. I had experienced that and I was satisfied. So I was stunned when I was told that I was going to umpire in the 1979 final.

The West Indies had proved what a great side they were by reaching the final for the second successive time and the occasion was given an additional appeal by the fact that their opponents would be England.

Hopes were high for the host nation when the West Indies were struggling at 99 for 4 in their opening knock, and I well remember Viv Richards saying to me, 'This is getting serious, Dickie. We're really struggling now. If they get another wicket, I reckon we've had it.' But, of course, England didn't get another wicket for a long time.

Collis King marched in to set a capacity crowd alight with one of the greatest one-day knocks I have ever seen. It eventually came to an end when he was caught on the boundary for 86 going for another mighty six. Man-of-the-match Richards, meanwhile, remained defiant to the last, unbeaten on 138, as the West Indies totalled a formidable 286 for 9 in their 60 overs.

It was too much for England. Mike Brearley and Geoff Boycott started too cautiously and although they put on 129 for the first wicket, that stand became a topic of heated debate. They had fallen well behind the necessary run rate and critics argued that England should have opened with Graham Gooch. It had crossed my mind as well, and when, to my amazement, Clive Lloyd dropped Boycott at mid-on early in his innings – a comfortable catch for such a fine fielder – I did wonder if he spilled it deliberately in order to keep Boycott in. I still can't make my mind up all these years later.

Whatever the whys and wherefores, the fact was that by the time the game entered its final phase the required run rate had reached eight an over, which was impossible against the West Indies' famed pace attack.

Joel Garner was the one who did most damage on this occasion. At six feet eight inches, he was so tall, and his arm so high at the point of delivery, that the ball came out of the trees at the Nursery End above the line of the sightscreen. When he pitched the ball well, it was almost impossible to pick up. 'Big Bird', as he was known, took five of the last seven wickets as the England batsmen went down like skittles and the West Indies duly completed a comfortable 92-run victory.

It had been claimed by some people that the heads of the West Indies players tended to drop when they were in trouble. They had definitely been in trouble in this game, as Richards had admitted to me, but, my goodness, they found the right man at the right time to lead a wonderful fight-back. They had confirmed their position as the best team in the world in what was another magnificent game, played in a great sporting spirit.

There was just one moment of anxiety for me. That was when the West Indian fans swarmed on to the field at the end, and I thought, Oh no, here we go again, better hang on to your cap, Dickie lad.

This time, however, I just won the race back to the safety of the pavilion, with my headgear still intact. The only problem was I pulled a muscle doing so.

England v West Indies   Prudential World Cup final

Lord's, London, 23 June 1979

West Indies innings (60 overs maximum)		Runs	Mins	Balls	4s	6s
CG Greenidge	run out (Randall)	9	31	31	0	0
DL Haynes	c Hendrick b Old	20	49	27	3	0
IVA Richards	not out	138	207	157	11	3
AI Kallicharran	b Hendrick	4	19	17	0	0
CH Lloyd*	c & b Old	13	42	33	2	0
CL King	c Randall b Edmonds	86	77	66	10	3
DL Murray†	c Gower b Edmonds	5	12	9	1	0
AME Roberts	c Brearley b Hendrick	0	8	7	0	0
J Garner	c Taylor b Botham	0	4	5	0	0
MA Holding	b Botham	0	7	6	0	0
CEH Croft	not out	0	6	2	0	0
Extras	(b 1, lb 10)	11				
Total	**(9 wickets; 60 overs)**	**286**				

Fall of wickets: 1–22 (Greenidge), 2–36 (Haynes), 3–55 (Kallicharran), 4–99 (Lloyd), 5–238 (King), 6–252 (Murray), 7–258 (Roberts), 8–260 (Garner), 9–272 (Holding).

Bowling: IT Botham 12–2–44–2; M Hendrick 12–2–50–2; CM Old 12–0–55–2; G Boycott 6–0–38–0; PH Edmonds 12–2–40–2; GA Gooch 4–0–27–0; W Larkins 2–0–21–0.

England innings (target: 287 runs from 60 overs)		Runs	Mins	Balls	4s	6s
JM Brearley*	c King b Holding	64	130	130	7	0
G Boycott	c Kallicharran b Holding	57	137	105	3	0
DW Randall	b Croft	15	36	22	0	0
GA Gooch	b Garner	32	31	28	4	0
DI Gower	b Garner	0	6	4	0	0
IT Botham	c Richards b Croft	4	7	3	0	0
W Larkins	b Garner	0	1	1	0	0
PH Edmonds	not out	5	14	8	0	0
CM Old	b Garner	0	4	2	0	0
RW Taylor†	c Murray b Garner	0	1	1	0	0
M Hendrick	b Croft	0	4	5	0	0
Extras	(lb 12, w 2, nb 3)	17				
Total	**(all out; 51 overs)**	**194**				

Fall of wickets: 1–129 (Brearley), 2–135 (Boycott), 3–183 (Gooch), 4–183 (Gower), 5–186 (Randall), 6–186 (Larkins), 7–192 (Botham), 8–192 (Old), 9–194 (Taylor), 10–194 (Hendrick).

Bowling: AME Roberts 9–2–33–0; MA Holding 8–1–16–2; CEH Croft 10–1–42–3; J Garner 11–0–38–5; IVA Richards 10–0–35–0; CL King 3–0–13–0.

Umpires: HD Bird and BJ Meyer

West Indies won by 92 runs

'We've got them now, Dickie, we've got them!'

So it was two World Cup finals out of two for the West Indies. Could they make it a hat-trick? Most people thought they could and would, especially when they won their way through to the 1983 final, but they were up against an Indian side who had already inflicted the first World Cup defeat on them in Group B, and I had a sneaking feeling that India might repeat that success in the final.

However, when India, who had knocked out England at the semi-final stage, were bowled out for only 183 on a perfect batting pitch, it looked odds-on that the West Indians would make it three in a row. It is true that the West Indians bowled well, but the Indians did not do themselves justice and, to be honest, I felt a bit sorry for them. Their captain, Kapil Dev, usually such a brilliant batsman, must take a lot of responsibility for the cavalier fashion in which he threw his wicket away when he should have been leading by example.

However, he certainly made up for it with the way he inspired his team in the dressing room. The players responded in dramatic fashion. While they were now mentally up for the battle, the West Indies seemed a little too relaxed, just as if they believed the game was already in the bag.

Gordon Greenidge, as Kapil Dev had done earlier, uncharacteristically gave his wicket away, padding up and being bowled, and another lapse of concentration saw Desmond Haynes caught. It was at that point that Kapil Dev sidled up to me and commented, 'Do you know, Dickie, we are going to win this. They think it's too easy. They'll get themselves out if we just keep the ball up to them and bowl straight.'

I was far from convinced. But then came the real turning point as the West Indies suffered two major blows. Viv Richards, the hero of the two previous finals, was tempted into a hook shot and was out for 33 as Kapil Dev took a blinding catch over his right shoulder, running back from midwicket, and Clive Lloyd pulled a groin muscle, which so restricted his movement that he, too, was dismissed cheaply.

At tea the West Indies were struggling at 76 for 5 from 25 overs and they never recovered. They abandoned their normal attacking style as Kapil Dev turned the screw. He captained that session to perfection and, added to his rousing interval speech, it more than compensated for his earlier rush of blood with the bat.

He kept saying to me, 'We've got them now, Dickie, we've got them.' He may have been trying to convince himself rather than me, but he was proved right.

It was left to me to effectively knock the World Cup crown off the heads of the West Indies when Michael Holding shuffled across, was rapped on the pad and was so plumb that even I had to give him out. As I lifted my finger, I announced, 'That's out, and thank you for a wonderful game, gentlemen.'

Then it was the usual race to the pavilion. I didn't even try to protect the stumps. In any case, I had switched one of them for an old one during the tea interval and kept the original in my dressing room as a memento.

India v West Indies Prudential World Cup final
Lord's, London, 25 June 1983

India innings (60 overs maximum)		Runs	Mins	Balls	4s	6s
SM Gavaskar	c Dujon b Roberts	2	14	12	0	0
K Srikkanth	lbw b Marshall	38	82	57	7	1
M Amarnath	b Holding	26	108	80	3	0
Yashpal Sharma	c sub (AL Logie) b Gomes	11	45	32	1	0
SM Patil	c Gomes b Garner	27	48	29	0	1
N Kapil Dev*	c Holding b Gomes	15	10	8	3	0
KBJ Azad	c Garner b Roberts	0	3	3	0	0
RMH Binny	c Garner b Roberts	2	9	8	0	0
S Madan Lal	b Marshall	17	31	27	0	1
SMH Kirmani†	b Holding	14	55	43	0	0
BS Sandhu	not out	11	42	30	1	0
Extras	(b 5, lb 5, w 9, nb 1)	20				
Total	**(all out; 54.4 overs)**	**183**				

Fall of wickets: 1–2 (Gavaskar), 2–59 (Srikkanth), 3–90 (Amarnath), 4–92 (Yashpal Sharma), 5–110 (Kapil Dev), 6–111 (Azad), 7–130 (Binny), 8–153 (Patil), 9–161 (Madan Lal), 10–183 (Kirmani).

Bowling: AME Roberts 10–3–32–3; J Garner 12–4–24–1; MD Marshall 11–1–24–2; MA Holding 9.4–2–26–2; HA Gomes 11–1–49–2; IVA Richards 1–0–8–0.

West Indies innings (target: 184 from 60 overs)		Runs	Mins	Balls	4s	6s
CG Greenidge	b Sandhu	1	11	12	0	0
DL Haynes	c Binny b Madan Lal	13	45	33	2	0
IVA Richards	c Kapil Dev b Madan Lal	33	42	28	7	0
CH Lloyd*	c Kapil Dev b Binny	8	32	17	1	0
HA Gomes	c Gavaskar b Madan Lal	5	18	16	0	0
SFAF Bacchus	c Kirmani b Sandhu	8	37	25	0	0
PJL Dujon†	b Amarnath	25	94	73	0	1
MD Marshall	c Gavaskar b Amarnath	18	73	51	0	0
AME Roberts	lbw b Kapil Dev	4	16	14	0	0
J Garner	not out	5	34	19	0	0
MA Holding	lbw b Amarnath	6	28	24	0	0
Extras	(lb 4, w 10)	14				
Total	**(all out; 52 overs)**	**140**				

Fall of wickets: 1–5 (Greenidge), 2–50 (Haynes), 3–57 (Richards), 4–66 (Gomes), 5–66 (Lloyd), 6–76 (Bacchus), 7–119 (Dujon), 8–124 (Marshall), 9–126 (Roberts), 10–140 (Holding).

Bowling: Kapil Dev 11–4–21–1; BS Sandhu 9–1–32–2; S Madan Lal 12–2–31–3; RMH Binny 10–1–23–1; M Amarnath 7–0–12–3; KBJ Azad 3–0–7–0.

Umpires: HD Bird and BJ Meyer

India won by 43 runs

England spoil the party

Having done three finals, I was very disappointed not to stand at a fourth in 1987. And the England team were to blame for that.

You see, the World Cup organising committee had called me in to the Taj Palace Hotel before the semi-finals to tell me that I was doing the final – because they were anticipating a game which would not involve England. It was obvious to me that they were convinced it was going to be an India v Pakistan final, but they had jumped the gun.

Perhaps I should explain here that times had changed since I had stood at the 1979 final in which England had played. We were now in the era of neutral umpires and, despite what the committee had told me, I knew that if Mike Gatting and the boys did get through, my dream of a fourth final appearance would be dashed.

So what did England do? They reached the final – spoilsports. Seriously, though, they had done so well, and it was nice to see them taking part in that final in Calcutta, with more than a hundred thousand people packed into Eden Gardens.

I have to tell you that the atmosphere there is out of this world. They really love their cricket, do the Indians. For some of them it is not so much a game as a way of life. And the noise they generate is unbelievable. That makes it especially difficult for umpires. With all that racket going on, it is very difficult to pick up nicks off the bat. You have to judge more by the way the ball deviates. There is the problem of pollution, as well – you get a lot of smog out there – and that makes it harder to see as clearly as usual. It can all be very intimidating, but you just have to concentrate on your job and try to blot out the clamour, which includes fireworks being let off continually.

What lessened my feeling of frustration and disappointment at not being allowed to umpire in that final was being told that Allan Border, captain of the Australian team who were to provide England's opponents, had pleaded with the organising committee, 'I want Dickie to do the final. I'm not bothered that he's English. That's the respect we have for him. And I speak on behalf of all the players and the Australian Cricket Board of Control.'

That, to me, was a tremendous compliment. And I've never forgotten it. To have the respect of the players like that is worth more than its weight in gold. And, you know, the great thing is that the same respect was shown to me wherever I travelled in the world. And that gives me a warm feeling. It makes me think that I really did achieve something in my career. I am able to look back on those days with a great sense of pride and satisfaction in a job well done.

A painful reminder

I have also been left with a rather painful reminder of that trip. I was in the taxi taking me to the airport when the crown came off one of my teeth as I was chewing a toffee. Worse still, I swallowed it. I didn't feel too bad until the flight, then a twinge of pain developed into a constant ache and by the time we landed at Delhi I was in absolute agony.

When I consulted the team doctor, Tony Hall, and told him what had happened he advised me to go straight back home.

'You must be joking,' I said. 'I've just flown halfway round the world to umpire in a World Cup. No way am I going back.'

I got no sympathy from the England players, either. 'One out, all out,' they chorused, and then fell about in further fits of laughter when the doctor said to me, 'Right then, if you're going have treatment here, you'll have to have an injection first. Get on the bed and drop your trousers.'

An appointment was made for me at a local dentist and my heart sank when I was directed to a very dilapidated building as far removed from the sterilised surgeries in England as you could possibly imagine. If I tell you that conditions were basic, that's very much an understatement.

However, the dentist was a very charming man and, after some rather painful poking and prodding, he said, 'Ah yes, I see the problem. Have you still got the crown?'

'I'm sorry,' I said, 'but I'm afraid I don't really know.'

'How do you mean, you don't know? You either have or you have not. Simple.'

'Not quite that simple,' I explained. 'You see, I swallowed it.'

'Well, didn't you look for it?' he demanded.

I could see that he was determined to get to the bottom of things, but it had never occurred to me to do this, so he finally agreed to make me a new crown. Do you know, that crown is still in place almost thirty years later. And I haven't had one moment's further trouble with that tooth from that day to this.

Just to crown it all, I never received a bill for the treatment, and I was certainly not going to ask for one. Either the Indian Cricket Board footed the bill, or the dentist let me have the treatment for free because of my celebrity status in his country. And I was happy to leave it at that.

The importance of saying the right thing

Another feather in my cap is that I was the first neutral umpire appointed by the ICC to officiate abroad. The match in question was also Zimbabwe's first Test match, against India in Harare, the capital city, in 1992.

There was the traditional presentation before the game as the teams and umpires were lined up on the field of play and the notorious Zimbabwean president, Robert Mugabe, was introduced to us all. I was surprised at how little he was; he looked much bigger on the telly. Anyway, he shook hands with everybody and when he came to me he said, 'They tell me you're from England, Mr Bird.'

I said, 'Yes sir.'

'Are you a friend of Margaret Thatcher?' he asked.

'I know her very well, sir,' I told him.

'Good. If you are a friend of Margaret Thatcher, you are very welcome in my country. Good day.'

And with that he marched off. I can't begin to tell you how relieved I was. His men were all round us with their machine guns. I would hate to have said the wrong thing. It could have been a premature end to my umpiring career. I'll never forget it.

'We've got a problem here, Shep!'

A Test match which caused me no end of problems was the one between England and the West Indies at Headingley in 1988.

It is not generally known, but before the game the Yorkshire grounds committee had a meeting at which they decided to block the drains so that the ground would retain its moisture. The idea was to prevent the pitch from drying out and cracking, which would have benefited the fearsome West Indies pace attack. They would have had the ball flying about all over the place in such circumstances.

That was all very well, but the committee men must not have listened to the weather forecast. The day before the Test was due to start there was torrential rain, which left the ground awash, and of course the water could not get away because of the blocked drains.

Several big squeegees were hurriedly brought in from Old Trafford, Trent Bridge and Edgbaston, and groundsman Keith Boyce and his groundstaff performed heroics battling through the night in a bid to get the pitch fit.

Next morning it was glorious – bright sun, blue skies – and, remarkably, we started on time. Curtly Ambrose opened the West Indian attack, bowling from my end to Graham Gooch, who comfortably dealt with the first four deliveries.

That's marvellous, I thought to myself. It looks as though the pitch is playing perfectly, with no ill effects from the soaking.

I relaxed and looked forward to a great game of cricket.

Then, as Amby was preparing to send down the fifth ball, I heard him shout, 'Oh, Mr Dickie, we've got big problems here, man.'

I said, 'There can't be any problems. It's all sorted. Come on, Amby, get on with it.'

He gestured to me. 'Come and have a look for yourself, man.'

So I did. And I couldn't believe what I saw. Water was oozing up over his boots, and he was paddling about in it.

'I don't believe it,' I gasped.

'You'd better,' retorted Amby.

I called to my umpiring colleague, David Shepherd. 'We've got a problem here, Shep,' I said. 'There's gallons of water oozing up.'

'Throw some sawdust down,' he suggested.

'Sawdust?' I replied. 'We'll need four lorryloads, and even then it might not be enough. Just come over here and you'll see what I mean.'

Shep ambled over and found the water splashing up over his boots. 'Hmm,' he said thoughtfully. 'See what you mean, Dickie. We've got to take them off.'

'What, and paddle about in stockinged feet?' I queried.

'Not the boots, you idiot,' he said. 'The players, of course.'

I looked at him, thunderstruck. 'What? Take them off at Headingley? In a Test match? In front of my home crowd? After only four balls? They'll lynch me.'

Shep insisted, 'I don't care; we've got to get this water away before we can carry on.'

My worst fears were realised. As soon as we began to leave the field they were at it.

'You're here again, Birdy. Every time you come to Headingley you bring them off for rain or bad light. It's not raining and the light's fine, so what is it this time?'

I was so angry and frustrated that I had a go back at them. 'There's nothing I can do about it. It's the drains. They couldn't take all that rain we've had. There's water oozing up all over the place. That's not my fault, is it? You don't need an umpire out there; you need a plumber.'

The spectators must have felt the same on a visit to the gents' toilets, which were inches deep in water, but the problem on the pitch was confined to that one area on the bowler's run-up and, thankfully, the groundstaff managed to squeegee all the moisture out in the space of about twenty minutes, time which we made up later in the day.

Even so, I wish now I'd had the presence of mind to have a T-shirt printed like the one unveiled by Manchester City's controversial Italian footballer Mario Balotelli last year.

It read, 'Why always me?'

Umpiring my first Test at Lord's

Now, it won't come as a surprise that Lord's has always been my favourite cricket ground. I don't think there is anywhere better. When you walk through the gates you get that special buzz. There is something about the place. It is steeped in history and all the legends of the game have played there. It is magnificent. For me it will always be number one. That is why I cherish the day in 1973 when I fulfilled my dream of umpiring a Test at the headquarters of English cricket.

It came at the end of my first season on the international panel and it was totally unexpected. Dusty Rhodes had originally been appointed to stand at the final Test between England and the West Indies, but I received a telegram from Lord's telling me that I was to take his place because he had an eye infection. I learned later that the real reason for the change was that the West Indies had specially asked for me to be one of the umpires.

Little did I know what I was letting myself in for. Just after lunch on the Saturday Billy Griffith, the then MCC secretary, announced on the public address system that there had been a warning from the IRA that a bomb had been planted somewhere in the ground. A cold feeling swept over me. This couldn't be happening. Not to me. Not at a cricket match. Not with a crowd of twenty-six thousand people.

The police wanted them all to leave and asked that they make for the exits in as orderly manner as possible. But do you know what they did? I can picture it now. I was still out there in the middle, with fellow umpire Charlie Elliott and the players, and suddenly thousands of spectators came swarming across the playing area to join us.

The covers had been brought on to protect the pitch and I thought the safest place would be sitting on them. After all, I knew there was no bomb under there. The spectators also obviously thought that it would be safe out there in the middle. None of us really knew what to do, and I just sat there, holding my head in my hands, worrying about what might happen if a bomb did go off.

However, the West Indian supporters around me didn't seem in the least bit concerned.

'Don't you worry about the bomb, Mr Dickie Bird,' they said to me. 'Just look at the total on the scoreboard and worry about that.'

I glanced across and it read West Indies 652 for 8. England eventually had to follow on and lost by an innings and 226 runs, then the second biggest defeat ever suffered by an England side, the worst having come in Brisbane during the 1946–47 tour of Australia.

There was no bomb, of course, but the authorities could take no risks, especially as a bomb had gone off in Baker Street that very morning.

A true gentleman

Billy Griffith, who was at the centre of that bomb scare, was a man I admired. A player with Sussex and England, he became secretary of the MCC in 1962, and he oversaw the abolition of amateur status, the introduction of one-day cricket and the creation of the Test and County Cricket Board (TCCB). MJK Smith used to tell a lovely story about him concerning an MCC tour of Australia in 1965–66. Apparently when Smith asked him when he should declare in a match against Western Australia, Griffith, a bold advocate of attacking cricket, replied, 'Now!' In the end the MCC scraped home by nine runs in the last minute and Smith remarked, 'That's the last time I take the ruddy manager's advice on a declaration.' The original wording, though, might have been a little bit more forceful than that.

Billy Griffith was a true gentleman, with great natural charm; such a nice, kindly man. He helped me enormously in the early part of my umpiring career. That is why I am particularly pleased that his son Mike succeeded Phillip Hodson as president of the MCC in October 2012. I'm so pleased for him; his father would have been so very proud.

Mike played cricket for Cambridge University and then for Sussex, where he stayed for twelve years, five of them as captain. He's the only person to have played both first-class cricket and international hockey at Lord's. He became a very fine chairman of the MCC cricket committee.

Other top-ranking officials who have done a great deal for the game include Donald Carr, Brian Langley and Tim Lamb.

I knew Donald mainly as secretary of the TCCB and I respected him very much. If I had any problem I would go and sit with him in his office at Lord's and talk to him about it. He was always only too pleased to help. The respect, I am glad to say, was mutual, not only as man to man, but as players. I had often played against him when he was with Derbyshire. He was a very good cricketer, who more often than not used to catch me out at slip. Many a scorebook entry read 'H.D. Bird, caught Carr, bowled Jackson'. And for not many runs, either!

Brian Langley was the umpiring coordinator at Lord's and I remember that one of his hardest tasks was trying to keep the rumbustious Cec Pepper and Bill Alley apart. Everyone knew that to have those two fiery and very outspoken characters officiating at the same match would be asking for trouble. It was Alley who once asked Billy Griffith, before a Middlesex v Essex game, whether anyone had ever been sent off at Lord's, because it was, he said, a distinct possibility that morning, as there were 'a few bad buggers in both teams'.

Griffith was appalled. 'Please, for God's sake, don't do that, Bill,' he remonstrated. 'It would be a slur on MCC. Tell me, what other ambitions do you have left?'

Alley thought for a second or two and then replied, 'I know it's getting a bit late for a place on the Test match panel, but I'd love to umpire an England–Australia Test at Lord's with Cec Pepper!'

Griffith recoiled in horror. 'Oh no,' he said firmly, 'We could never have that!'

Tim Lamb played for Middlesex and then Northamptonshire before retiring in 1983. The following year he became secretary and general manager of Middlesex, and four years later he joined the TCCB, becoming chief executive in 1996. One of the things he said that has stuck in my mind was, 'I'm not a revolutionary. The problem with revolution is that it inevitably leads to counter-revolution. We know there are many things wrong with the English game, but my message is that there is far more right than wrong.'

All the administrators I've mentioned were professionals who knew the game inside out, and I am pleased to say we now have another in the current chief executive of the England and Wales Cricket Board (ECB): David Collier, who was appointed in 2004. He worked for four counties – Essex, Leicestershire, Gloucestershire and Nottinghamshire – before landing the top job, which had been vacated by Tim Lamb. You could say he's always been a bit of a high-flyer because – and I wasn't aware of this until recently – he has held a glider pilot's licence since the age of 16.

Still on the subject of administration, Yorkshire CCC owes a huge debt of gratitude to entrepreneur Colin Graves, who became chief executive in 2012. He was raised on a farm at Thorne in South Yorkshire, and went to Goole Grammar School before founding the Costcutter chain of convenience stores in 1986, until stepping down as chairman in 2012. If it was not for him, we might not have a club. He was Yorkshire's saviour financially at a time when the club was in serious difficulties.

The finest Test I've umpired

But back to the Tests. The finest I ever stood at was Pakistan v Australia in Karachi in 1994.

Australia won the toss, elected to bat and scored 337, thanks mainly to Michael Bevan (82), Steve Waugh (73) and Ian Healy (57), and Pakistan could manage only 256 in reply, opener Saeed Anwar top-scoring with 85.

In their second innings, despite a stubborn 114 not out from number three batsman David Boon, Australia collapsed from

171 for two to 232 all out as Wasim Akram claimed 5 for 63 and Waqar Younis 4 for 69, but that still left Pakistan needing 315 to win on a turning wicket waiting to be exploited by Shane Warne, so the Aussies were still clear favourites.

Anwar again batted well for his 77 and Salim Malik took up the gauntlet with 43, but when Mushtaq Ahmed went out as last man to join Inzamam-ul-Haq, Pakistan still needed 57. It seemed a lost cause, but 'Mushy' stuck it out with an unbeaten 20 to help 'Inzy' (58 not out) clinch an unlikely victory. The winning runs came when Healy missed the stumping of Inzamam off Warne and the ball went for four byes.

It was a remarkable effort. The Australians could not believe they had lost that match. It was a particularly disappointing game for Australian opener Mark Taylor, who bagged a pair on his debut as captain.

After that Test the Pakistan Cricket Board presented me with a carpet which I still have in front of the fire in my sitting room. It is wearing well – probably better than me.

Mark Waugh, an excellent batsman who got stacks of runs, played for Australia in that game and last summer I had a phone call from him, in which he made an unusual request. His wife is a racehorse trainer and he got in touch to see if I minded having a racehorse named after me. I said I had no objection and I hoped all went well.

They called the horse Umpire Bird. I've heard no more. Maybe, as the old joke has it, it started at ten to one and was still running at half past four.

Pakistan v Australia 1st Test

National Stadium, Karachi, 28 September – 2 October 1994

Australia 1st innings		Runs	Mins	Balls	4s	6s
MJ Slater	lbw b Wasim Akram	36	103	63	3	0
MA Taylor*	c & b Wasim Akram	0	13	4	0	0
DC Boon	b Mushtaq Ahmed	19	42	34	2	0
ME Waugh	c Zahid Fazal b Mushtaq Ahmed	20	28	25	3	0
MG Bevan	c Aamer Sohail b Mushtaq Ahmed	82	189	146	12	0
SR Waugh	b Waqar Younis	73	109	85	13	0
IA Healy†	c Rashid Latif b Waqar Younis	57	151	92	5	0
SK Warne	c Rashid Latif b Aamer Sohail	22	69	52	2	0
J Angel	b Wasim Akram	5	27	27	1	0
TBA May	not out	1	13	5	0	0
GD McGrath	b Waqar Younis	0	3	3	0	0
Extras	(b 2, lb 12, nb 8)	22				
Total	**(all out; 88.2 overs)**	**337**				

Fall of wickets: 1–12 (Taylor), 2–41 (Boon), 3–75 (ME Waugh), 4–95 (Slater), 5–216 (SR Waugh), 6–281 (Bevan), 7–325 (Warne), 8–335 (Healy), 9–335 (Angel), 10–337 (McGrath).

Bowling: Wasim Akram 25–4–75–3; Waqar Younis 19.2–2–75–3; Mushtaq Ahmed 24–2–97–3; Akram Raza 14–1–50–0; Aamer Sohail 5–0–19–1; Saleem Malik 1–0–7–0.

Pakistan 1st innings		Runs	Mins	Balls	4s	6s
Saeed Anwar	c ME Waugh b May	85	190	124	13	1
Aamer Sohail	c Bevan b Warne	36	97	97	7	0
Zahid Fazal	c Boon b May	27	103	72	4	0
Saleem Malik*	lbw b Angel	26	104	76	4	0
Basit Ali	c Bevan b McGrath	0	14	10	0	0
Inzamam-ul-Haq	c Taylor b Warne	9	44	39	1	0
Rashid Latif†	c Taylor b Warne	2	8	9	0	0
Wasim Akram	c Healy b Angel	39	107	77	5	1
Akram Raza	b McGrath	13	47	37	2	0
Waqar Younis	c Healy b Angel	6	23	10	1	0
Mushtaq Ahmed	not out	2	10	7	0	0
Extras	(lb 7, nb 4)	11				
Total	**(all out; 87.1 overs)**	**256**				

Fall of wickets: 1–90 (Aamer Sohail), 2–153 (Saeed Anwar), 3–154 (Zahid Fazal), 4–157 (Basit Ali), 5–175 (Inzamam-ul-Haq), 6–181 (Rashid Latif), 7–200 (Saleem Malik), 8–234 (Akram Raza), 9–253 (Waqar Younis), 10–256 (Wasim Akram).

Bowling: GD McGrath 25–6–70–2; J Angel 13.1–0–54–3; TBA May 20–5–55–2; SK Warne 27–10–61–3; SR Waugh 2–0–9–0.

Australia 2nd innings

		Runs	Mins	Balls	4s	6s
MA Taylor*	c Rashid Latif b Waqar Younis	0	12	7	0	0
MJ Slater	lbw b Mushtaq Ahmed	23	66	51	3	0
DC Boon	not out	114	336	220	10	0
ME Waugh	b Waqar Younis	61	174	132	3	1
MG Bevan	b Wasim Akram	0	3	1	0	0
SR Waugh	lbw b Wasim Akram	0	2	1	0	0
IA Healy†	c Rashid Latif b Wasim Akram	8	45	27	0	0
SK Warne	lbw b Waqar Younis	0	5	3	0	0
J Angel	c Rashid Latif b Wasim Akram	8	15	14	1	0
TBA May	b Wasim Akram	1	17	12	0	0
GD McGrath	b Waqar Younis	1	14	7	0	0
Extras	(b 7, lb 4, nb 5)	16				
Total	**(all out; 78 overs)**	**232**				

Fall of wickets: 1–1 (Taylor), 2–49 (Slater), 3–171 (ME Waugh), 4–174 (Bevan), 5–174 (SR Waugh), 6–213 (Healy), 7–218 (Warne), 8–227 (Angel), 9–229 (May), 10–232 (McGrath).

Bowling: Wasim Akram 22–3–63–5; Waqar Younis 18–2–69–4; Mushtaq Ahmed 21–3–51–1; Akram Raza 10–1–19–0; Aamer Sohail 7–0–19–0.

Pakistan 2nd innings (target: 314 runs)

		Runs	Mins	Balls	4s	6s
Saeed Anwar	c & b Angel	77	290	179	9	1
Aamer Sohail	run out	34	64	44	5	0
Zahid Fazal	c Boon b Warne	3	37	22	0	0
Saleem Malik*	c Taylor b Angel	43	130	122	7	0
Akram Raza	lbw b Warne	2	25	22	0	0
Basit Ali	lbw b Warne	12	61	43	2	0
Wasim Akram	c & b Warne	4	19	9	0	0
Inzamam-ul-Haq	not out	58	155	89	7	0
Rashid Latif†	lbw b SR Waugh	35	62	56	6	0
Waqar Younis	c Healy b Warne	7	38	28	1	0
Mushtaq Ahmed	not out	20	42	30	2	0
Extras	(b 4, lb 13, nb 3)	20				
Total	**(9 wickets; 106.1 overs)**	**315**				

Fall of wickets: 1–45 (Aamer Sohail), 2–64 (Zahid Fazal), 3–148 (Saleem Malik), 4–157 (Akram Raza), 5–174 (Saeed Anwar), 6–179 (Wasim Akram), 7–184 (Basit Ali), 8–236 (Rashid Latif), 9–258 (Waqar Younis).

Bowling: GD McGrath 6–2–18–0; J Angel 28–10–92–2; SR Waugh 15–3–28–1; SK Warne 36.1–12–89–5; TBA May 18–4–67–0; ME Waugh 3–1–4–0.

Umpires: HD Bird and Khizer Hayat

Pakistan won by 1 wicket

10

THE MEN IN
WHITE COATS

As I reflect on my career, I am more convinced than ever that there are five qualities which are vital for an umpire to reach the top of his profession – honesty, concentration, application, dedication and confidence.

It is also important to gain the respect of the players – and there is no doubt that a thick skin helps as well. It is those umpires who can live with the pressure who go on to officiate at Test level.

When it comes to making decisions, there are two golden rules as far as I am concerned: if in doubt, give not out; and if you realise you have made a mistake, never try to atone for it. Two wrongs never did make a right. I would advise any budding official to concentrate totally on the next delivery and forget what has passed.

It can be a lonely place out there in the middle. When it comes to the crunch, you are the one who has to make those difficult decisions, although I do not believe the pressure is as great these days as it used to be, because now an umpire can call on the third official to make a ruling.

Everyone knows what a worrier I am – my mannerisms give that away – and that was particularly true when I was a player.

It wasn't unknown for me to walk to the wicket with the gloves on the wrong hands and, as they were the old-fashioned type with the wrap-round thumbs, it was almost impossible to switch them over. It must have looked as though I had broken bones in both hands.

Now, Michael Parkinson and Geoffrey Boycott like to tell the story of how they used to put my pads and gloves on for me because I was so nervous. They have even claimed that they tied my left and right pads together, so that when I got up to walk out to the middle I fell straight back down again. Very funny! They also say that I used to chew through the end of my gloves and then start on my nails. You can take those stories with a pinch of salt. You know what ex-cricketers – and umpires – are like when it comes to telling tales about other ex-cricketers and umpires!

But, yes, I was known for being nervous. So, you might ask, whatever possessed me to think that I might make a good umpire?

The truth is I never did give it a thought. When my first-class career ended I continued to play at weekends for Paignton CC while taking up a coaching position at Plymouth College, an independent school in Devon, and I was quite content with that.

Then, one day in the summer of 1969, we were playing a touring team rejoicing in the name of Heffle Cuckoos, captained by former Middlesex and England pace bowler J.J. Warr, who had become a member of the MCC committee, and he asked me if I had ever thought about becoming an umpire. I fell about laughing.

'What, me?' I said. 'You've got to be joking.'

But the seed had been sown. It had never entered my head to be an umpire, but the more I thought about it, the more the idea appealed to me. I sought the advice of some of my former Yorkshire colleagues and the majority of them said, 'Go for it, Dickie.' So go for it I did.

He would have been so proud

Mind you, some of the people who knew me really well – Ray Illingworth, Michael Parkinson and Geoffrey Boycott, for example – still shook their heads in disbelief. They all said I had such a nervous nature that never in a million years would I make a good umpire.

It was important for me to find out what my dad thought. He had advised me all the way through my career. Unfortunately, he was ill in hospital back in Barnsley at the time, but I managed to travel up to see him. When I told him I was thinking of becoming an umpire, he did not say a word. He just looked at me.

When I left I felt a bit hurt. It was the first time he had failed to offer me some encouragement or advice. It was so unlike him. It was almost as if he hadn't recognised me. However, I very quickly realised how ill he was. He died the next day.

It is a great sadness to me that he never saw me umpire. I would have given everything if he had been able to live to see what I achieved. He would have been so proud. But it made my mind up for me. Somehow I knew it was what he would have wanted. So I applied to Lord's to become a first-class umpire and three months later I heard that I had been accepted.

The amazing thing is that when I became an umpire the nerves I experienced as a player never affected me. If I got a couple of low scores as a player I could not sleep at night, worrying where the next run was going to come from. With umpiring it was different. Once I was out there in the middle I did not worry about the decisions I made because I knew that I was giving an honest, totally unbiased opinion on what I had seen. I was also determined to enjoy myself, while at the same time seeking to earn the respect of the players.

I was often accused of not giving many lbw decisions. It may be true, it may not. But I'll tell you what my criterion was for making a judgement. Unless I was absolutely convinced that the ball, having pitched on an approved line, would have hit the stumps, I would turn down any appeal. Simple as that.

'No, Goody, no. Get back!'

I have to admit that there were times when, as an umpire, I was caught up in the excitement of the game. There was an instance when Lancashire were playing Hampshire at Southampton in the early 1970s – doesn't that sound an awfully long time ago now? – and wicketkeeper Keith Goodwin pushed the ball through midwicket. He ran one very quickly, obviously with an eye on a second, but I could see, from my position at square leg, that he had no chance of beating the throw. Forgetting my completely neutral role for a split second, I shouted,

'No Goody, no. Get back.' He did not take my advice and was comfortably run out, leaving the Hampshire players in stitches as I put up the finger of fate to send him on his way.

I wasn't the only one

People always said I was a character. But there were others amongst the umpiring fraternity, none more so than former leg-spinner and leg-puller Cec Pepper, who were just as deserving of that description. It was quite ironic when he joined us in the middle because in his playing days umpires had been the butt of many of his barbs and jibes, although none, it must be said, bore any real malice.

For example, I am told that he once apologised to umpire Harry Wood, a dyed-in-the-wool Lancastrian, for his raucous, over-zealous appealing, which was always littered with some extremely colourful language. Wood told him not to worry as 'it were all part o' t' game', but then retorted after the next appeal, 'Not out, you fat Australian bastard!'

No doubt today Harry would have found himself in trouble, but it was the kind of riposte Cec would have loved.

There was no one quite like another Australian, Bill Alley, who at one time had been a professional boxer, which accounted for his rather battered features. He must have been pretty good in the pugilistic arts as well, because he told me he won every one of his twenty-eight welterweight fights. Finally, however, he did receive a knock-out blow – from a cricket ball during net practice. It was that which forced him to give up boxing.

He was born in Sydney but settled here in the West Country and played cricket in the Lancashire leagues. Remarkably, it was not until he was 38 that he first played County Championship cricket with Somerset, but he continued with them until he was 49, when he turned to umpiring.

In his playing days he particularly revelled in his confrontations with Fred Trueman. In one game he drove Fred's first ball to the boundary and hooked the next for another four. You can imagine Fred's reaction. The next two deliveries were vicious bumpers, which brought a storm of boos from the home crowd. At the end of the over Bill strode down the pitch towards Fred, bat raised. The spectators went quiet, wondering what was going to happen, especially when Fred marched down to meet him halfway. There they were, the two of them, staring each other out like boxers in the build-up to a bout.

Fred then pushed his face right into Bill's and whispered, 'First pint's on me tonight, Bill.'

When he became an umpire Bill admitted to me that, as a player, he had once been a very naughty boy. Only once? I thought to myself.

The incident he recalled was at Bournemouth when he borrowed the umpire's penknife and began, quite openly, to lift the seam, which, of course, was illegal. The umpire was appalled. 'I'm going to have to report you to Lord's,' he fumed at Bill. To which Bill replied, 'You'd look pretty foolish, having handed me the knife and then standing and watching while I picked the seam.' Needless to say, nothing more was heard of the matter.

You never know when it might come in handy

It occurs to me that you might be wondering what an umpire was doing with a penknife. Well, it was part of his stock-in-trade. I always had in the pockets of my umpire's jacket the following items – and you might be surprised at the length of the list:

- **Six miniature beer barrels.** Used as ball counters.
- **A pair of scissors.** These came in handy if the stitching on the ball had worked loose, and it's remarkable how often a player needed a fingernail trimming. At Old Trafford in 1974 I even cut the hair of India's Sunil Gavaskar, who was having problems because it kept falling into his eyes.
- **A penknife.** Mainly for cleaning the dirt out of spikes.
- **Needle and cotton.** I may be a very poor cook, but I have always been able to put in a neat stitch when the need arises, and I have done a lot of running repairs on trousers. This could be embarrassing when they split in sensitive places, and I am glad to report that I did not have to do any sewing when I stood at the women's World Cup.
- **Safety pins.** Also used for patching up little tears.
- **A rag.** For drying the ball.
- **A spare bail.** This was in case one got broken, which did happen when there were a lot of really quick bowlers about. It sometimes occurred to me that we ought to carry a stump as well, but to avoid walking stiff-legged with it stuck down

a trouser leg, we used to leave one handy by the pavilion or in the groundsman's quarters.

- **Chewing gum.** Not only for myself. I used to calculate that it cost me a few pounds each year to keep the players supplied.
- **Spare balls.** In case the one in use went out of shape. There was a box in the dressing room containing a number of balls in plastic bags, labelled to indicate how many overs had been bowled with each. Out in the middle we umpires would probably have three spare balls. For example, I often had a nearly new one, and one which had been used for between 20 and 35 overs, while my colleague had one which had gone through 50 to 65 overs. Anything between would mean a trip back to the dressing room and a little discussion with both teams in order to reach agreement over a replacement.

So, you see, every one of those items came in very handy on many occasions.

Tales from the umpires' room

Batsmen are notorious for never thinking they are out. It's just a natural reaction. Even if all three stumps have been spread-eagled, they'll claim it should have been called a no-ball. Bill Alley was umpiring one match when David Steele was clean-bowled but claimed that the bails had been dislodged by a gust of wind. As he began to trudge slowly back to the pavilion Bill told him, 'Just be careful, David. You never know, the wind might blow your cap off.'

Graham 'Budgie' Burgess, the former Somerset player who became an umpire, was another nice bloke, but I didn't think so kindly of him after standing with him at a County Championship match at Hove. After the second day's play I was still in the shower when Budgie shouted 'Cheerio' to me as he left for his hotel. 'Cheers, Budgie, see you tomorrow,' I yelled back. I finished my shower, got dressed, picked up my bag – and found the door to the umpires' room was locked. I couldn't get out. Panic stations. I shouted like mad, but nobody heard me. I tried the phone but couldn't get a line because all the office staff had gone by this time. I was still there at midnight when, by pure chance, the nightwatchman walked past on his rounds and heard me shouting. You can imagine my relief when he opened the door.

When Budgie came in next morning he said, 'Sorry, Dickie, but I think I might have locked you in.'

'Think? There's no think about it. You did lock me in good and proper,' I told him. 'I could have been there all night!'

I don't think he did it on purpose. He couldn't have. He wouldn't have. Would he?

When Barrie Leadbeater played for Yorkshire he was renowned for just sauntering about at times, so when he became an umpire I should have known what to expect. We were standing together at a County Championship match at Colwyn Bay and everything on the first day had gone without a hitch until we were preparing to go back out after tea. I lined up with the teams but there was no Leadbeater to be seen.

One of the players said, 'What are we going to do, Dickie?'

I said, 'We've got to start on time, so we can't wait any longer. I'll just have to stand at both ends, that's all.'

With that, we set out from the pavilion and on to the green. Just as we had all taken up our positions, Barrie ambled over to join us, apparently without a care in the world.

'Where have you been?' I muttered angrily.

'Having my tea,' he replied. 'Why, is there a problem?'

That was typical Barrie. But I made it my business to ensure that it didn't happen again. Whenever we were umpiring together I'd insist he joined the early Bird and was ready and waiting at least five minutes before every session.

Shep was a tremendous companion

I was devastated in October 2009 when I heard that my long-time colleague David Shepherd had died at the age of 68 after a long battle against cancer. He was a fine umpire, and we spent many happy hours together. He was a great man and a tremendous companion. He also had some rather quirky superstitions, most notably his little jig when the score reached 111 – known as Nelson – or multiples thereof.

Strangely, though, one of my abiding memories of Shep came off the field and not on it. We were in Madras for a World Cup group match between Australia and India. On arrival, after a tiring flight, we decided to go for a stroll on the nearest beach to cool off. As we walked contentedly along the water's edge I said, 'By, Shep, this is the life. Sea, sand, sun and all this wonderful scenery.'

As I spoke Shep grabbed hold of me and gasped, 'Here, just look at your feet.'

I looked, and I was rather alarmed to see some distinctly unpleasant stuff covering them. We had not been warned that this part of the beach was used for the area's sewage disposal system. It was awful – all over my training shoes and my legs. So it was back to the hotel, strip off, have a bath, splash it all over and come up smelling of roses.

If you are a follower of cricket, you will know that Shep was built for comfort rather than speed, so in one of his last seasons as a player with Gloucestershire, he was horrified to discover that the club had decided to adopt a new phys-ical-fitness approach to the game and had arranged a series of long cross-country runs as part of its pre-season train-ing. He protested, to no avail. And from the start he found it too tough. Before long he was way behind the rest of his colleagues. In fact, quite a number were on the return leg of the out-and-back course while he was still puffing and panting on the outward leg. Then Shep saw a chap on a milk float. He waved him down and gasped, 'You don't happen to be going anywhere near the county ground, do you?'

'As a matter of fact, I am,' came the reply. 'I've just one more street to do and then I'm on my way back to the depot, which takes me right past the ground.'

So Shep said, 'Do you mind if I hitch a lift?'

'Not at all,' said the milkman, who turned out to be a keen cricket enthusiast. 'It'll be a pleasure.'

When his weary team-mates arrived back at the ground, Shep was already there – handing out pints of milk!

'I had to buy something,' he explained, 'after he'd been so good to me.'

I gather he had a standing order with the milkman for a few days afterwards.

He'd got a lot of bottle, had Shep.

My first Test match

Another umpire with whom I shared memorable occasions was Charlie Elliott. He was my colleague when I stood at my very first Test match, England v New Zealand, at my home ground of Headingley in the summer of 1973.

I was really nervous as I walked out to the middle with him on that first day, but I felt much better when I looked up and saw a familiar face as I was putting the bails on the stumps. It was Stan Bulmer, a photographer from my local newspaper, the *Barnsley Chronicle*.

'Mind if I take a picture, Dickie?' he asked.

'I don't mind at all, Stan,' I replied, 'but someone else might. You're not supposed to be out here. We're just about to start a Test match.'

How Stan managed to get to the middle before being stopped by an official, I don't know. But he did. And he got the picture he wanted. He was another larger-than-life character, sadly no longer with us.

I felt even better after making my first lbw decision. I knew it was the right one, and I felt a little flash of annoyance, as well as amusement, to see all the players on the balcony rush into the dressing room to check the action replay on television.

The tension vanished completely that first morning when an opportunity presented itself for me to indulge my habit of offering my white coat to any barracker who thought he could do a better job. It never occurred to me that I would have the nerve to do it in front of the cameras and the game's top brass, but I couldn't resist it.

Ronald Griffiths was a West Indian from London who was a regular and popular figure at Test matches. You could not miss him. He used to walk round the boundary edge, in front of the crowd, shouting and bawling. On that first day he saw fit to criticise my decision to signal for a wide by Yorkshire's Chris Old. 'Give the lad a chance,' yelled Ronald at the top of his voice.

Instinctively I took off my umpire's jacket, walked over to where Ronald was sitting and invited him to put it on. The crowd howled with laughter. Now I really did feel at home in the Test match arena. And from that moment on I began to enjoy myself.

Ronald was also a big fan of Geoffrey Boycott and he always addressed him as 'Sir Geoffrey'. After that Headingley incident I became 'my son'. 'Good decision, my son,' he would yell, or 'Come on, my son, get that finger up, he's got to be out.'

He certainly helped to liven up the proceedings and cricket is all the richer for characters such as Ronald Griffiths.

As for the match itself, there were no controversial decisions, no bad light, no rain – in fact, it could not have gone better. Add to that a magnificent century by Boycott, some excellent bowling by John Snow and an England win, and it was all I could have dreamed of.

I could see that my colleague was very upset

It was Charlie Elliott who was standing with me again for that bomb-scare Test at Lord's later that summer. In between, I had partnered Arthur Fagg at the second match of the England v West Indies series at Edgbaston and that was one of the blackest times I experienced as an umpire.

On the third morning there was a big appeal for a catch behind the wicket as Geoff Boycott played forward to a ball from Keith Boyce. When Arthur gave a not-out decision Rohan Kanhai went mad and I could see that my colleague was very upset by the West Indies captain's reaction.

In the umpires' room at close of play I said to him, 'Look, Arthur, I know you've far more experience than me, but try not to worry about it.'

He didn't reply. He simply packed his bag and left.

The following morning I was shocked when I strolled down for breakfast in my hotel and saw the newspaper headlines – 'TEST UMPIRE IN "I'LL QUIT" THREAT'. I learned that the previous evening Arthur had been hijacked by the press and said some things that he must have regretted.

When I met Arthur back at the ground on that third day he

said to me, 'Dickie lad, I'm going to take no further part in this game unless I get an apology from Rohan Kanhai for his behaviour yesterday. If he doesn't apologise, then they can get someone else.

'If they won't accept decisions, there is no point carrying on. Why should I? I'm nearly sixty. I don't have to live with this kind of pressure. I had to live with it for two and a half hours out there. People don't realise how bad it has become.

'I just don't enjoy umpiring Test matches any more, nor Sunday League matches, come to that. There is too much at stake. The players shout for things, and when they don't get the decisions, they react in the way Kanhai reacted yesterday. The game has changed. And not for the better, I'm telling you. Umpires are under terrific pressure these days. Players will have to learn to accept decisions, otherwise there is no point in people like me continuing.

'We make mistakes. But so do the players. We are all human. It shouldn't matter whether Boycott was out or not. It was an umpire's decision, honestly given. Boycott signalled with his arm that the ball had brushed his leg and looked at me for the decision. You know that when players are trying it on, they don't look at you. I didn't see any deviation. What could I do but give him not out?'

As I listened, it was clear that Arthur was in a very emotional state, and when no apology was forthcoming he said, 'Right, that's it. I'm packing my bags. I'm off.'

Half an hour before the start, Arthur was still hanging around, with officials trying unsuccessfully to make him change his mind. For me, new to the Test scene, it was like a bad dream. At first I hardly knew what to do and sought out Leslie Deakins, the secretary of Warwickshire CCC, and Alec Bedser, the chairman of selectors, for their advice. In the end we decided that I should take both ends, with Warwickshire coach and former Sussex and England batsman Alan Oakman press-ganged into standing at square leg. Alan was far from keen on the idea and took some persuading, but eventually he agreed.

As you can imagine there was quite a buzz when the two of us walked out to the middle, but when we got there I had another shock. Alan turned to me and said, 'I don't quite know how to tell you this, Dickie, but I've forgotten the bails.' So he had to go back off to fetch them, with the crowd wondering what on earth was going on.

I took the first over, with Alan at square leg, as had been arranged. As I walked to the other end, wondering how I would be able to manage to do both ends all day, there was a sudden roar from the crowd. I looked up and saw Arthur strolling out to the middle. A feeling of relief flooded over me. I was told afterwards that Alec Bedser and West Indies manager Esmond Kentish had managed to make him change his mind. But he looked tired and drawn.

There were also some problems with time-wasting and intimidatory bowling during that match, but I thought Arthur and I handled that well and there was no further trouble. At the end of the game Arthur and Kanhai shook hands and I thought that would be the end of the matter. However, Arthur never got over it. In fact, he became ill shortly afterwards and did no more Tests.

It was so sad – and unnecessary. Normally Arthur would have shrugged his shoulders and taken no notice of Kanhai's tantrum. But something just snapped that day; I don't know why. After all, his decision may well have been the correct one. Knowing Arthur, it probably was. It is true that from my square leg position I heard a noise, but that could have been pad, or bat on pad.

I am, however, glad that Arthur had the courage to come back out. That must have taken some doing.

The Centenary Test

The other low point for me came in what should have been one of my proudest occasions – the Centenary Test between England and Australia at Lord's in 1980.

The Saturday of that game proved to be a nightmare for me and fellow umpire David Constant. The previous day we had torrential rain, so much so that spectators were diving into deep puddles at the Tavern end of the ground and practising their swimming strokes.

It was still bucketing down when we arrived on the Saturday morning, but it stopped at about half past nine and the sun came out. We kept making inspections but each time it was obvious to us that the ground was still not fit for play. The crowd became more and more restless and started hurling abuse when we went out to the middle to have another look, but we eventually decided, after consultation with the two captains, that we should give it a go.

I was still out there with the groundsman, Jim Fairbrother, when there appeared to be a bit of a rumpus around the members' enclosure. When I reached the dressing room I was shocked to find David, tie askew, looking very distressed and dishevelled. He told me that he had been grabbed by the tie and pushed and jostled in a very ugly scene.

With the hindsight of all the intervening years, I do feel it might have been better had Conny and I decided, as it was a very special occasion, to start play earlier than we did and take the slight risk of a player getting injured. At the time, however, we played it by the book, which said that the pitch was not fit for play. It was a great pity that there was all this controversy, because there were so many good things to remember in that game – top-class batting, bowling and fielding; and a sporting spirit displayed by two great sides.

'If you don't enjoy it, it will put nails in your coffin!'

I learned a lot from both Charlie and Arthur, as well as from people like Tommy Spencer, Syd Buller and Dusty Rhodes, and have always remained grateful to them for the help they gave me in the early days of my umpiring career.

Syd was the number one as far as I was concerned, and it was a tragedy when he collapsed and died at Edgbaston. He was a fellow Yorkshireman, a hell of a nice chap and a top-class umpire. It was shortly after his death that his widow gave

England v Australia Centenary Test
Lord's, London, 28 August – 2 September 1980

Australia 1st innings		Runs	Mins	Balls	4s	6s
GM Wood	st Bairstow b Emburey	112	363	295	10	0
BM Laird	c Bairstow b Old	24	83	64	3	0
GS Chappell*	c Gatting b Old	47	138	115	9	0
KJ Hughes	c Athey b Old	117	205	209	14	3
GN Yallop	lbw b Hendrick	2	11	11	0	0
AR Border	not out	56	96	80	7	1
RW Marsh†	not out	16	48	32	3	0
Extras	(b 1, lb 8, nb 2)	11				
Total	**(5 wickets dec; 134 overs)**	**385**				

Fall of wickets: 1–64 (Laird), 2–150 (Chappell), 3–260 (Wood), 4–267 (Yallop), 5–320 (Hughes).

Bowling: CM Old 35–9–91–3; M Hendrick 30–6–67–1; IT Botham 22–2–89–0; JE Emburey 38–9–104–1; GA Gooch 8–3–16–0; P Willey 1–0–7–0.

England 1st innings		Runs	Mins	Balls	4s	6s
GA Gooch	c Bright b Lillee	8	14	13	1	0
G Boycott	c Marsh b Lillee	62	193	146	5	0
CWJ Athey	b Lillee	9	34	22	0	0
DI Gower	b Lillee	45	120	100	7	0
MW Gatting	lbw b Pascoe	12	53	37	2	0
IT Botham*	c Wood b Pascoe	0	15	14	0	0
P Willey	lbw b Pascoe	5	6	11	1	0
DL Bairstow†	lbw b Pascoe	6	29	18	0	0
JE Emburey	lbw b Pascoe	3	29	18	0	0
CM Old	not out	24	19	15	2	2
M Hendrick	c Border b Mallett	5	4	6	0	0
Extras	(b 6, lb 8, nb 12)	26				
Total	**(all out; 63.2 overs)**	**205**				

Fall of wickets: 1–10 (Gooch), 2–41 (Athey), 3–137 (Gower), 4–151 (Boycott), 5–158 (Botham), 6–163 (Willey), 7–164 (Gatting), 8–173 (Bairstow), 9–200 (Emburey), 10–205 (Hendrick).

Bowling: DK Lillee 15–4–43–4; LS Pascoe 18–5–59–5; GS Chappell 2–0–2–0; RJ Bright 21–6–50–0; AA Mallett 7.2–3–25–1.

Australia 2nd innings

		Runs	Mins	Balls	4s	6s
GM Wood	lbw b Old	8	40	35	0	0
BM Laird	c Bairstow b Old	6	69	45	1	0
GS Chappell*	b Old	59	134	115	7	0
KJ Hughes	lbw b Botham	84	141	99	11	2
AR Border	not out	21	34	29	1	1
Extras	(b 1, lb 8, nb 2)	11				
Total	**(4 wickets dec; 53.2 overs)**	**189**				

Fall of wickets: 1–15 (Wood), 2–28 (Laird), 3–139 (Chappell), 4–189 (Hughes).

Bowling: CM Old 20–6–47–3; M Hendrick 15–4–53–0; IT Botham 9.2–1–43–1; JE Emburey 9–2–35–0.

England 2nd innings (target: 370 runs)

		Runs	Mins	Balls	4s	6s
GA Gooch	lbw b Lillee	16	21	15	2	0
G Boycott	not out	128	316	252	12	0
CWJ Athey	c Laird b Pascoe	1	36	21	0	0
DI Gower	b Mallett	35	95	63	4	0
MW Gatting	not out	51	158	153	7	0
Extras	(b 3, lb 2, nb 8)	13				
Total	**(3 wickets; 82 overs)**	**244**				

Fall of wickets: 1–19 (Gooch), 2–43 (Athey), 3–124 (Gower).

Bowling: DK Lillee 19–5–53–1; LS Pascoe 17–1–73–1; RJ Bright 25–9–44–0; AA Mallett 21–2–61–1.

Umpires: HD Bird and DJ Constant

Match drawn

me a bit of advice. 'You've just got on the list, Dickie, and you're doing pretty well. So enjoy it. If you don't enjoy it, it will put nails in your coffin.' I've never forgotten those words. And enjoy it I did.

I took great pleasure, for example, in an incident at an England v Australia clash at Old Trafford. It was a typical Manchester day – blue skies, sun belting down! – and as I led the two teams off the field one member, who had obviously paid several visits to the bar, yelled at me, 'You're here again, Bird. It's the same every time; you bring the teams off the field for something or other – bad light, rain. What's your problem now on the hottest day of the year?'

I said, 'There are no problems, sir, it's lunchtime.'

Arthur Jepson was another first-class umpire who had been a very good county player. He opened the bowling for Nottinghamshire over a long period, toiling away manfully on those perfect pitches at Trent Bridge, which were a batsman's paradise – and he also played in goal for Stoke City.

During a rain-stopped-play period when I was umpiring with him one day, he told me of the time when Stoke were drawn against Middlesbrough in the sixth round of the FA Cup. Well, you got to talking about all kinds of things at such times. I told him a few stories about Barnsley as well. Anyway, Arthur informed me that, as he learned afterwards, the Middlesbrough team talk the day before the tie concentrated on the need to get him to lose his rag. They were convinced that they could do so if they riled him sufficiently, and that, they thought, might just be enough to swing the result in their favour.

The match remained goalless until a few minutes from time, when Middlesbrough won a corner. As the ball came over, the Middlesbrough centre-forward clattered into Arthur, who fell to the ground under the challenge. He was not down for long. He was so enraged by what he felt was a clear foul on him that he jumped up and chased the centre-forward downfield. While he was doing so, Wilf Mannion, one of the great inside-forwards, controlled the loose ball and slotted it into the net for the only goal of the game. Boro's tactics had worked to perfection.

It has just occurred to me, though. Arthur never did tell me whether or not he caught up with the opposition striker.

Arthur and I were the two umpires at the semi-final of the Gillette Cup between Lancashire and Gloucestershire at Old Trafford in 1971 when the light became so bad that David Hughes suggested that it was getting too dark to carry on playing, to which Arthur replied, pointing to the skies, 'Can you see the moon up there?'

'Of course,' said David.

'Well then,' Arthur put it to him, 'how far do you want to see?'

Former Yorkshire spin bowler Jack Birkenshaw also went on to become a Test umpire and he tells the story of a match at Leicester when Ray Illingworth looked to have Gloucestershire and England's Arthur Milton caught off bat and pad just before lunch. Arthur, who was renowned as a walker, this time never budged, and was given not out.

When they went in for lunch Milton's partner said to him, 'Bloody hell, Arthur, you hit that one.'

Illingworth sent down the first delivery of the afternoon,

Arthur ran down the pitch, deliberately missed the ball, shouted, 'Sorry, lads', and kept on running to the pavilion.

Those were the days, eh? Could you see that happening in 2013? Thought not.

They don't know they are born today!

Jack Birkenshaw not only played with me at Yorkshire, but also moved, like me, to Leicestershire later in his career. Way back in 1959, we shared quite an experience when we were on duty with Yorkshire second team against Cheshire at Hull. It was the third and final day when the word came through from the selection committee that we were required to travel down to Bournemouth in order to play for the first team against Hampshire the following day.

The second-team captain, Ted Lester, told us that we had to be on the six o' clock train that evening. As Cheshire had declared in order to give the match a chance of achieving a result other than a draw, Jack and I were told to open the innings and 'get on with it'.

As we walked out to the middle Jack said to me, 'We can't hang about, Dickie. We've got to get out pretty sharpish or we're going to miss that train.'

I said, 'I'm not getting out deliberately. No way.'

So Jack had a slog, got out, and I was left in limbo. In the end I knew I had to follow him, but I thought, I'm not giving my wicket away. So I 'retired hurt'.

Then, still in our whites, pads, gloves and boots, complete

with spikes, bags taken hurriedly in hand, we made a mad dash by taxi to the train station. As we scurried along the platform we were slipping and sliding all over the place because of our spikes, and I was thinking that if I wasn't really hurt when I retired hurt, I might be hurt any time now!

The railway line ran past the ground in those days and all the lads had said they would give us a wave as we chugged past – and they were as good as their word. We eventually made it to Bournemouth and played in the first-team game, but Jack and I still wonder how we managed it. We were talking about it only last year when we met up for a players' reunion evening at Leicestershire's ground.

Something else that occurs to me about those days was that if you were an uncapped player in the first team you were responsible for the baggage of all the other players – and Jack and I both suffered the toils and tribulations of that. Say Yorkshire were playing at Headingley and then had to travel to Southampton, Hove or somewhere else in the deep south. If you were an uncapped player, you had to make sure that all the bags were bundled into a taxi, taken to the railway station and unloaded into the guard's van. Then you had to hop on board yourself, travel down with all the equipment and oversee their safe passage from the station to the hotel by taxi. After all that, you had to play in the match as well!

Usually there were a couple of uncapped players available, but sometimes you had to do it all by yourself – as I know to my cost.

They don't know they are born today!

I didn't know where to look

When I was appointed to my second World Cup final in 1979 I was delighted to learn that standing with me would be former Gloucestershire wicketkeeper Barrie Meyer, another dual sportsman, who once scored four goals playing football for Bristol Rovers against my beloved Barnsley at Oakwell – a fact he has never allowed me to forget.

But Barrie had an even greater claim to fame as a footballer. He was in the Rovers side which beat Manchester United's so-called Busby Babes – including my old mate Tommy Taylor, Duncan Edwards, Dennis Viollet, Eddie Colman and Bill Foulkes – in an FA Cup tie at Bristol. It was a massive shock. Yet Barrie never boasted about it. In fact, I had to drag the story out of him.

He was a very good umpire and it was always good to stand with him. When he retired he went to South Africa to coach in Durban and he's still living in Natal.

He was yet another of those white-coated characters who could always see the funny side of things and never let anything upset him. Take that Test match between England and India at Edgbaston in 1986. It was on the Saturday afternoon and play was being televised live. I was standing there in the middle, minding my own business, when a young woman, dressed only in panties and bra, ran towards me. Well, being a confirmed bachelor, quite naturally I didn't know where to look. Much to my relief, she totally ignored me as, chased eagerly by a posse of stewards, she made a beeline for Barrie, who was at the bowler's end.

She then took one of the bails off the top of the stumps and put it down her panties. Barrie never blinked. Cool as you like, he reached inside the aforementioned undergarment, pulled out the missing bail and, with a remarkable air of nonchalance, put it back where it belonged. By this time a female special constable had arrived on the scene and the young lady was marched off to the waiting police van.

Afterwards someone asked me if she'd got bail. I said, 'No, Barrie got it back.'

11

COUNTING TO SIX

I'VE never hidden the fact that I have my reservations about electronic aids and third umpires. I expressed them quite forcefully when I was still actively involved in first-class cricket – and I have not changed my mind now that I'm merely spectating.

I do think that generally the third umpire system has been a tremendous help for close run-outs, close stumpings and hit wickets. These are very difficult decisions to have to make when it is purely down to the human eye. The third umpire can also probably help with decisions on the boundary. But that is where I would draw the line.

To think that I spent so much time at Barnsley FC, with the professionals there, doing sprints, just so that I was capable of getting in position to judge run-outs. Now all the umpires have to do is draw a make-believe square in the air calling for the third umpire to play with his technical contraptions.

I well remember one incident just after the introduction of electronic aids when I was standing at the Test match between Australia and Pakistan in Hobart, Tasmania. It was the first morning and, as I had just travelled thirty hours, I was still somewhat jet-lagged. I was therefore very relieved when the first hour passed quite uneventfully.

Then, however, Australia lost a wicket and David Boon came to the crease as the new batsman. He was going along quite nicely when there was a call for a quick single. Now, David was never the quickest between the wickets and he struggled to make his ground. There was a loud roar of 'Howzat' and my immediate reaction was 'That's out.' However, bearing in mind the pressure that there was on umpires to use the new system and the acknowledged difficulty in making such close calls as this, I felt obliged to go to the third umpire. After all, it was a piece of cake now, wasn't it? No need to think. Just signal and the decision would be made for me.

I waited for the judgement – a green light for not out, a red light for out. I waited and waited and waited. Nothing happened.

What on earth's going on? I thought to myself. The 38,000 people in the ground were obviously thinking exactly the same thing, and they started shouting, 'Come on, Dickie, get on with it.'

Much to my relief, a light eventually flashed up on the scoreboard. Was it green? Or was it red? It was neither. It was white.

In exasperation I shouted up to the little room where the third umpire was sitting.

'What the dickens does that mean?'

'It means,' came the reply, 'that the system has broken down. So the decision's up to you.'

That, I thought, was how it should be. So I told Boon he was out, he accepted the decision and that was that. No fuss, no palaver, no problem.

When I went in at lunch I was told that the television people had played the incident back several times and Boon was definitely out – by six inches. Mind you, it was a good job I did get it right, because can you imagine the outcry if those pictures, being beamed all over the world, showed that I had got it wrong!

Then there was the time when South Africa were playing in a one-day international series in Pakistan and they were in a position to win the game when a run-out appeal was referred to the third umpire. Again red and green buttons were in operation. This time the third umpire pressed the wrong one. The batsman, David Richardson, was well in – that's to say not out – but the red button was pressed by mistake and so out he had to go.

After the match the third umpire went up to Richardson and said, 'I am so sorry, Mr Richardson, I do apologise. I pressed the wrong button. I pressed the out button instead of the in button. You should have been in and I pressed out. I apologise a thousand times.'

It might have been better if he had said nothing at all.

The problem with Hawk-Eye

It was in 2001 that television networks began using the Hawk-Eye system to improve coverage for their viewers. That sparked off an eight-year debate, during which the system's accuracy was questioned and scrutinised, as to whether or not it might be used by the ICC to reduce the number of 'mistaken' decisions made by umpires.

Hawk-Eye was first used in the 2009 Test match between New Zealand and Pakistan at the University Oval, Dunedin, and now it has become a fixture, although the Decision Review System is still one of the most talked-about aspects of cricket. The arguments for and against continue unabated.

I am unashamedly in the camp of those who question whether the system is in keeping with the history of the game. I am all for helping umpires as much as possible, but I still maintain that all the authority is being taken away from them and being handed to a machine. It has now come to the ridiculous stage where the machine decides on everything – even no-balls! All the umpire has to do is count to six.

There are three areas that give me particular cause for concern. I am dead against electronic aids being used to adjudicate on lbw, caught behind and bat-pad decisions. So many things have to be taken into consideration for these three types of dismissal. Electronic aids cannot tell the state of the pitch, how much the ball is moving in the air, how much it is moving off the seam, how much the ball is turning when the spinners are on. They can't differentiate between the different types of bowler – right hand, left hand, over the wicket, round the wicket, fast, medium, spin. You also have to take into account the point from which the bowler delivers the ball – the return crease or the back line.

Say a batsman plays right forward and the ball hits him on the pad. In reality, it might well have deviated yards after that. I have yet to be convinced that Hawk-Eye can make a true assessment of that.

There are so many things to take into consideration. And only the umpire out there in the middle is in a position to judge them all. A batsman may be in front of his stumps and look plumb in the television pictures, but when all contingencies are taken into account, the ball could be missing the leg stump by eighteen inches by the time it has finished its flight.

The unfortunate effects of the review system

Of course, this is only my opinion. Not everyone will agree with me. But I am very sad that this has come into the game. I really do have a lot of sympathy for today's umpires. Ask them what they would prefer and they would tell you they would plump for the old days when it was the umpire who had the last word.

It is clear that more batsmen at international level are being given out lbw than ever before thanks to the review system. Consider this: Derek Underwood, one of the finest spin bowlers of his time, took only 8 per cent of his wickets as a result of leg-before; Graeme Swann's figures show that 30 per cent of his Test wickets come by the same method – a staggering difference.

You do wonder how all this affects cricket in the local leagues around the country. They can't afford to set up the kind of system which operates at professional level. But, subconsciously, having seen lbw decisions escalate so much, will league umpires be more inclined to uphold a borderline appeal that they would previously have turned down?

It is all becoming very complicated. Too complicated, in my opinion. Cricket has to try to make sure that the umpire's position retains the respect that it always had, and I do not think this is happening. DRS and what we see on television doesn't help at all. Just the opposite, in fact.

Maybe umpires ought to have the courage of their convictions and give their own decision instead of reverting to the camera at every opportunity, but with the so-called referral system they have no option. Therefore electronic contraptions – those infernal machines – are making all the decisions, and, for me, that's simply not cricket.

The referral system is a stain on the game, in my opinion, and it sounds as though former Australian wicketkeeper Ian Healy feels the same way. He was commentating on an Australia v South Africa Test in 2012 when the Aussies ran out of referrals, so it was left to the umpires to make the decisions, and Healy reflected, 'It's so nice to see we are back to normal.'

The Board of Control for Cricket in India (BCCI) are also totally against the concept. They say it should be left to the umpires to make the decisions. They are concerned that by using technology the roots of their national sport are being crippled. Good for them, I say.

You just watch when replays are shown on the screen. The ball always goes on a straight track. It seems as if nearly every one is deemed to be hitting the wicket. And that's clearly not possible. Ray Illingworth – a former England captain and an off-spin bowler, of course – said to me only last year, 'Do you know, Dickie, if I was bowling now, I'd easily pick up 5,000 wickets – mostly lbws.'

Spot on!

This is why the BCCI do not like referrals, because they claim that the system which makes the decisions is not accurate. There was one match involving India in which three lbw appeals were turned down by the umpires that would have been given out had they been judged by the simulation system, and they would have been having a cup of tea instead of still toiling to take wickets. So did the Indians change their minds? They did not. And you have to admire them for that. They stuck to their guns. They still maintain that the umpire is the only person who is in a position to make such decisions.

Australian Simon Taufel is a very good umpire and highly respected. Yet in the 2012 Test series between Pakistan and England, played in the United Arab Emirates, just about every decision that was referred went against him. Needless to say, he didn't like it! Neither would I if I had been in his boots. Talk about the authority of the umpire being undermined! It is interesting to note that Taufel has now retired from umpiring to become umpire performance and training manager with the ICC.

I'm glad I umpired when I did, because I got a lot of satisfaction – as did all the other umpires in those days – in making the right decisions. It is true that we all make mistakes, but the man who makes fewest mistakes goes to the top. That's how it should be in any profession.

When we did make a mistake, people talked about it in the pubs and clubs and on the terraces; there were discussions in the press, on radio and television. It was all part of this wonderful game. It provided a talking point – a focus. But now? How do you argue about a decision made by a machine?

Seeing the light

There is, however, one electronic aid that does meet with my approval, and that is the light meter. Those of you who remember my occasional problems with that kind of situation will fully understand why that is so. I used to get down on my knees every morning and pray, 'Please, dear Lord, no bad light today.'

Did you know that it was a chance remark by a photographer that led to the introduction of light meters?

It was in 1978, following England's victory over New Zealand by an innings and 119 runs at Trent Bridge in the second Test, that there was a big debate about the conditions in which New Zealand had to bat. A photographer just happened to mention that, according to his light meter, there was no difference between when play went ahead in the afternoon and when it had been called off in the morning.

And suddenly the light obviously dawned in some official minds. Just the job! Why not have meters for umpires?

Guess who was standing at the third Test at Lord's when the light meters were used for the first time. Dead right. Dickie Bird – the bad-light specialist. Barrie Meyer and I were given a brief talk on how the meters worked by well-known cricket photographer Patrick Eagar, and that was that.

Needless to say, we had five days of brilliant sunshine and the light meters never came out of our pockets.

From then on, however, light meters were the norm. I always got the same reaction when I checked mine. 'Put it away, Dickie,' the crowd would yell. But there is no arguing with the system.

Even so, I have witnessed some memorable games in conditions that the light meter would have told us were unplayable, the prime example being that famous 1971 Gillette Cup semi-final between Lancashire and Gloucestershire at Old Trafford. We finished at nine o'clock and it was really dark. The game ended in moonlight. Yet it was one of the greatest games I have ever umpired. Even now, it seems like only yesterday.

I also remember that there was a famous occasion when I had to bring the players off because the light was too bright! It was in the summer of 1995, when England were playing the West Indies at Old Trafford.

Michael Atherton was batting and he complained to me he couldn't see the ball because of the sun shining in his eyes. I walked up to where he had been receiving and he was dead right. It was impossible to see because of the blinding sun. It was also a problem for the slip cordon. So I said, 'Oh dear me' – or words to that effect.

I thought the problem might stem from some greenhouses a little way from the ground and wondered whether or not to send someone down there to cover them up in some way. But

Lancashire v Gloucestershire Gillette Cup semi-final

Old Trafford, Manchester, 28 July 1971

Gloucestershire innings (60 overs maximum)		Runs
RB Nicholls	b Simmons	53
DM Green	run out	21
RDV Knight	c Simmons b Hughes	31
MJ Procter	c Engineer b Lever	65
DR Shepherd	lbw b Simmons	6
M Bissex	not out	29
AS Brown*	c Engineer b Sullivan	6
HJ Jarman	not out	0
Extras	(b 2, lb 14, w 1, nb 1)	18
Total	**(6 wickets, 60 overs)**	**229**

DNB: JB Mortimore, BJ Meyer†, J Davey.

Fall of wickets: 1–57, 2–87, 3–113, 4–150, 5–201, 6–210.

Bowling: Lever 12–3–40–1; Shuttleworth 12–3–33–0; Wood 12–3–39–0; Hughes 11–0–68–1; Simmons 12–3–25–2; Sullivan 1–0–6–1.

Lancashire innings (target 230 runs from 60 overs)		Runs
D Lloyd	lbw b Brown	31
B Wood	run out	50
H Pilling	b Brown	21
CH Lloyd	b Mortimore	34
J Sullivan	b Davey	10
FM Engineer†	hit wicket b Mortimore	2
JD Bond*	not out	16
J Simmons	b Mortimore	25
DP Hughes	not out	26
Extras	(b 1, lb 13, nb 1)	15
Total	**(7 wickets, 56.5 overs)**	**230**

DNB: P Lever, K Shuttleworth.

Fall of wickets: 1–61, 2–105, 3–136, 4–156, 5–160, 6–163, 7–203.

Bowling: Procter 10.5–3–38–0; Davey 11–1–22–1; Knight 12–2–42–0; Mortimore 11–0–81–3; Brown 12–0–32–2.

Umpires: HD Bird and A Jepson

Lancashire won by 3 wickets

then we realised that the sun was shining on to the press box at one end of the ground, reflecting on to the hospitality boxes at the other and then back on to the pitch.

What to do about it was another matter entirely.

I tried to get the people in the hospitality boxes to do something but they just shouted back, 'What are you going on about, Dickie? Calm down, man. Come up here and have a beer.'

I wouldn't have minded. I could have murdered one right then.

Changes at Old Trafford

Incidents like that are now a thing of the past at Old Trafford, because they have changed the pitch round completely to avoid batsmen having to stare straight into the sun. The dressing rooms are also at the opposite side to where they used to be, but I am pleased that the old pavilion has retained its unique character. The front still looks very much the same, all the alterations having come at the back.

Old Trafford was always a fine ground, but the alterations have made it even better. It is a magnificent arena and is ready to make a welcome return as a venue for Test cricket in 2013. The transformation owes a great deal to the very hard-working committee, headed by chief executive Jimmy Cumbes, who, sadly, is retiring from the role. He has done so much for Lancashire cricket and everyone is sorry to see him go.

I have always got on well with Jimmy, who was a bowler for Lancashire, Surrey, Worcestershire and Warwickshire, as well as a goalkeeper for West Brom and Aston Villa, but he always complained that I never gave him any lbws. There was one game in particular when he was feeling very aggrieved because I had turned down three confident appeals against Graham Roope.

When he took my sweater from me after the third shout he complained, 'When are you going to give me an lbw, Dickie? I can't remember ever having even one.'

I tried to explain why that was the case. 'Jimmy, just listen to me, lad, and learn. Tha's bowling nip-backers, and tha can't possibly get lbws wi' nip-backers. Now if you were to hold one up, then tha's got a chance.'

He nodded in the direction of the huge gasometer next to The Oval. 'See that, Dickie? I reckon if he was in front of that bloody gasometer, you still wouldn't give him out.'

'Not if it were a nip-backer, Jimmy,' I agreed, 'not if it were a nip-backer.'

Snow stops play

Bad light, rain, bright sun – they've all caused me problems. But I couldn't believe it that day at Buxton in June 1975, when snow stopped play in the middle of one of the hottest summers on record.

Lancashire had made 477 for 5, which was a record for the 100-over first innings of a County Championship match, before a sudden blizzard covered the pitch to a fair depth. It didn't last long and as the snow quickly melted we were able to resume, but conditions were as bad as I've ever experienced. Even good-length balls shot up head-high and Derbyshire were skittled out twice, for 42 and 87.

The batsmen were fearful for their well-being and one of my abiding memories is of Ashley Harvey-Walker handing me his false teeth wrapped in a handkerchief when he came out to bat. 'Look after these, Dickie,' he said. 'I won't be long.'

He was right. In quick sticks he got an edge and was snapped up round the corner. He looked at me eagerly. 'Is that out?' he asked. ''Fraid so,' I told him. 'Thank goodness for that,' he exclaimed, and with that he reclaimed his teeth and hurried off to the safety of the dressing room.

12

LADIES' MAN

I TAKE some pride in the fact that I am the only umpire to have stood at both the men's and women's World Cup finals. My involvement with the latter is largely due to a woman called Mary Britto, who I first came across when she was the driving force behind the Wakefield youth team at the time when I was playing for Barnsley.

To be honest, I had forgotten all about her until I received a letter from her some years later, when she had become chairman – she still preferred that title rather than chairwoman and the dreadful chairperson – of the New Zealand Women's Cricket Council, asking if I would umpire in a World Cup competition for women that they were promoting over there in 1982. I jumped at the offer. I don't like our cold winter weather and this was a chance to escape to warmer climes.

My recollections of the details of the event are a little hazy, I have to admit, but I do know that I was struck by the pace of Sharon Tredrea, the Australian captain from Victoria, especially in the final, when Australia beat England by three wickets. She was genuinely quick for a woman. In fact, I would go so far as to say she was as fast as Paul Allott, of Lancashire, and Hampshire's Tim Tremlett, who were very good bowlers on the county circuit back home at that time.

I actually remarked to her about the speed of her bowling and she told me, 'You should have seen me three years ago, Dickie – I was even quicker then.'

There was no one else to come anywhere close to her in the pace-bowling department, but there were one or two useful spinners and most of them were good fielders. Maybe they did not have the arm strength of the men, but they were accurate with their throwing and neat and tidy with their catching and ground fielding.

On the whole, the standard of cricket was pretty high. There was some excellent stroke-play and very little was given away in the field. In fact, many of the players looked good enough to hold down a place in a reasonable league team in England.

Jan Brittin stood out amongst the English girls. The Surrey all-rounder, who had also represented English schools at athletics, displayed a wide range of quality strokes and scored 391 runs in the competition, which featured teams from England, Australia, India, New Zealand and an International XI, which was drafted in after the West Indies and Holland had withdrawn.

One other thing sticks in my memory about that World Cup series – and you will see why in a moment. I was umpiring a game between England and Australia, who had Denise Alderman, sister of Australian men's team seamer Terry, as their opening batsman. Early on in her innings the England bowler, wicketkeeper and close fielders all let rip with an almighty shout for caught behind.

Hmm, I thought. It didn't sound like bat; it didn't sound like glove. So I called, 'Not out.'

The next time she got to my end, Denise smiled and said, 'Good decision that, Dickie. The ball hit my metal chest protector.'

That was a first for me. I didn't even know they wore them. Still, I always did like to keep abreast of the times.

Some years later I was umpiring back home and Terry Alderman was playing for Kent at the time. I mentioned the incident to him and he said, 'I know all about it, Dickie. Denise never tires of telling the story.'

I must say I enjoyed being with the ladies – and I discovered another advantage. When I showered I always used to put on floppy sandals to prevent myself from slipping. Once, in New Zealand, I forgot to put them on and, sure enough, down I went, landing quite heavily and bruising my right elbow. Suddenly I found the place full of budding Florence Nightingales and I could not help but make a speedy recovery.

All the teams and the umpires were invited to a big reception given by the prime minister, the Right Honourable Sir Robert Muldoon, at Parliament House in Wellington, which is known as the Windy City, and when I was there it lived up to its name. During the matches, even the weighted bails would not stay put. Sometimes the players could hardly stand up straight as the wind whistled straight down the pitch, and bowling into it was a feat in itself. But there were no complaints from the teams. They battled away with great spirit and it was a joy to umpire them.

New Zealander Fred Goodall was the other male umpire who joined women officials for the competition, which was won by Australia, who retained the trophy by beating England with three wickets to spare in the final.

Here we go again

Something always seems to happen to me on my journeyings abroad, and that New Zealand trip was no exception. While there, I was due to travel with the England team from Auckland to New Plymouth, and when I arrived at the airport I was a little bit concerned, to say the least, when I saw the propeller-driven contraption that we were to fly in, and my worries increased greatly when the captain couldn't get it started.

What happened next? Well, we all got out and we gave it a good push. And it burst into life. Honestly! It's a good job there were no photographers around. They would have had a field day taking a shot of me and the girls putting our shoulders to the wheel – or should I say the wing.

But that wasn't the last of my flying adventures. When I flew home at the end of the competition the captain of the plane turned out to be a cricket fanatic, so when he discovered that I was one of his passengers he invited me to join him on the flight deck, which was a great thrill. We talked a little bit about flying and a lot about cricket and afterwards he told a steward to give me a couple of bottles of wine with his compliments.

I put the bottles in my bag but, as I changed planes at Los Angeles airport, I dropped it – and the bottles were smashed to smithereens. The wine soaked into everything in my bag, including some souvenir programmes I was bringing back with me. I still have them. They are very crinkled and discoloured. But you can just about still smell the wine.

The impressive England women's team set new standards

Women's cricket has continued to come on in leaps and bounds since those days and the progress made by England in T20 cricket has been quite astonishing in recent years.

From July 2010 until the World T20 finals in Colombo in 2012, England were beaten only twice in 33 matches, which meant that captain Charlotte Edwards was arguably the nation's most prolific leader of them all and wicketkeeper-batsman Sarah Taylor had a claim to be the best female cricketer.

Edwards has also become the first female to sit on the MCC World Cricket Committee. In 2012 she was one of four additions to this select group, the others being West Indies captain Jimmy Adams, former Australian wicketkeeper Rodney Marsh and former England captain turned commentator and analyst Michael Vaughan.

On her election Edwards said, 'I'm passionate about the game of cricket and feel I've got plenty to add to the discussion. It will be an amazing experience just to pick these guys' brains. On a broader level, it's great for the women's game that I've been given this opportunity.'

It is a deserved reward for Charlotte and a big shot-in-the-arm for women's cricket, which is definitely in the ascendancy.

Clare Connor, the former England captain and now the ECB's director of women's cricket, has overseen a remarkable transition which has seen the number of clubs with women's sections increase from 93 to 560 in the last decade. Every one of the 39 county cricket boards now has girls' teams competing at Under-13, Under-15 and Under-17 levels and there is fierce competition to earn a place in the national team.

I am told that England run rigorous training camps which cover all aspects of the game and the improvements have been there for all to see. That in itself creates a problem, though. I am not the best person to comment on the current standard of women's cricket, because I have seen too little of it, but I am aware that both England and Australia have very good teams, while all the rest are comparatively weak, which means that there is little real competition. England and Australia dominate, with the West Indies, India and New Zealand playing catch-up, and all the others even further behind.

I have to say that there were very few spectators at the World Cup final when I umpired in New Zealand, and although things have improved in that regard, women's cricket has continued to struggle to draw the crowds. What they have been doing in more recent times to increase interest is playing matches just before one of the men's T20 fixtures, and that seems to be working well for them.

The decision of the ICC to put the women's T20 immediately prior to the men's World T20 event in October 2012 was inspired, because not only did it result in greater press and television coverage, but it also meant that many people were watching the women's game for the first time and quite a few were so impressed that they expressed a desire to see a lot more of it.

As you might expect, the final in Colombo was between England and Australia, with the latter coming out on top.

What is a particular delight as far as I am concerned is the fact that a Barnsley lass has been a regular in the England side for the last few years. Katherine Brunt started her career where I started mine – at Shaw Lane, home of Barnsley CC. Her dad played for the second team, and she got interested in the playing side through joining her brother in the nets.

A fast-medium bowler, she went on to play for Yorkshire Under-15s and Under-17s, but packed it in at the age of 17 because she had stopped enjoying her cricket. Two years later, however, she was back, leaner and fitter than ever, and it was not long before England beckoned.

You might say, as has been suggested, that she has a lot in common with Andrew Flintoff, who also had fitness problems during his career, yet both of them played vital roles in helping England regain the Ashes in 2005. She has continued to suffer from back ailments, but her grit and determination have always pulled her through and she remains an important member of the England team.

My irresistible charms

So much for the international scene. There have also been domestic occasions when you could say I was a bit of a ladies' man. For instance, it was a very kind lady who came to my rescue in a match between Yorkshire and Somerset at Harrogate. I do know that Somerset were batting, but I can't for the life of me remember the batsman's name. It might even have been Viv Richards. Anyway, whoever it was, he complained that the sun was reflecting off a car and into his eyes.

'Is there anything we can do about it, Dickie?' he begged. 'Because I just can't pick the ball up when they're bowling from that end.'

I told him, 'I'll see what I can do.'

So I strolled to the area where the car was parked, and on the front row I noticed a lady wearing a very big white sun-hat.

'Excuse me, ma'am,' I said, 'could I borrow your white hat?'

'Certainly, Dickie. What do you want it for?' she asked.

'I want to use it as a sightscreen,' I told her.

I then held it up and shouted to the batsman, 'Is that all right?'

And I got a thankful thumbs up from the middle.

Another day I even had an eager miss on the boundary edge clamouring for a kiss from yours truly. It happened at Hastings during a Sunday League match between Sussex and Kent, where this young woman, who, it has to be said, did appear to be slightly worse for wear in the drink department, tottered on to the pitch and refused to leave.

Kent captain Chris Tavaré persuaded me and Alan White-head, the other umpire, to go over and try to persuade her to vacate the playing area.

'I won't go until Dickie Bird gives me a kiss,' she said. So, naturally, I obliged. And very pleasant it was, too.

Jealousy is a terrible thing

I always used to enjoy standing with Alan Whitehead. He umpired a handful of Test matches but he should have done more. They claimed he was a bit too abrasive with the players – too officious is probably the word I'm looking for – but he wasn't. However, he was a strong umpire, and there's a differ-ence between being strong and being officious. Alan never let anything get out of hand. If he sensed there was any danger of that, he would step in quickly and nip it in the bud. I always admired him for being straight and honest.

He would never let a fellow umpire down, either. If you were standing with him you could trust him 100 per cent. He would support you all the way. And that's how it should be. You're a team out there, you work together, and he was brilliant for me. I'm just sad that I never did a Test match with him.

He had previously played for Somerset as a slow left-arm bowler and we both got on the first-class umpires' list at the same time. He lives in Wells, Somerset, now, and he is the one umpire I still keep in contact with.

But, do you know, he's still jealous that the fair damsel at Hastings chose to kiss me instead of him!

13

CHARACTER BUILDING

THESE days people keep asking me, 'Where are all the characters, Dickie?'

I have to confess that I can't think of any. At least, none to match the ones when I was umpiring. And that's not just an old man looking at the 'good old days' through rose-tinted glasses. I do truly feel that the characters have disappeared from the game, and a lot of the enjoyment has disappeared with them. There doesn't seem to be as much fun. It's all too serious.

Mind you, it wasn't easy in my era, you know. There was the same pressure on the players. There was pressure on me as an umpire. Especially in Test matches. But I found that having a smile and cracking a few jokes helped to ease that tension, and the players responded. They liked to have a bit of a laugh as well.

That playful Mr Lamb

Of the many characters who were around in my day there was none greater than Allan Lamb. He was always playing practical jokes on people – usually me – and while I could have throttled him on more than one occasion, I always saw the funny side of it afterwards and we have remained good friends.

One famous incident involving Lamby that I love recalling also involved another of the game's characters, Ian Botham – now, of course, Sir Ian. The two of them teamed up to have a laugh at my expense during a Test match between England and New Zealand at Trent Bridge. When it was Lamby's turn to come out to bat he asked me to look after his mobile phone. He said to me, 'Put that in your pocket and keep it safe.' Then he added, as an afterthought, 'Oh, and if it rings, answer it.'

I looked at him, scarcely believing what I'd just heard. 'You must be joking,' I told him. 'We're in the middle of a Test match, man. You'll get me shot. I'm not putting that phone in my pocket, and that's that.'

But he argued, 'I can't very well carry it about while I'm batting, can I? Look, stuff it in your pocket like the good chap you are, and just hope it doesn't ring.'

Well, what could I do? I could see the crowd was getting restless, wondering what was going on, so into my pocket it went, and the game finally restarted.

Lamby had been out there for ten minutes or so, pottering about and getting nowhere fast, and all this inaction lulled me into a false sense of security – until suddenly I heard a phone ringing. I looked round, wondering who had been daft enough to bring their mobile into the middle with them, when the penny dropped and I realised the ringing was coming from my pocket.

I didn't know what to do. Oh, no, now I'm for it, I thought. Whatever will Lord's think? A Test match umpire out there with a mobile phone!

So I shouted across in desperation to the innocent-looking batsman at the other end. 'Lamby, phone's ringing.'

'Well, answer it then,' came the prompt reply.

I pulled the damn thing out of my pocket, trying desperately not to let anyone see what was happening, and whispered, 'Hello, this is Dickie Bird speaking on Allan Lamb's phone. Who's there?'

A voice answered, 'This is Ian Botham ringing from the dressing room. Would you please tell that fellow Lamb to start playing a few shots or get out.'

Lamby was at it again in a game between Lancashire and Northamptonshire at Old Trafford. I was sitting in the umpires' room with my colleague, Raymond Julian, waiting for the bell which signalled the resumption of play after lunch. When it rang we got up to go, only to find the door locked from the outside. Worse was to follow. We then saw smoke billowing underneath the door. Our cries for help were heard by Ron Spriggs, the Lancashire attendant who looked after the umpires and players. He unlocked the door and came to the rescue of two very grateful umpires, who emerged coughing and spluttering, to be greeted by the two Lancashire batsmen and a giggling Northampton team led by Lamby. We didn't need three guesses to identify who had locked the door and then put a couple of smoke bombs against the bottom of it. They reckon you could still smell the smoke a year later.

Mind you, Lamby did apologise at the end of the game. 'I'm sorry about that little prank, Dickie,' he said. 'No hard feelings, I hope.'

I'd calmed down by this time and was just starting to see the funny side of it, so I answered, 'Of course not, Alan. You know I don't mind a little joke now and again.'

'Well, now, that's very good of you, Dickie,' said Lamby. 'I always knew you were a sport. See you later.' And off he went.

I went to the dressing room, had a shower, changed, packed my bags and went to the car park ready to drive home. But I couldn't. Because there were no wheels on my car. Lamby had jacked it up, taken all four wheels off and left them stacked up neatly at the side of the car park railings.

And there, on the windscreen, was the message, 'All the best, Dickie. Have a good journey home.'

He caught me out again when I was officiating at the 1987 World Cup finals in India and Pakistan. I had managed to avoid the dreaded 'Delhi belly' by sticking to my usual diet, but a fever knocked me for six and I was confined to my bed for three days. The England lads kept popping in to try to cheer me up, but succeeded only in making me feel worse, and I thought the end had come when Lamby walked in to my room.

'Now then, Lamby,' I muttered weakly, 'have you brought me some flowers? Or, better still, some chocolate?'

'Sorry,' he said. 'No flowers. No chocolate. But I do have something for you.'

'Oh? What's that, then, Lamby?'

'This,' he exclaimed, and flung the door wide open.

The corridor of the hotel was full of army guards, with rifles, all on security duties. Lamby brought six or seven of them into the room, lined them up at the foot of the bed and barked, 'Right. Put the poor bugger out of his misery. Ready! Aim! Fire!'

I'll tell you one thing. It cured me of my fever! But I did suffer a bit from diarrhoea!

It would have taught Lamby a lesson if I'd hit back with a few lbw decisions to send him packing in double-quick time, but it honestly never occurred to me to do anything like that. You see, although we used to give and take the banter, the pranks and the jokes, we also had a lot of respect for each other. Lamby knew that, no matter how much he teased me, I would never let it affect my decision-making.

For my part, although he might have had me calling him all the names under the sun at times, I always had the greatest respect for him as a cricketer and a fun-loving human being.

Lamby was born in South Africa, and Newlands, one of the most picturesque Test grounds in the world, is his home ground. With Cape Town and the imposing Table Mountain in the background, Newlands is a glorious sight to behold – quite breathtaking.

It was there that he first became notorious as a serial prankster, and Eddie Barlow, who was his captain at the time, became so irritated with his antics in one game that, as a punishment, he had him operating on the third-man boundary – at both ends. That is a very long walk on any ground and before long Lamby decided he had had quite enough of that, thank you very much. Having caught sight of a man with a bike on the boundary edge, he asked if he could borrow it. At the end of that over Lamby then proceeded to cycle from one third-man position right across the pitch to the other boundary at the opposite end of the ground. On the completion of his epic journey, to wild applause from the crowd, he dismounted, put the bike down and waited in anticipation of the biggest rollicking of his life from Barlow.

But nobody could be angry with Allan for long, and Barlow saw the funny side of it. 'Okay, Lamby,' he said, 'you've made your point. Forget about third man.'

Beefy keeps me on my toes

There were times when Ian Botham had me hopping about in indignation, never more so than in the 1983 Test series between England and New Zealand.

As we were taking the field at Trent Bridge, I said to him, 'Which end are you opening from with the new ball?'

'We're opening at the Pavilion End, then I'm coming on for the second over at the Radcliffe Road End,' he told me.

I was at square leg for the first over, and then strolled in to take up my position behind the stumps at the Radcliffe Road End, where Botham was preparing to bowl. With every step I took, there was a series of loud explosions which had me jumping about like the proverbial cat on a hot tin roof. Only this time it was a Bird on a cool grass field. It turned out that Both had sprinkled some Chinese crackers all over the place and I was conveniently putting my foot in it as usual. Typical Botham.

In the 1984 Test against the West Indies at Old Trafford, Both was bowling when he noticed that I was hopping about even more than usual between deliveries and he asked me if anything was wrong. I told him I was desperate for a pee and there was still an hour to go before the break. Now, if a player finds himself in that predicament, he can slip off the field on some pretext or other, a substitute fielder comes on and nobody takes any notice. But if it's the umpire . . .

There was no sympathy from Both on this occasion. Not that I was expecting any. He made a scraping motion with his foot and asked, 'Shall I dig you a little hole?'

'No thank you,' I said, 'but you can hold the fort while I pay a visit.'

With that I ran off, returning a few moments later to a tremendous ovation from the crowd. On regaining my position at the bowler's end, I announced to the players, 'Gentlemen, for this relief, much thanks,' and play resumed.

I still see Ian and Lamby quite regularly during the cricket season. In fact, Lamby turned up unexpectedly when I was invited into one of the boxes at Lord's when England played South Africa in 2012. I had just settled in nicely, along with Sir Tim Rice, Sir Michael Parkinson, Sir David Frost, Ronnie Corbett and Mark Austin, the journalist, when who should walk in but Lamby.

I said, 'Oh, no, who invited him? Get him out.'

He started with his antics and I feared the worst. However, as luck would have it, we were all very fortunate, because his wife was sitting in the next box – and she's the boss. She kept him under control.

He was as hard as nails

Brian Close was a character of a different kind. Not so much fun and games with him, more pure grit and determination. He was as hard as nails. When he was fielding, it was Close all right – as close to the wicket as possible in order to intimidate the batsman. He is fond of telling the story, to anyone who is willing to listen, of the time when Fred Trueman sent down a rare long hop, which Gloucestershire batsman Martin Young met with the full meat of the bat and pulled to leg with great power. It bounced off the side of Brian's head into the hands of slip. Brian never flinched.

At the close of play a concerned spectator asked him how he felt after suffering such a blow on the head, and he replied, 'I'm alreight.'

'But what if the ball had hit you between the eyes?' asked the fan.

'Oh, that would've been different,' admitted Brian. 'In that case, t' catch would most likely have gone to cover.'

I saw another illustration of his bravery – some might call it foolhardiness – at first hand, when I was umpiring a match between Somerset and Australia at Bath. Greg Chappell hit a half-volley which flew like a rocket towards Close at short leg. The ball hit him on the shin, but he just stood there as if nothing had happened. He didn't even bend down to rub the spot where he had been hit.

A bit later I caught him rolling up his trouser leg to have a sneaky look at the damage. I could hardly believe what I saw.

His shin was twice its normal size – it looked like a rotten tomato – and blood was oozing from the wound. I said to him, 'You'd better go off, Brian, and let someone take a gander at that. It looks pretty bad to me. You must get it treated.'

'I'm alreight, lad,' he replied. 'It's nowt ter worry about. Just get on wi' t' game.'

One thing that Brian lacked was patience. And he ran out of it one day after the side had been guilty of a poor morning session in the field. Consequently, as captain he gave them a fiery pep talk during lunch. He railed at them, 'There are three things we've got to do. The bowlers must get their act together and cut out the rubbish they've been sending down. Secondly, the fielders have got to be more alert. We've been giving runs away all over the place. So, come on, let's get out there and do the job properly.'

Wicketkeeper Jimmy Binks was the only one who dared ask him, as they marched out for the start of the afternoon session, 'By the way, skipper, what was the third thing?'

'Oh, I don't know,' snapped Closey. 'You think of something.'

The man behind the moustache

In 1993 Australia were playing England at Old Trafford in a Test match and their team included Merv Hughes, a fast bowler who, with his flamboyant moustache and colourful language, was another great character of his time. He played the game hard – and I do mean hard.

On this occasion he was bowling to Graeme Hick, who kept playing and missing. Merv's language was terrible. I thought to myself, I've got to have a word with him about this. So I called him to one side and said, 'I want you to be a good boy, Merv, and stop this swearing. It's not nice and it's not necessary.'

He stared at me and then said, 'Dickie Bird, you're a legend. For you, I won't swear again.'

There, I thought, feeling pleased with myself, that's done the trick. And I took up my position for the next ball. Merv came tearing in, Hick played and missed – and I've never heard such language in all my life!

But he was a great bloke was Merv – I can vouch for that.

You see, when I travelled to Australia all those years ago to promote my first autobiographical book and take part in a series of signing sessions, I did too much – far too much, in fact. I ended up with repetitive stress syndrome. The problem is that when I sign books I don't just scribble an illegible signature; I add a message to the person the book is intended for, and that's why it took me such a long time to sign them all.

They queued in their thousands in Sydney. In fact, the model Naomi Campbell was higher up the street at a shop selling scents and perfumes, that kind of thing, and she was more than a bit miffed that all the people were waiting to see me rather than her. And, looking at the two of us, you can understand why! She didn't complain to me personally, though, which was disappointing. I wouldn't have minded having a long chat with one of the world's most beautiful women.

Still, that might have sent my blood pressure soaring even more. I am convinced, you see, that the illness I suffered as a result of all that book signing was the start of my blood-pressure problems. I felt really poorly and the doctor ordered me to take a week's complete break.

I was lying in bed in my hotel room one day, feeling really depressed, when there was a knock at the door. I called, 'Come in, it's not locked,' in what I imagine was a very weak, plaintive voice, and who should bounce in, absolutely full of life and energy, but Merv Hughes. I hadn't seen him for ages, but here he was trying to cheer me up with a bunch of flowers and a box of chocolates.

That's the kind of man he is. And he didn't swear once!

Meeting Keith Miller, an Australian great

I eventually got back on my feet, largely thanks to the influence of my old mate Mike Parkinson. I was very fortunate that he was also out in Australia at the time. He visited me regularly in my hotel and he was the one who persuaded me to get out and about again. He took me right up the coast from Sydney to see another cricketing character, Keith Miller, who had been one of the Australian greats when I was just beginning my playing career. In fact, I was twelfth man for Yorkshire at Bradford Park Avenue in 1953 when Miller was playing for the tourists.

Miller was a wonderful man. He went through the war as a bomber pilot and that experience helped to make him the devil-may-care individual he became. I asked him that day if he had ever worried, either in the run-up to a Test match, just before it started, or during it, and he replied, 'Dickie, after the war I didn't think there was anything to worry about. I got through the war and said then that I was going to live life to the full. The time to worry is when you've got half-a-dozen Messerschmitts up your arse.'

In later years Miller was involved in correspondence with Mike Kemp, a former RAF pilot from Bournemouth, and in 1995 he wrote the following letter to him, a copy of which I have in my possession:

As a pilot in the RAF and the fact that you live in Bournemouth brought back mixed memories as I shall explain.

In 1943 a large contingent of Australian aircrew were billeted in many hotels in Bournemouth – Durley Dene and Highcliffe Towers were two places I was in and I suppose they are gone, rebuilt these days.

Anyway, I was ordered to London to play in a cricket match at Dulwich. It was a Sunday. On returning the same night Bournemouth was in chaos. Focke-Wulf planes did a hit-and-run raid on Bournemouth. I then learned seven RAAF mates of mine had been killed. One bomb exploded on a church spire which crashed down on a pub next door and killed them. The pub was called The Carlton (opposite Norfolk Arms Hotel).

I've returned to Bournemouth over the years and on the site of The Carlton is the newspaper *Bournemouth Echo*.

The mates who died were the little group I drank with all the time. So talk about life and luck. I suppose the order to go to play cricket saved my life. The attack on Bournemouth was at 12.50 p.m. – lunchtime. I'll never forget the time as a lot of clocks around town were stopped at 12.50. It was the only time Bournemouth was bombed.

Miller apologised for his handwriting as he had had a stroke three years earlier.

Perhaps this explains a remarkable act of generosity which did not come to light until after his death in October 2004 at the age of 84.

Ian Wooldridge, a top sports writer with the *Daily Mail*, was inundated with letters after he had written an obituary notice. Every one, he said, 'extolled the sporting brilliance he brought into their lives, or had personal recollections of his extrovert kindness in giving autographs or, in various cases, an artefact like a ball or a batting glove. He couldn't care less about where the next was coming from.'

There was one story, however, that Wooldridge admitted really knocked him out. In his days as a cricket reporter for the *Daily Express*, Keith visited many of the county grounds, where he got to know the first names of every gateman and groundsman.

'Where's old Charlie?' he asked one day at a Midlands ground of a pensioner turnstile operator whom he had known for years. 'Alas, got too old and muddled about handling money,' he was told.

Casually, during the day, Miller went to the secretary's office and obtained Charlie's address. That evening, after play, he drove round to Mr and Mrs Charlie's modest two-up two-down. They were thrilled that he had remembered them.

But Miller had noticed one thing. During his short stay he realised they had no television set. Next day a TV was delivered to their home. There was no covering note to suggest where it had come from. But they knew. That's the kind of man Keith Miller was. And that's why he's one of my sporting heroes, as well as being one of the greatest characters cricket has ever seen.

Keeping things interesting

Then there was John Snow, one of the finest bowlers England has produced and also a crafty blighter, as I noted at first hand when standing at a Test between England and the West Indies at Trent Bridge in 1976. Understandably, I am often asked to retell this story. England were in a spot of bother, as they often were when the cavalier cricketers from the Caribbean were in their pomp, so Snow hit upon an imaginative idea to try to slow the game down and put the visiting batsmen out of their fluent rhythm.

After lunch he went out to the middle with his pockets stuffed with breadcrumbs, which he sprinkled all over the ground. Within seconds we were invaded by what seemed to be hundreds of pigeons. It certainly did the trick. It didn't just slow the game down, it brought it to a full stop. I flapped my arms about even more extravagantly than usual, but it was a dickens of a job to get those pesky pigeons off the square.

Dealing with one prankster is bad enough, but when two get together you can expect some fireworks, and so it was in a match between Yorkshire and Kent at Headingley when Richard Hutton was about to bowl to Stuart Leary, Kent's South African batsman. As he waited for Richard to run in and bowl, Stuart said to me, 'Just watch out, Dickie, I'm going to hit his first and fifth balls over midwicket for six.'

'Bet you won't,' I retorted.

In ran Richard, Stuart swung his bat and the ball soared many a mile over the leg-side boundary for a massive six. I raised both arms, not only to signal the six, but in mock surrender to the batsman. The next three were dot balls. Richard raced in for his fifth delivery and I was muttering to myself, 'Nah, he'll not do it again – he can't do it again.' But he did. And there was this excitable white-capped umpire jumping up and down in amazement.

'Ee, just look at that,' I cried out. 'Would you believe it. He's bloody done it.'

There must have been something about those Yorkshire v Kent matches, because I well remember another clash between the two counties when Richard was bowling to a young batsman who kept playing and missing. Finally, Richard could stand it no longer. He strode down the wicket to the batsman and asked him, 'Excuse me, young man, would you mind telling me what you are in the side for? Is it your bowling?'

'Er, well, no, not really,' he replied. 'I wouldn't say it was for my bowling particularly.'

'Your fielding, then?' persisted Hutton.

'No. Not just for that,' said a bewildered batsman.

'In that case,' Hutton scolded him, 'I simply can't understand why you're in the side at all, because you can't bloody well bat.'

Caught in the act

Bishan Bedi is a former Indian captain who was also one of a famous spin quartet, and he became well known for always wearing a colourful patka, or turban as I called it. He was also very outspoken and forthright in his views.

One day Northants were playing Hampshire at Bournemouth and when the match had finished I had a shower in the players' dressing room. As I came out Bishan Bedi went in. I started putting on my clothes and when I got to my socks and shoes I noticed that he had hung his turban on a peg. I looked at it, then at my shoes, and decided to borrow it to give them a bit of a polish. He'll never know, I thought to myself. However, he was out of the shower quicker than I anticipated and he caught me at it.

He glared at me and snarled, 'And what do you think you are doing with my turban?'

I said, 'I'm sorry, Bish. I thought it was a rag that had been left for people to polish their shoes.'

Thankfully he saw the funny side of it and laughed it off. I saw him in India when I went out there for the ICC a few years ago and he still reminded me of that day.

The race of the century

You know how sometimes you let slip a remark and immediately wish you hadn't? It was like that when I was chatting with South African all-rounder Mike Procter and the subject of fitness cropped up. I told him that I did sprint training at Barnsley FC so that I could get in position as quickly as possible to judge run-outs.

'That's interesting,' he said. 'How do you think you would go in a race against Andy Stovold?' he asked.

Now, Andy was a decent bowler but had always carried a bit of weight, so I replied, 'I reckon I could beat him.'

By this time the other players in the dressing room had homed in on the discussion, and it dawned on me that I'd been caught, hook, line and sinker.

'Are you down to umpire any more games here this season?' Procter asked.

I looked in my diary. 'Yes,' I told him. 'Last match against Northants at Bristol.'

'Right,' said Proccy. 'I'll sort it, then. On the last day you two can have a race and we'll be there to cheer you on.'

I felt sure that it was just a bit of banter. They wouldn't go ahead with it. Would they? The answer was a resounding 'yes'. When I arrived at Bristol that September Procter was waiting for me.

'Morning, Dickie,' he greeted me. 'Looking forward to your race with Andy.'

Just before the last over was due to be bowled the club made an announcement over the Tannoy system: 'Would members of the public please stay behind at the end of the game as there will then be a race between Andy Stovold and Dickie Bird.'

Enticed by this free post-match entertainment, it seemed to me that they all must have stayed. In fact, by the time the ground-staff had marked out a track with flags it looked very much as though people were actually coming into the ground rather than leaving, because the crowd was getting bigger. Despite the fact that I was nearly twice as old as Andy, most of the players fancied me to beat him and I am pleased to say that the favourite stormed home. All that sprint training came in very handy.

Could you see something like that happening today?

Characters, you see. Lots of them.

Pulling a fast one

Take Ray East, a left-arm spinner who played for Essex. He was renowned for being a bit of a prankster in the Allan Lamb mould. For example, if a car backfired in the distance he would fall to the ground clutching his heart, as if he'd been shot. I even remember seeing him bowl with a piece of fruit he'd picked up from the lunch table – an orange, maybe. Or, on some occasions, it was a peach of a delivery.

But on this particular occasion he surpassed himself. He was given out lbw by umpire Jack van Geloven off the last ball before the tea interval, and all the way back to the pavilion he chuntered on at Jack about the decision.

'You didn't really give me out, did you?' Ray pleaded. 'You're kidding, surely. I mean, that ball would have hit another set of stumps, it was that wide.'

Jack was having none of it. 'Stop moaning, Ray. You're out, and that's that.'

When play resumed after tea the crowd were surprised to see an unfamiliar figure striding out to replace Ray at the crease. He had a droopy moustache, sported a beard and wore an old-fashioned ringed cap. He fussed about taking his guard, the bowler charged in – and at the last moment the batsman stepped away from the crease, raising one hand in the air. He then pulled off his moustache, beard and cap – to reveal none other than Ray East!

The ground was in uproar. People fell about laughing. Only Jack wasn't amused. 'East,' he snapped, 'I've told you once and I shan't tell you again, you're out. Now bugger off.'

For me this is what cricket should be all about: comradeship, friendship, banter, and a fun-filled fund of remarkable stories to pass on when you reach your eighties.

Now, did I tell you about . . .

14

THE GREATEST

The greatest team

Looking back, I have come to the conclusion that Ian Chappell's Australians of the early 1970s was the greatest Test team I ever had the privilege to umpire, followed by the West Indies from 1975 and into the 1980s. I also thought, going back a lot further – even before the start of my professional playing career – that the England team of 1953 under Peter May was worthy of being called 'great'. Just think of some of the members of that team – Denis Compton, Len Hutton, Freddie Trueman, Brian Statham, Tom Graveney, Godfrey Evans, Jim Laker, Tony Lock, Johnny Wardle. What a line-up!

Then there was the South African side in the late 1960s, littered with so many outstanding all-rounders – Eddie Barlow, Trevor Goddard, Tiger Lance and wicketkeeper/batsman Denis Lindsay, with Peter Van der Merwe as captain. The problem is, it is not really possible to compare them, because the South Africans were lost to apartheid. They were able to pit their skills only against Australia and England, and that was a tragedy, because they had so many magnificent players. In addition to that all-star cast of all-rounders, they had Barry Richards and

Graeme Pollock, who would both be in my World XI. Richards played just four Tests, averaging 72.57, while Pollock averaged 60.97 in his twenty-three Tests, which included a record 274. What would they have done, had they played Test match cricket regularly against all the competing nations?

Just consider the array of talent in that Australian side – Dennis Lillee and Jeff Thomson the opening attack; Maxie Walker first change; the best off-spinner in the world at the time, Ashley Mallett; wicketkeeper Rodney Marsh; and then of course batsmen of the calibre of Doug Walters – what a player! – Ian Redpath and the Chappell brothers.

If that Aussie side was the greatest of them all, then the West Indies under Clive Lloyd must come a close second. It had a master batsman in Viv Richards, backed up by openers Gordon Greenidge and Desmond Haynes, and a wonderful array of fast bowlers in Michael Holding, Andy Roberts, Malcolm Marshall and Joel Garner.

What a battery of quickies that was. It was easy for the captain. He could have a couple of them resting down at third man and fine leg while the other two peppered the batsmen, and then change them round after a few overs so that the bullets never stopped firing. It must have been frightening for the batsmen to face up to that non-stop bombardment of genuinely fast bowling.

The West Indies have been in the doldrums for quite a few years now, but there were signs in 2012, at least in the T20 game, that they could be on their way back. And wouldn't that be a treat?

The Australian side of the late 1990s wasn't bad, either – the Waugh brothers, Mark and Steve, Justin Langer, Matthew Hayden, Shane Warne, Glenn McGrath, Brett Lee, Jason Gillespie, Adam Gilchrist and so on.

Just imagine – wouldn't it be wonderful if all those great teams could play against each other in a clash of the titans, so that maybe, just maybe, we really could decide which was the greatest of them all?

The greatest captain

Any great team needs a great captain and the greatest I have seen are Ian Chappell, Ray Illingworth, Michael Brearley, Richie Benaud, Imran Khan and Kapil Dev. They were all astute readers of the game; all could suss out the opposition, working on the weaknesses of individual players; and all were great thinkers.

Chappell had every quality required in a captain. He was a man born to lead. He captained the Australian teams which toured England in 1972 and 1975 and he had also been a member of the 1968 team. Despite the so-called burdens and pressures of captaincy, on all three occasions he reached 1,000 runs on tour. He scored three double centuries and, as well as England, he toured South Africa, the West Indies, India and Sri Lanka, playing in seventy-five Tests from 1964 to 1980.

Yet Ian once told me that he so admired Ray Illingworth that he used to invite him out for a drink just so that he could pick his brains and learn from him. Needless to say, he was a damn good pupil.

He was also a very good batsman. I have always said that if I had to choose two players to bat for my life in the trenches facing enemy fire, it would be Ian and Steve Waugh. How extraordinarily lucky Australia were to have two sets of brothers like that – Ian and Greg Chappell in the 1970s, followed in the 1990s by Steve and Mark Waugh.

Illingworth was undoubtedly one of the game's deep thinkers. His knowledge of the strengths and weaknesses of every single opponent was incredible, and he was the master when it came to field placings and bowling changes. He was hard, he was tough, but his methods brought success and earned him the utmost respect worldwide. He captained his country in thirty-one out of the sixty-one Tests in which he played, and lost only five of those matches, winning twelve and drawing fourteen.

Brearley is one of those people who was looked upon as a captain first and foremost. Mike took a lot of stick, particularly from the press, who claimed that he was not a good enough batsman to warrant his place in the side. I don't agree. But if there was any deficiency in the run-gathering department, he more than made up for it by the way he led the side in thirty-one of the thirty-nine Tests in which he played, including four overseas tours. Of those thirty-one matches he lost only four.

If there was one criticism I had to make of Brearley, it was that I was not always sure what he was talking about. I remember him saying to me one evening, 'Dickie, there is no such thing as an absolute certainty, only the certainty that befits the subject. What is certain or accurate for a carpenter is not certain or accurate for a geometer.'

Now what was all that about?

And how about this? He once complained that I was neurotic. He said I was the kind of person who had to keep going back to the front door to make certain he had locked it. Well, I mean to say, anyone who knows me will tell you that I am not a bit like that . . .

Benaud was the only one of my top five who captained Test teams before I was appointed to the international umpiring panel, but I was privileged to see him in action while I was a player, and there is no way I could leave him out. Do you know, he captained Australia in twenty-eight out of sixty-three Tests in which he played, and never lost a series. How about that?

I include Imran Khan in that list mainly because of the marvellous job he did keeping the peace within what is often a volatile Pakistani camp. He never had any trouble with his players – and there were some outstanding individuals at that time. He kept them together and got them playing as a team, which was no mean feat.

You have to bear in mind that captains in cricket have a far more important role to play than those in football. They have much more responsibility. Captains in football are ten a penny. In cricket the captains have to go to all the selection meetings; they have a say in the make-up of the team; they have to speak at functions, home and abroad; and they have so many things to work out in the dressing room as well as out there on the pitch. It is a truly vital role.

As for Kapil Dev, there was that one game in particular where I learned at first hand what a great captain he was – that World Cup final of 1983 against the West Indies, when he demonstrated such inspirational leadership qualities

Which brings me to the current England team

Thinking about it, I believe that Andrew Strauss could now be added to that list of great captains. I rated him highly as captain of England. Where he was particularly good was in the dressing room. All the players thought the world of him and they all supported him, although who is to say whether or not his decision to stand down in 2012 came about partly because of the Kevin Pietersen episode.

I don't know the ins and outs of it, so I make no judgement. I was not a party to what went on. The only people who really know are the team players – England on the one hand, South Africa on the other. They could tell you what happened. The South Africans know what he said. He apparently sent them the messages. They could clarify the situation. But not one of them has come out with it. Until you get to the truth, you cannot start to apportion blame. That is why I think it was right that Pietersen was welcomed back into the team after making an apology.

It seems that, one way and another, thoughtless use of Twitter has also caused a number of problems for the England team. I have to say that I think the whole business is rubbish. It should be stopped. I don't know how, but we've got to find a way. There is no place for it in sport. It leads to all kinds of unnecessary trouble. And not just in cricket. It has caused huge upsets in the personal lives of people in society as a whole. It cannot be allowed to go on unchecked.

It was a real shame that all this cropped up at the end of Strauss's time as captain, because the lad did so much for English cricket. There are those who claim that he had run out of form towards the end and he was struggling to prove his place in the team, but I don't accept that. He would always have been the first on my team sheet. I know he would eventually have started to get me runs again. Everybody has a lean spell, but the best players always come out of it, and he was one of the best.

I think he was at the peak of his game when he retired. But then, that's the best time to go. At the top. It's the only way, as I know from experience. Leave them saying you went too early and wanting more, rather than muttering that it was about time the old bugger packed it in. You know, in your own mind, when it's time to bring down the curtain.

Anyway, I believe that in Alastair Cook, Strauss's successor, England have someone who could develop into one of the all-time greats himself – both as a batsman and as a captain. I rate him very highly.

There are some players who are adversely affected by the burdens of captaincy. Ian Botham is a prime example. He hardly took a wicket or scored a run when he was made

England captain, but as soon as he was relieved of that role he immediately returned to his swashbuckling best as an inspirational match-winner.

However, this lad Cook has a marvellous temperament. He is calm and assured and he proved that the captaincy will not affect him as he steered England to a magnificent winter series victory in India in 2012. He showed his ability to lead by example with some extraordinary performances, epitomised by his inspirational batting in the first Test, when England were in a right old spin in their opening knock and were facing an innings defeat as India piled on the runs and made them follow on. In the second innings, having already made 41 in the first, Cook defied the Indian spin attack on a turning pitch for more than eight hours with a superb 176. It showed patience, dedication, concentration and immense mental strength. It was very reminiscent of Michael Atherton's marathon ten-hour stint which saved the Test match against South Africa at the Wanderers ground in 1995.

Cook went on to become the only man to make a century in his first five Tests as captain – he had previously scored two tons against Bangladesh when standing in for Strauss in 2010. He also overhauled Wally Hammond, Geoff Boycott, Colin Cowdrey and Kevin Pietersen as England's leading century-maker – his record-breaking 23rd coming in Kolkata – and earned the distinction of being the youngest player to pass the milestone of 7,000 runs in Test cricket. When you think how young he still is, if he remains fit he could go on to break all kinds of records.

He can handle other players as well, and I am certain he has their respect, which is important.

On top of all that, Captain Cook has a lovely ring to it, don't you think?

Incidentally, I think that in Andy Flower England now has the best cricket coach in the world today. He and Strauss worked really well together. This fellow's man-management is the best I have ever seen – and I go back a long time. You only have to hear him speak about the game on television. He comes across so well. He knows the game inside out and it is largely because of him that England reached number one in the world.

I was interested to learn in November 2012 that former left-arm spinner Ashley Giles had been appointed to take over as limited-overs coach. I thought that was a very good move, and a very good choice. It takes some of the immense pressure off Flower and leaves him to concentrate on the wonderful job he is doing with the Test team. As director of cricket, Giles had led Warwickshire to the County Championship crown the previous season.

England managing director Hugh Morris, another man for whom I have a very high regard, was confident that Giles would prove himself at the highest level. He told the press at the time, 'Ashley has done a terrific job at Warwickshire and has had an enormous amount of experience over the last five or six years. He also has a huge amount of respect within the game. We have seen him go through our coaching programme over the past four years. There are some talented people around the world but we are confident we've got the right man for the job.'

It was stressed, however, that Flower would still retain overall control of preparation and playing strategy for all three forms of the game. It looks an excellent set-up to me, and, with the backing of the chief executive at Lord's, David Collier, and Giles Clarke, the chairman of the ECB, I think England can get back to the top spot after being temporarily knocked off by South Africa.

I do wish Strauss had stayed on a bit longer to take on the Australians, but Cook is a first-class replacement and English cricket remains in good hands.

Where was I?

So then, Illingworth, Brearley and Strauss were, for me, the best three captains England have had, although, if you go back to the time when I was nobbut a lad then you have to say that Peter May was both a fine captain and a great batsman.

The best of them all? I really couldn't put my head on the block for this one. It's too close a call. I could not separate the six I have already mentioned.

The greatest batsman

So, what about batsmen? The list of candidates for the title of greatest is seemingly endless. For starters there are Viv Richards, Sachin Tendulkar, Brian Lara, Sunil Gavaskar, Garry

There's only one Fred Trueman! A *This is Your Life* greeting from a Yorkshire and England legend in 1992.

Sir Garfield Sobers, the greatest all-round cricketer of them all, flew from the other side of the world to be there when Michael Aspel produced the famous red book.

What a moment when I meet up again with Alf Broadhead, the man who took me under his wing at Shaw Lane after I was turned away as a youngster.

In the Royal Box at Wimbledon with Sir Bobby Robson in 2003.

The White Rose of Yorkshire and the Red Rose of Lancashire are on display as I meet up with jockey Willie Carson at Royal Ascot.

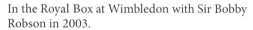

Batman or batsman? A playful moment prior to receiving my honorary degree at Leeds University.

Come on you Reds! With my old friend Michael Parkinson in the West Stand at Barnsley Football Club's Oakwell ground.

Another proud moment as I receive the Freedom of the Borough of Barnsley, my home town. With me are the Council's chief executive, Phil Coppard, and the Mayor, Councillor Arthur Whittaker.

Surbir Sajdewa shows me, Chris Silverwood and David Byas some of the cricket equipment he was able to obtain as the result of a grant from the Dickie Bird Foundation in 2004.

Life's a beach! Umpiring the England v West Indies semi-final in the Tri-Nations Beach Cricket tournament in Sydney, in 2007.

Parky and me again, this time receiving our honorary degrees at Huddersfield University's Barnsley campus in 2008.

That's how I gave them out, sir! A jovial chat with Prince Charles when he pays a visit to my statue in Barnsley in January 2012.

A proud moment as I show the beefeaters my OBE after receiving it from Prince Charles at Buckingham Palace in May 2012.

England women's cricket star Katherine Brunt, who, like me, began her career at Barnsley's Shaw Lane ground.

Jonny Bairstow, fulfilling my prophecy as he plays in the Lord's Test against South Africa in 2012.

Below: Nick Compton, following in the footsteps of a famous grandfather.

Left: Yorkshire's Adil Rashid, who, as a leg-spinner, is a rarity in modern first-class cricket.

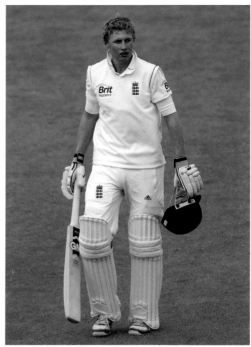

Jonny Bairstow enjoying the Yorkshire v Northamptonshire County Championship match at Headingley in 2012.

Is this England's next captain? Joe Root, who has already begun to make a name for himself in the England team.

Root batting for England Lions against the West Indies at Northampton in May 2012.

Reliving the past while enjoying the present. Chatting with Brian Close and Ray Illingworth during the second Test between England and South Africa at Headingley in 2012.

A colony of Birds! Fans dressed as yours truly at the England v South Africa Test at Edgbaston in 2003.

Sobers, Greg Chappell, Graeme Pollock, Barry Richards, Rohan Kanhai, Majid Khan – and that's just scratching the surface of my era.

My choice, as I indicated earlier, might surprise a lot of you. I go for Barry Richards, of South Africa, as the best I have seen. He was a brilliant right-hand opening batsman who was, sadly, lost to international cricket because of apartheid. I know that people will argue that you cannot judge a man on four Tests, but there is no doubt in my mind that he was the best. This, you have to bear in mind, was also the player who scored 325 not out in a single day when playing for South Australia against Western Australia at Perth. Imagine that!

Unable to play at international level, Richards eventually became bored with the county game in England. I watched as he scored a superb hundred for Hampshire before turning to me and saying, 'That's enough from me, Dickie. Time I gave somebody else a chance.' And he hit one in the air quite deliberately to get out.

But what really sticks in my mind is the day he said to me, 'Dickie, I think I've had enough of this. I find it difficult to get out of bed in a morning to play in yet another game. There's really nothing left for me to play for, is there? Nothing more to achieve.'

I replied, 'Well, Barry, if you really feel like that, you'd better pack it in. Once the enjoyment of the game has gone, that's it, as far as I am concerned.'

I'll never forget the way he paused, just for a moment, then said, 'That's exactly what I'm going to do.' And he did. His departure was a big, big loss to cricket. He was just unfortunate to have been born in the wrong place at the wrong time.

One batsman who has stood the test of time is India's Sachin Tendulkar. He was still playing Test cricket in 2012 and, for me, was still one of the best players on the international scene.

I just cannot believe how long ago it was when I first met him. I was umpiring a one-day international in Sharjah and this lad came up to me, aged about 16 or 17, and said, 'I've always wanted to meet you, Mr Dickie Bird. I am a big admirer of yours.'

I said, 'That's very kind of you, son. You seem very young. What's your name?'

'Sachin Tendulkar,' came the reply. 'My headmaster has given me permission to have time off school to come here to Sharjah and play for India.' Then he added, 'I would like you to watch me and tell me what you think. I would value your opinion.'

I said, 'Well, I'll certainly have a look at you,' and wished him all the best.

He took guard facing a West Indian attack which included Courtney Walsh and Curtly Ambrose and made well over 50. It was a quite magnificent innings, especially for one so young and inexperienced. I know there is a big difference between a one-day international and Test match cricket, but I recognised the sheer class of a potential world star that day.

Afterwards he asked me, 'Well, what did you think, Mr Bird?'

'My boy,' I said, 'you'll put your name in the record books.'

So he did. And how!

The greatest all-rounder

There have been a good number of outstanding all-rounders I have had the pleasure of watching from my privileged vantage point out there in the middle: Imran Khan (Pakistan); Richard Hadlee (New Zealand); Kapil Dev (India); Jacques Kallis (South Africa) – still playing in 2012 and better than any of his contemporary rivals; Mike Procter (South Africa); and, of course, our own Ian Botham.

However, as I have said many times, for me the greatest all-rounder of them all, without any shadow of doubt, was Garry Sobers of the West Indies. He was three cricketers in one: superb left-handed batsman, arguably one of the best new-ball bowlers of his type – left arm over the wicket – and a brilliant close-to-the-wicket fielder.

I'll not bore you with all his statistics, but here are just a few to give you some idea of the extraordinary talent of the man. His most famous feat was hitting six sixes off a six-ball over delivered by M.A. Nash of Glamorgan at Swansea in 1968; he took a career-best 9 for 49 against Kent at Canterbury in 1966; hit 1,000 runs in an English season nine times; captained the West Indies on thirty-nine occasions; and was skipper of the Rest of the World team in five matches against England.

On top of all that, he was a supreme gentleman. Who else but Garry would have flown from the other side of the world just to appear on *This is Your Life* when I was featured in that television programme? I can't begin to tell you what that meant to me. And whenever I've been to the Caribbean he's always been the first to ring and invite me for a meal and a drink. Money can't buy that kind of friendship and mutual respect, can it?

The greatest wicketkeeper

As for the specialist position of wicketkeeper, Alan Knott, of Kent, was the doyen of them all as far as I am concerned. He was also quite a character. One of his most embarrassing moments came in the fifth Test against Australia at Old Trafford in 1981. He had just caught Martin Kent off John Emburey and was having a natter with a colleague while the new batsman, a certain Dennis Lillee, was striding to the crease. There was an announcement over the public address system which Knotty did not catch but, assuming it was something to do with the great Australian fast bowler, he joined in the applause.

Ian Botham called out to him, 'Oh, for goodness' sake, stop being such a show-off, Knotty.'

'How do you mean?' countered the puzzled stumper.

'Oh, come on,' retorted Both. 'Don't tell me you didn't hear that they've just announced that you've just broken the record for wicket-keeping dismissals against Australia.'

There was another red-faced occasion for Knotty when a dog wandered on to the pitch during a Sunday League game against Warwickshire at Edgbaston. He didn't notice the dog cocking its leg against one of the stumps, giving it a drenching, so he couldn't understand why the Kent players fell about laughing every time he crouched down behind the wickets. It was not until he saw the television highlights that evening that he realised what had caused such merriment.

Knotty himself also told me the tale of the time he wore a helmet for the first time as a batsman, against the West Indies in a World Series game. With the visor pulled down, the poor lad could hardly see. Not only that, because the helmet covered his ears he couldn't hear, either. He somehow survived one ball, then, more by good luck than management, turned the next down the leg side. Unfortunately, he failed to hear Tony Greig's call for a single and was run out by half the length of the pitch. I had to smile at a radio interview afterwards when he was asked if he had heard Greig's call and he replied, 'Pardon?'

Knotty, incidentally, was the one who commented, after a streaker had interrupted a Test match at Lord's in 1975, 'It's the first time I've ever seen two balls coming down the pitch at the same time.' Cheeky!

Close behind Knotty would be another Englishman, Jack Russell. As well as being outstanding behind the stumps, Jack, like Knott, was also a good batsman. One of his most memorable Test-match knocks came during the winter tour of South Africa in 1995–96 when he stuck with Michael Atherton to save the match against all the odds in Johannesburg. While his skipper continued his marathon innings, Jack defied the attack at the other end to enable England to hold out for a remarkable draw.

It was Jack, incidentally, who provided me with my last victim in Test cricket, lbw to Sourav Ganguly. Jack came up to me afterwards and said, 'Don't say I never do anything for you, Dickie. That was a present for you after all these years. I've got to admit it was plumb – but, of course, it had to be for you to give it, hadn't it?'

I can't help but remember Jack, because he did a painting of me which hangs on the wall just to the left of where I sit in my cottage, so it's looking down on me every single day. He took up painting in 1987 after he decided to pass the time away during a rain interruption by doing sketches. He never looked back. He has painted cricket scenes, landscapes and seascapes, including many of the places he has visited on his travels, and done superb sketches of wildlife. He is also keen on military history and has enjoyed creating detailed paintings of famous military operations. He's a very talented man is Jack Russell.

One of the best of the overseas contingent behind the stumps was Farokh Engineer, who was a magnificent wicket-keeper-batsman, as well as having a mischievous sense of fun. He played county cricket for Lancashire and was once asked by the club chairman, Cedric Rhoades, if, in view of the continued hostilities between India and Pakistan, there was any likelihood that he would be returning home.

'Only if the fighting reaches my village,' replied Farokh. 'Then, of course, I will have to go to protect my wife and children.'

'Which village is that?' Rhoades asked.

'Altrincham,' came the reply.

The greatest fast bowler

I have no doubts at all about the best fast bowler – Australia's Dennis Lillee. When Yorkshire people hear me say that, they are sometimes upset. 'What?' they cry. 'Better than Freddie Trueman?' Much as I admired Fred and numbered him among my best friends, I have to say, 'Yes.'

In later years, when I told Freddie what I thought, he snapped back, 'Tha must be joking. I'm better off five paces now than he ivver was. I thowt tha were a mate o' mine.'

I told him, 'Look, Fred, I played with you. It was a pleasure to go on to a cricket field with you, and a great honour for me to field in the gully for you when you were bowling flat out. You will always rank in my book as one of the greatest.'

He stared at me for a moment, then replied, 'Oh, all reight then, in that case I might buy thee a pint.'

I do think that my honesty struck a chord with Fred. When he knew he was dying, he asked me to do the eulogy at his funeral. He told me, 'I don't want people in t' pulpit praisin' me when they've criticised me throughout my career.'

So why did I rate Lillee above Yorkshire's hero? Several reasons. He had a beautiful approach to the wicket; he stood up in his delivery stride, left knee stiff as a poker; his fellow-through was perfection; in fact his whole action was poetry in motion. He had so much control and variation. For me it was wonderful just to stand there and watch him.

Dennis was also one for having a laugh and a joke, often at my expense. With all the similar characters I came into contact with during my career, it's a good job I can laugh at myself, I'll tell you. On one occasion I was preparing to go out to umpire a match between Lancashire and the Australian tourists at Old Trafford in 1972 when some of the Aussies pushed their way into my room.

'Hey, I'm not having this,' I shouted at them. 'What do you think you're playing at? We're about to start a game of cricket. Get yourselves out of here. Now.' And they did.

I thought no more about it until I was going through the ritual of my usual last-minute check to see if everything was in place and put my hand in my pocket to make sure that all my counters were there. Yes, counters accounted for. But there was something else. Something that felt strange to the touch. I pulled it out. To my horror I saw that it was a snake. In panic I hurled it across the room and yelled for the attendant. 'Help, help,' I cried. 'There's a snake in here.'

I was still feeling all shook-up at lunch. I sat down hungrily and could hardly wait to start on the tureen of hot soup that was on my plate. But when I lifted the cover off, there it was again. I jumped many a mile in the air and ran off yelling, 'There's a snake in my soup.'

Somebody – it could well have been Lillee – shouted back, 'Don't tell everybody, Dickie, they'll all want one.'

But I wasn't taking any chances. I'd heard what snake bites could do. So I legged it out of there quicker than any Olympic sprinter. When I eventually plucked up enough courage to return to the dining room, the snake had disappeared – and so had my soup.

The players burst into another bout of raucous laughter when they saw me, but Lillee said, 'Don't worry, Dickie. It was only a rubber one.'

I knew then who the snake in the grass was.

Lillee was also involved in an on-the-pitch incident with me and his skipper, Ian Chappell. It happened at The Oval, again in 1972, when Lillee asked me to change a rather battered ball which, in his opinion, was badly out of shape. I gave it a brief inspection, handed it back and told him to complete the over. I could tell he wasn't impressed, because the next ball was so unlike him. It lacked pace, length, direction, the lot.

He then tossed the ball over to Chappell and said, 'What can I do with that, skipper? I'm a fast bowler, not a miracle worker.' Expletives, as you can imagine, deleted.

Chappell's response was, 'Look, Dennis, I realise the ball is out of shape, but just get on with it until the end of the over, then I'll have a chat to Dickie about it.'

But that didn't suit Dennis either. He showed his disgust by sending down two good-length, well-flighted off-spinners, spelling a clear message to all and sundry, but particularly me, that here was a ball that could be used only by the slower bowlers.

I just stood there, with a deadpan expression, and said nowt. When Chappell came up at the end of the over to ask for the ball to be changed I told him, 'I wouldn't change either the ball or the bowler, Ian. He's the best off-spinner I've seen all season.'

However, being the fair and reasonable man that I am, I did what he had asked.

I have to say that I never had any problems with Dennis. He played hard, of that there is no doubt, but he has always been a very friendly character and whenever I've been over to Australia we've always met up, had a meal and a drink, and wallowed in memories of those good old days.

One of those memories involves one of my favourite cricketing people, Bill Bowes, who was writing for the *Yorkshire Evening Post*. In those pre-computer times, Bill had to telephone his daily reports to a copy-taker back at the office. One day he was in the old press box at Bradford, which was a low narrow room with windows that looked out on to the rows of members' seats, so that when they were open in warm weather that part of the crowd could hear a lot of what was going on behind them. Yorkshire were struggling for runs against a Warwickshire side who had been very much to the forefront in signing overseas stars, and were pretty formidable opposition. However, the bowlers were not having much joy either, so the outcome was a boring stalemate.

Bill's regular copy-taker was a woman called Lillian – Lilly for short – but she was temporarily unavailable when he phoned in his report, so he had to dictate to someone else – who had little knowledge of cricket and its short legs, long legs, square legs, silly mid-ons and maidens being bowled over. Much of the time, she simply couldn't understand what Bill was on about and she was forever interrupting to question what he was saying.

Gradually his normal good temper gave way to sheer frustration as he was forced to repeat each sentence slowly and clearly several times, very often spelling out the words as well. Finally he cracked. 'Oh, for heaven's sake, put Lilly on,' he yelled down the phone in a very loud voice.

On hearing this, one of the members turned and shouted, 'Blimey! Don't tell me they've signed him an' all.'

The greatest spin bowler

It was a bit of a headache making my choice as the greatest spinner.

There was Lance Gibbs, of the West Indies, an off-spinner of rare quality, who was probably the biggest spinner of the ball of his type I have ever seen, and Australian legend Shane Wane, with his superb control of leg-spin, the flipper and the googly.

He was bowling from my end on that memorable occasion at Old Trafford in 1993 when he pitched the ball a yard outside leg stump and Mike Gatting saw it turn almost square, beat him all ends up and clean-bowl him middle and off. Gatting could not believe it. He just stared at Warne, then at his stumps, in sheer amazement. It was a truly remarkable delivery. I do not think I have ever seen a ball turn so much, and it has become known as 'the ball of the century'.

On a turning pitch, there was nobody to beat our own Derek Underwood, who was virtually unplayable in such conditions. However, he rarely troubled batsmen on a good pitch, despite the fact that he still varied his flight and bowled an immaculate length.

Taking everything into consideration, the best spinner has to be Abdul Qadir, of Pakistan. He didn't turn the ball as much as Warne, nor was he as devastating on a turner as Underwood, but his variation was without equal. He could bowl leg-spin, googly, top-spin, flipper – and all with an impeccable line and length and masterly control. The tragedy is that he had problems with the Pakistan Cricket Board and consequently at least five years were lopped off the end of his international career.

So there you have it:

Greatest Test team: Ian Chappell's Australia

Greatest captains: Ian Chappell, Ray Illingworth, Mike Brearley, Richie Benaud, Imran Khan and Kapil Dev

Greatest batsman: Barry Richards (South Africa)

Greatest all-rounder: Alan Knott (England)

Greatest fast bowler: Dennis Lillee (Australia)

Greatest spin bowler: Abdul Qadir (Pakistan)

Okay, go on then, argue about it!

And what about my other favourite sports?

I have also enjoyed watching great players in other sports. In football, for example, for me there have been none better in my lifetime than the legendary Manchester United and Northern

Ireland winger George Best, England winger Tom Finney – the 'Preston plumber' – and the current Argentinian international Lionel Messi, of Barcelona, who is simply magical.

In tennis, for me it has to be the Swede Bjorn Borg and American Pete Sampras. Roger Federer has a great record, but I would still place those other two above him. Between 1974 and 1981 Borg, whose stamina was exceptional, won eleven Grand Slam singles titles – five consecutive Wimbledon singles titles and six French singles titles; while Sampras won fourteen Grand Slam titles, including seven at Wimbledon and five in the US Open.

As for boxing, there is no doubt in my mind that the best three exponents I have seen are Rocky Marciano, Muhammad Ali and Sugar Ray Robinson.

I actually met Marciano in Johannesburg while I was coaching in South Africa. He had retired by then, after defending his world title six times and remaining undefeated in forty-nine professional fights, and he had been invited over to be a guest at a world light heavyweight championship bout between Pierre Fourie and Bob Foster at the Rand Stadium in front of a crowd of more than 40,000. I was also at that fight, which Foster won on points.

Marciano was staying at the Skyline Hotel in Hillbrow, which was just down the road from me, so I thought I would pop along to see if I could meet him. As it happened, he was just getting out of a taxi when I arrived, so I went up to him, introduced myself and said, 'I'm a big boxing fan; do you think I could have a photograph of you?'

He willingly agreed and I even managed to get someone to take a photograph of the two of us together, arms round each other's shoulders – although I have to say I could barely reach round his. What irritates me is that I can't find those photographs anywhere. I just don't know what has happened to them.

There was more to come from Marciano, though. He invited me into his hotel to share a bite to eat with him and that was a big thrill for me. I plucked up the courage to ask him if he thought he would have beaten Ali, or Cassius Clay as he then was, and he said, 'Dickie, for thirteen rounds he would have been well in front on points, but I tell you this: I would have caught up with him in round fourteen and I would have knocked him out.'

I believed him. He had been in a similar situation when he fought Jersey Joe Walcott for the world title. He described it to me. 'By the thirteenth round my nose was a mess. There was blood everywhere and I could hardly breathe. They wanted to stop the fight, but I said to my trainer, you give me one more round, that's all I want. Just one more round. So they gave me that one round. And I knocked him out.'

Muhammad Ali the greatest? Not quite. Rocky gets my vote.

Michael Parkinson disagrees with me. He says Ali was the greatest sportsman ever, despite the fact that the one who 'floated like a butterfly and stung like a bee' threatened him on his television chat show. Parky's dad was in the audience that night, and afterwards he went into the dressing room in fighting mood.

'What do you think you were playing at, son?' he stormed. 'I wouldn't have put up with that.'

Parky said, 'But what could I do?'

To which Parkinson senior replied, 'Do? I'll tell you what I would have done if he'd spoken to me like that. I'd have dropped him one straight on his bloody chin.'

Knowing him, I believe he would have as well – although it might also have been the last thing he did!

The greatest football managers

I have known a fair few football managers in my time and, being aware of my lifelong interest in that sport, people often ask me who I consider to be the greatest.

Bill Nicholson of Tottenham Hotspur springs to mind. When he was appointed manager they were sixth from bottom of the old First Division; two years later they completed the first domestic double of the 20th century, winning both the league title and the FA Cup. They went on to carry off the FA Cup three times in seven years, and added two League Cup successes as well. Under Nicholson's guidance, Spurs also became the first British club to win a major European trophy, lifting the European Cup Winners' Cup in 1963, before winning another, the Uefa Cup, in 1972.

Then, of course, Brian Clough has to come into the frame. He completely transformed the fortunes of not one but two clubs. First of all, partnered by Peter Taylor, he joined Derby County when they were in Division Two, led them to the title and, on gaining promotion to the top flight, gave them the first Division One title of their 88-year history.

It was a similar story at Nottingham Forest. They were promoted to Division One in his second full season, and twelve months later they completed a Championship and League Cup double. Clough then took the club an exciting step further with two successive European Cup final successes with a team of virtual unknowns. The only domestic trophy that eluded him was the FA Cup.

It was often said that Taylor was the brains in that partnership, whilst Cloughie provided the motivation. Whoever did what, it certainly worked!

Brian was also a cricket fanatic and I got to know him well. He was always at Trent Bridge, where he not only watched the cricket but played on the squash courts. If I was umpiring I would go out to make an inspection of the pitch and sometimes find Cloughie already in the middle. I'd say, 'What do you think you're doing here out on the square?' He'd say, 'Sorry, Mr Bird, I shall leave immediately.' And I'd tell him, 'Don't you worry about it, Brian. Stay as long as you like, providing you've gone by the time we lead out the teams.'

Arsenal's Arsène Wenger has had a lot of success, but he has not yet won anything in Europe. That's where you have to give credit to Roberto di Matteo, who won the European Champions League for Chelsea in 2012 after stepping in as caretaker manager. He also won the FA Cup, but was rewarded by being given the sack after only six months in charge. Incredible. But that European success is forever on his CV, isn't it?

Manchester United's Matt Busby had considerable domestic success with his 'Busby Babes' before Munich, and ten years later won the European Cup with the side he rebuilt after that disaster. A remarkable achievement.

Bob Paisley's record at Liverpool is also remarkable. Under Paisley the Anfield club won the league title six times in nine seasons, the European Cup three times, the UEFA Cup once and the League Cup three years in a row.

This is what Kenny Dalglish had to say about him: 'There was only one Bob Paisley and he was the greatest of them all. He went through the card in football. He played for Liverpool, he treated the players, he coached them, he managed them and then he became a director. He could tell if someone was injured and what the problem was just by watching them walk a few paces. He was never boastful but had great football knowledge. I owe Bob more than I owe anybody else in the game. There will never be another like him.'

Paisley was also such a modest, down-to-earth chap – a real gentleman – and I had great respect for him. He enjoyed watching and playing cricket and I was sitting next to him at Headingley one day, just after he had won the European Cup, when he said to me, 'I think I'm going to try to buy a little bungalow for me and the missus. What do you think?' I said it sounded a good idea, although I was surprised he was thinking of something so modest. He went on, 'Yes, I still live in a terraced house and I'm happy there. But perhaps it is time for a bungalow.' And we left it at that.

The first manager of a British side to win the European

Cup was Jock Stein with Celtic in 1967. Add to that nine successive Scottish League titles with Celtic and two excursions with Scotland into World Cup finals and it is obvious what a great manager he was before his untimely death, when he collapsed with a heart attack at a World Cup qualifying game at Ninian Park.

His assistant at that time was a certain Alex Ferguson. Now, of course, Sir Alex. And, exceptional as all those other managers were, none can quite match up to the current Manchester United boss. It would take up too much space to list all his achievements in the three decades he has spent at Old Trafford, not to mention his successes with Aberdeen prior to that. Suffice to say that he has so far won forty-seven trophies with the two clubs, including two Champions League titles, a UEFA Cup Winners' Cup and a UEFA Super Cup with United. No wonder they unveiled a bronze statue to him in 2012.

What makes Fergie stand out is the fact that he has built a number of teams during his years at Old Trafford, and he keeps on doing so. Although he has spent a lot of money bringing in star players such as Ronaldo, he has also put his faith in the club's own youth system, which has produced local talent like the Neville brothers, Paul Scholes and Nicky Butt to name but four.

It was reported that Fergie was close to calling it a day a few years ago, but as I write he's still going strong. When he does go, I would like to see Martin O'Neill take his place. Although he had a difficult time at Sunderland in the 2012–13 season, I still rate him very highly and think he would be the ideal successor, although whoever takes on the job has a thankless task in filling the boots of the master.

On a much smaller scale, my choice as Barnsley's greatest manager would be Angus Seed, the man who signed me from school – and most old-timers will agree with me – but there will always be a soft spot for Danny Wilson, who brought Premiership football to Oakwell for the first and only time in the club's history.

The name's Bird – Dickie Bird

Talking of football reminds me of an occasion when I donned my boots again – despite my dodgy knee. It was in 1959, and at that time Yorkshire used to play football matches for charity in the winter months. We had a good side, including Brian Close and Willie Watson, who had both played professional football, Ray Illingworth, Don Wilson, Bryan Stott and Bob Platt in goal.

This particular day we were playing against a Showbiz XI at Odsal Stadium, home of the Bradford Rugby League team, and we were amazed when a crowd of 23,000 turned up.

Closey was our centre-forward and he scored a hat-trick against former Wolves and England centre-half and captain Billy Wright, who had just retired, and Brian was a bit miffed when Platt, who had a blinder in goal, got all the headlines. Pop star turned actor Tommy Steele was also in the Showbiz XI.

I played with my knee strapped up and I have to admit I didn't do an awful lot. I was inside-left, and in the hospitality suite after the match I got talking to the young man who had played directly opposite me at right-half for the Showbiz side. I asked him what part of show business he was from and he said, 'I'm an actor. You've probably never seen me, though, because it's very difficult to get work, you know.' I shook his hand and wished him all the best. Twelve months later he was given a movie role which was to launch him to stardom.

His name? Sean Connery.

Since then I have fondly imagined myself meeting up with him again, going up to him and saying, 'Remember me? The name's Bird – Dickie Bird.'

15

REGRETS? I'VE HAD JUST TWO

SOMETIMES you look back at something in your life and you think, If I had my time over again I wouldn't have done that. My moment was my decision to quit Yorkshire and join Leicestershire in 1960.

It was a massive mistake. Probably the biggest I ever made. But I had reached the end of my tether. I felt I just couldn't take any more knock-backs.

I suppose my feeling of discontent started, strangely enough, immediately after I had made my highest score in first-class cricket – 181 not out against Glamorgan at Bradford in May 1959. I had been recalled to the side because Ken Taylor was playing for England and I was just a bit apprehensive in view of the fact that Glamorgan were a very good side, featuring England internationals Gilbert Parkhouse, Allan Watkins, Peter Walker, Jim McConnon and Jimmy Pressdee. Their spin attack was second to none and it was the kind of pitch that should have suited them, but it was largely thanks to a quickie, Freddie Trueman, that they were bowled out twice and we won by an innings.

And there was Dickie Bird, with this career-best unbeaten 181. Not many people are aware of the fact, but I was out there throughout the entire game. We fielded first, bowled Glamorgan out, then I opened and batted through to a declaration with nine wickets down, took off my pads and went straight back out to field as we bowled them out for a second time.

I got back to the dressing room tired but feeling on top of the world, and when chairman Brian Sellers came in I expected him to sing my praises. However, all he said was, 'Tha's played well, Bird, but we've decided ter drop thee for t' next match. Tha's back in t' second team.'

As he turned to walk out, I called after him, 'Mr Sellers, I'm so proud to be part of a great Yorkshire squad.' He didn't know what to say. It was true. I was proud. Still am. But I was a little bit hurt by the chairman's attitude. And the resentment began to grow.

In Sellers's defence, people claimed that the side had already been picked for the next three matches before my Bradford innings. But it wasn't. When I was on 154 I looked up to the balcony at Valley Parade and I saw the Yorkshire selection committee going in for their meeting. And I was thinking, Surely I'll be in for the next game; surely they'll give me a place – after this knock on a poor pitch. But no.

The next time I played for the first team was against Hampshire at Bournemouth in July and I got 68. It still didn't earn me a regular place, and I was in and out of the side for the rest of the season. I was playing the best cricket of my life, yet they kept leaving me out of the first XI.

Even so, I was extremely proud to be twelfth man when a

very young Yorkshire side clinched the County Championship by beating Sussex at Hove and I was able to share in the
celebrations.

After that we travelled back to Scarborough, where we were
due to play in the annual cricket festival. There were no motor-
ways then – hard to imagine, I know, but it is true – so it was a
long journey and we didn't arrive at the east-coast resort until
four o' clock in the morning. We tried to snatch a few hours'
sleep before going to the ground on the Saturday morning,
when we found thousands and thousands of people lining the
roads. The ground itself was also chock-a-block and they had
to close the gates. The game should have started at eleven
thirty – but we were still having our photographs taken at that
time.

It was all very exciting, but for me things were about to
come to a head. Having watched from the pavilion as my
mates ended the seven-year reign of the Surrey invincibles, I
was back in the side for the Scarborough Festival match against
the MCC, who included the fastest bowler I have ever come
across – Frank 'Typhoon' Tyson.

Opening the innings against him, I was determined to show
the selectors how wrong they had been to leave me out on so
many occasions, and I hit Frank's first three deliveries through
the off side for four. I might have known that the next ball
would be a bouncer, but cocky little me went on the front foot
and as the ball hurtled down Frank yelled, 'Hit that bastard for
four.' The bowler had dropped it short and it bounced up wick-
edly and hit me on the point of the chin. It was just as if I'd

Yorkshire v Glamorgan   County Championship
Horton Park Avenue, Bradford, 23–26 May 1959

Glamorgan 1st innings		Runs
WGA Parkhouse	b Platt	18
B Hedges	b Trueman	1
JS Pressdee	b Trueman	23
PM Walker	c Stott b Trueman	8
AJ Watkins*	c Trueman b Close	20
LN Devereux	lbw b Birkenshaw	39
DJ Ward	c JV Wilson b Birkenshaw	6
JE McConnon	lbw b Platt	13
DGL Evans†	not out	1
DJ Shepherd	c Stott b Trueman	0
F Clarke	b Trueman	0
Extras	(lb 8)	8
Total	**(all out, 59.4 overs)**	**137**

Fall of wickets: 1–11, 2–34, 3–48, 4–61, 5–84, 6–116, 7–135, 8–137, 9–137, 10–137.

Bowling: Trueman 17.4–2–56–5; Platt 22–6–33–2; Close 11–7–21–1; D Wilson 3–0–9–0; Birkenshaw 6–2–10–2.

Yorkshire 1st innings		Runs
WB Stott	b Clarke	19
HD Bird	not out	181
DEV Padgett	lbw b Shepherd	38
DB Close	c Ward b Walker	12
JG Binks†	b Clarke	8
PJ Sharpe	b Watkins	45
JV Wilson*	b Shepherd	27
J Birkenshaw	c Evans b Shepherd	8
FS Trueman	b Walker	11
D Wilson	not out	35
Extras	(b 2, lb 19)	21
Total	**(8 wickets declared, 135 overs)**	**405**

DNB: RK Platt.

Fall of wickets: 1–20, 2–106, 3–123, 4–146, 5–237, 6–294, 7–318, 8–335.

Bowling: Clarke 25–4–108–2; Watkins 25–10–49–1; Shepherd 42–11–106–3; Walker 38–7–103–2; McConnon 5–0–18–0.

Glamorgan 2nd innings

		Runs
WGA Parkhouse	c Binks b Birkenshaw	66
B Hedges	c D Wilson b Close	50
JS Pressdee	c Sharpe b Close	0
PM Walker	c D Wilson b Birkenshaw	23
DGL Evans†	run out	28
AJ Watkins*	c Binks b Close	4
LN Devereux	c & b Birkenshaw	0
DJ Ward	st Binks b Birkenshaw	29
JE McConnon	c Close b Birkenshaw	5
DJ Shepherd	not out	8
F Clarke	b Trueman	0
Extras	(b 13, lb 7)	20
Total	**(all out, 80.2 overs)**	**233**

Fall of wickets: 1–89, 2–89, 3–132, 4–166, 5–171, 6–174, 7–197, 8–205, 9–232, 10–233.

Bowling: Trueman 12.2–3–24–1; Platt 12–3–27–0; Close 23–3–74–3; D Wilson 8–2–34–0; Birkenshaw 25–8–54–5.

Umpires: JH Parks and WFF Price

Yorkshire won by an innings and 35 runs

been punched by Frank's world champion boxing namesake, Mike.

There was blood all over the place. I saw stars. I heard bells ringing. Those, I was told afterwards, belonged to the ambulance which carted me off to hospital, where I had several stitches inserted in the wound. I still carry the scar to this day.

I did, however, return a little later to resume my innings. Tyson was immediately recalled to the attack to put the fear of God into me, but I had the satisfaction of hitting his first delivery straight back over his head for four. I went on to make 50 or 60 – I can't remember the exact total – which I reckoned was pretty good for a man who had been knocked unconscious. So I thought that I would at least be in the squad to make the trip down to The Oval, where Yorkshire were to complete their triumphant season by playing a team selected from the rest of the County Championship sides.

Imagine my disappointment – despair even – when I was left out yet again. Even the rest of the Yorkshire lads thought it disgraceful. So what did they do? They had a collection for me and took me down with them. That's the kind of people they were. Brilliant.

Afterwards I had a long chat with Sellers to try to clear the air and he said, 'I know tha's a bit upset cos tha's been in and out o' t' side all summer, Birdy. And tha's played some good innings. So tha's a good chance o' startin' next season in t' first team. Vic Wilson's at the end of 'is career and 'is place is likely to go to you.'

I felt much better after that. The chairman had given me hope that regular first-team days were just around the corner.

Then, in January, I had a call from the skipper Ronnie Burnet, who had done so much to mould the young players into a first-rate team in a very short space of time. He was actually crying down the phone.

I said, 'What's up, skipper?'

'Dickie,' he said. 'You're not going to believe this, but I've been sacked as Yorkshire captain.'

I was shell-shocked. 'You're joking,' I said. 'They can't sack you. You've just won the County Championship.'

'That's what I thought,' he replied tearfully. 'I was certain I'd be given at least another season. What's more, you'll never guess who they've made captain in my place.'

'No idea, skipper.'

'Vic Wilson.'

'Never!' I gasped. 'Then that's it for me as well. There goes my chance of getting a regular place in the side. And after all Sellers said to me at the end of last season.'

I was seething by this time. Wilson had scored a century in that final game at The Oval, which might have had something to do with the decision to delay his retirement. But to be made captain as well! I couldn't believe it.

I was still feeling down in the dumps when I reported back in the nets in April, but I was determined not to let the situation upset me and I had a good month. I made some big scores in the practice matches and I was confident my form was good enough to earn me a place in the party for the southern tour, which preceded the County Championship season in those days. I was also encouraged by the fact that both the coaches, Arthur Mitchell and Maurice Leyland, told me that they had been so impressed with the way I had played that they had recommended that I should be in the side.

I was feeling quite chirpy as I attended the pre-season lunch, when Mr Sellers was due to announce the squad of fourteen names for the southern tour, confident that mine would be amongst them. I was sitting next to Ted Lester, the second-team captain, and he said, 'I hope I won't be seeing you again this season.' He wasn't being rude; he simply thought that I ought to be a first-team regular.

Finally, Sellers began reading out the names in alphabetical order, so I didn't have long to wait. But I wasn't in the Bs. Strange, I thought, perhaps he's overlooked it, or maybe he's saving the new names until later. But no. There was no H.D. Bird. I couldn't take it in. I just sat there. In tears.

What made it worse, as I learned afterwards, was that the final place had been between me and another lad, and the chairman of selectors who had used his casting vote to make the decision was Clifford Hesketh, who just happened to be the Barnsley rep-resentative on that committee. It was the last straw. I had thought throughout my time with Yorkshire that Hesketh would give me his support as a Barnsley lad. But he did nothing for me. Only last year, at the 150th anniversary of the Shaw Lane Club, I got to reminiscing about this with Hubert Padgett, another former Yorkshire cricketer from Barnsley, and he said, 'Funny you should mention that, Dickie. He did nothing for me either.'

I believed I'd done well enough to earn my place. I'd averaged 40-odd in my first-team appearances the previous season, when I was playing better than I had ever done, so I said to myself, I'm never going to crack it here; time to move on. It hurt me to come to that decision, but what else could I do?

Joining Leicestershire

When I told my dad I was going to ask for my release he said, 'Fight it out, son. Fight it out.'

I now wish I had listened to him. Instead, I took the advice of Willie Watson, a former Yorkshire player who had become captain of Leicestershire, and he assured me that there would be a place for me in the team at Grace Road.

So in 1960 I joined a team at the bottom of the County Championship table after being with a side that had just won the title. I once described it as 'graveyard cricket'. It was certainly a big step down the ladder and unfortunately I was never the player I had been with Yorkshire.

The press built me up as some sort of saviour, the very man to turn the tide; someone who could get among the runs regularly and give the side greater stability higher up the batting order. I thought I handled the pressure well in my first season, when I scored more than a thousand runs and was awarded my county cap. Then came the change which sent my fortunes into a bit of a nosedive. Maurice Hallam, a Leicestershire man through and through, replaced Watson as captain – and he didn't much care for Yorkshiremen because the England selectors, in their wisdom, had picked Yorkshire's Ken Taylor rather than him.

In my opinion the selectors got it wrong. Hallam had scored a thousand runs at the end of May; Taylor had managed only 450 or so. But why should Hallam choose to make the four Yorkshiremen at Leicestershire – Jack Birkenshaw, Jack van Geloven, Peter Broughton and me – suffer for it? It wasn't as though we had been responsible for picking the England team. Yet Hallam stated publicly that he would make it very difficult for us; and he did.

Nevertheless, there were still some magical moments. There was the time Hallam and I put on 277 for the first wicket against South Africa in July 1960, the county's best opening stand since the war. The story goes that a late arrival at Grace Road blinked at the scoreboard, shrugged his shoulders and muttered, 'Two hundred for none, eh. Ah, well, I suppose we couldn't expect anything else.' Then he took his seat and could not believe his eyes when he realised the tourists were actually fielding. Surely, he thought, that can't be Maurice Hallam and Dickie Bird out there piling up the runs against the tourists. But it was.

On another occasion I was 98 against Sussex at Grace Road and confident of completing my century. I stroked the ball to mid-off and called to my batting partner for a comfortable single to take me one run closer. He let me get right up to him – then sent me back. There was no way I could regain my ground and I was run out by a mile. I've never forgotten, nor forgiven, the man responsible for robbing me of an almost certain ton. His name was Pratt.

I can, however, boast of creating a record at Leicester which I believe still stands. I bagged a pair between tea and close of play on the first day of a match.

What happened in that encounter in 1960 was that Sussex batted first and were all out for 239. When we replied I was dismissed for a duck and we were bowled out for 42, so we had to follow on. There was time for only one over before close of play, but that was long enough to see me out again, in exactly the same way, caught by Hubert Doggart round the corner at leg slip off a Thomson inswinger without troubling the scorer.

That maybe summed up my time at Leicestershire. I did not enjoy it. I have to be honest about that. I struggled, the team struggled, and it became a bit of a grind.

It has to be said, however, that a few years after I left them the club underwent a dramatic change for the better when Michael Turner took over as chief executive and Ray Illing-worth was drafted in as captain. They did so much for that county. They took Leicestershire from being a struggling side – and I mean struggling – to the County Championship title in 1975. It was an amazing achievement. Turner produced the goods off the pitch and Illy on it. He got the players he wanted – only ordinary cricketers, you might have thought, but they were all-rounders who could do a bit of bowling and a bit of batting – and he moulded them into a winning side. Now I am a life member and proud to be associated with what is a magnificent set-up.

As I look back now, however, it just makes me regret even more the error I made on leaving Yorkshire when I did. If I

Leicestershire v Sussex County Championship
Grace Road, Leicester, 3–4 August 1960

Sussex 1st innings		Runs
ASM Oakman	c Watson b van Geloven	46
DV Smith	b Spencer	13
ER Dexter*	b Boshier	3
JM Parks†	c & b Boshier	14
KG Suttle	c Spencer b Pratt	1
GHG Doggart	b Savage	39
Nawab of Pataudi	b van Geloven	38
NI Thomson	b van Geloven	25
RV Bell	not out	12
DL Bates	c Julian b Spencer	1
RG Marlar	c Pratt b van Geloven	38
Extras	(b 4, lb 3, w 1, nb 1)	9
Total	**(all out, 74.4 overs)**	**239**

Fall of wickets: 1–21, 2–26, 3–48, 4–59, 5–99, 6–127, 7–175, 8–189, 9–196, 10–239.

Bowling: Spencer 24–8–78–2; Boshier 12.1–2–37–2; Pratt 19–3–50–1; Savage 8–0–31–1; van Geloven 11.3–1–34–4.

Leicestershire 1st innings		Runs
W Watson*	b Dexter	1
HD Bird	c Oakman b Thomson	0
D Kirby	c Dexter b Thomson	9
MR Hallam	lbw b Thomson	1
J van Geloven	b Bates	1
PA Munden	b Bates	5
RL Pratt	not out	16
R Julian†	b Thomson	0
CT Spencer	b Thomson	8
JS Savage	b Thomson	1
BS Boshier	absent hurt	–
Extras		0
Total	**(all out, 24.1 overs)**	**42**

Fall of wickets: 1–1, 2–3, 3–11, 4–12, 5–12, 6–21, 7–22, 8–38, 9–42.

Bowling: Thomson 12.1–3–23–6; Dexter 4–2–3–1; Bates 8–4–16–2.

Leicestershire 2nd innings (following on)   **Runs**

W Watson*	b Dexter	3
HD Bird	c Doggart b Thomson	0
D Kirby	run out	59
MR Hallam	c Parks b Dexter	14
J van Geloven	c Oakman b Dexter	5
PA Munden	run out	12
RL Pratt	c & b Smith	11
R Julian†	b Smith	1
CT Spencer	not out	38
JS Savage	b Thomson	15
BS Boshier	absent hurt	–
Extras	(b 5, lb 12, nb 1)	18
Total	**(all out, 50.4 overs)**	**176**

Fall of wickets: 1–7, 2–8, 3–40, 4–50, 5–80, 6–99, 7–105, 8–149, 9–176.

Bowling: Thomson 19.4–5–55–2; Dexter 13–4–40–3; Bates 15–3–50–0; Smith 3–0–13–2.

Umpires: CS Elliott and JG Langridge

Sussex won by an innings and 21 runs

had just carried on a bit longer, I could have made the move with Illy and I know things would have worked out well for me then.

Such wonderful friends

Anyway, the top and bottom of all this is that if I could have my time again, I'd have stayed with Yorkshire; at least for a little while longer. Despite the knock-backs, those days at Headingley were amongst the happiest of my life and I had such wonderful, wonderful friends.

Among them were Don Wilson and Phil Sharpe and all three of us were big fans of the Black and White Minstrel Show. We would go all over the place to watch them – the Victoria Palace in London, the Futurist in Scarborough – and sometimes we were invited into the dressing room to chat with the lead singers, Tony Mercer, Dai Francis and John Boulter, who all had beautiful voices; Reg Thompson, the resident comedian; and the famous compère Leslie Crowther. They were all cricket fanatics and we got on famously.

When they were at Scarborough for the summer season we were regular visitors during the cricket festival in September. They were great times. We used to go through their routine with them from start to finish. Don said I was quite brilliant at 'Abba Dabba'. People always said that my signalling and arm movements were quite theatrical. Maybe it was because of those happy days in theatre with the Black and White Minstrels.

Even though I was in and out of the side, I was on good terms with the other lads as well – Bryan Stott, Ken Taylor, Doug Padgett, Brian Close, Raymond Illingworth, Ronnie Burnet, Jimmy Binks, Jack Birkenshaw, Fred Trueman, Bob Platt, Brian Bolus, Mel Ryan and Vic Wilson.

The more I look at the names in that team, the more I begin to feel that maybe I did well enough just to join them occasionally during that historic Championship-winning season. To be even a small part of a squad of players like that – I rate it as the greatest county side in history, and I don't care what anybody else says – was truly an honour. And an achievement in itself.

I mentioned Trueman and Platt in that line-up and I believe that was as good an opening attack as Yorkshire had in that era. Platt was a very good bowler, but his batting left a great deal to be desired. He went in at number ten or eleven, and that is exactly where he deserved to be. However, strange as it may seem, one of my abiding memories of him is as a batsman.

We were playing Derbyshire at Chesterfield in July 1959 and Derbyshire batted first, making a big score of 351 for 8 declared. When we replied it looked as though we would have to follow on as wickets tumbled right, left and centre, including that of H.D. Bird for a solitary run. I kept my pads on, ready to go in as night-watchman if we were asked to bat again.

Then Bob went in at number ten and hit an unbeaten 57 to take us to 275 and well clear of the follow-on total. We couldn't

believe it. Neither could that highly respected cricket corre-
spondent, E.W. Swanton, who wrote in his report for the *Daily
Telegraph*,

> The surprise was Platt's batting. Anyone arriving late on the
> ground and watching him stroking handsomely through the
> covers could have taken him for a reputable No 5 bat. He went
> on to make 57 not out, his previous best having been 17, and I
> cannot begin to explain why it was not many more.

I still talk to Bob quite often and he always brings up the
subject of his great knock in that game. When all the old players get together he makes sure to give us a reminder of his
batting prowess.

That innings at Chesterfield was Bob's one claim to fame
as a batsman – but as a bowler he was the perfect foil to
Fiery Fred. He presented a totally different kind of threat for
the batsman. He was the only right-arm bowler in 150 years
who bowled inswingers and late-cutters for Yorkshire, who
had always insisted on bowlers who could make the ball
leave the bat.

If Bob had taken the advice of Dai Davies, a former Glamorgan player who went on to become an umpire, he would
have been lost to Yorkshire. While doing his National Service,
Bob played for the Combined Universities against county
teams and during one of these encounters Davies said to him,
'Bob, lad, I feel I've just got to tell you something. Yorkshire
will never entertain you bowling inswingers and late-cutters.

My advice is to leave Yorkshire; try somewhere else where you will be more appreciated.'

But Bob stuck it out, earning his county cap and making quite a name for himself with Yorkshire. In fact, he eventually became cricket chairman at the club and it was during his tenure in 2001 that Yorkshire, captained by David Byas, won the County Championship for the first time in thirty-three years. Sadly, another decline followed until 2012, when they won promotion from Division Two to regain their First Division status.

One of Bob's best performances came in a match against Surrey at The Oval in June 1959, when Surrey were 36 for none at tea and going like a train. During the interval Freddie played hell about the pitch, and almost everything else, suggesting that Surrey had prepared a strip to suit their bowlers. He was going berserk. Not a happy chappie at all.

Bob sat there, cool as a cucumber, and said, 'Calm down, Freddie. That gasometer over there is beginning to rise. It could be a sign. It might mean our fortunes will rise after tea.'

And guess what? Freddie and Bob went on to skittle Surrey, taking 5 for 51 and 5 for 31 respectively. Bob went up to his colleague when the last wicket fell and said, 'Told you so.'

That was one of three occasions when Bob out-bowled his more famous partner with a ten-wicket haul, the others being against Middlesex in 1960 and Worcestershire in 1962.

Mention of Worcestershire reminds me of the time Bob and I planned to arrive early at the Star Hotel in Worcester, where the Yorkshire team was staying. The hotel was situated next to a railway bridge and near the bus station, so there was always a lot of noise, and we were determined to get the one quiet room.

However, when Fred turned up he said, 'Who do those two buggers think they are? I'm having the quiet room. Put them in the back.'

So he turfed us out and we had to put up with the rattle and roll of the trains thundering past on the main line. He also said to Bob, 'I'll tell you something else, young man, and I'm telling it to you straight, if there's a wind tomorrow it will be behind me when I open the bowling. You'll be at the other end.'

Freddie must have seen the weather forecast, because, sure enough, it was windy next morning and while he steamed in with it behind him, Bob toiled all day long into it. Then we had to go back to our noisy room without getting a wink of sleep while you-know-who dropped off as soon as his head hit the pillow.

The Star Hotel is not there any more – which may have come as a relief to others in our situation.

Playing for Worcestershire around that time was the West Indian Vanburn Holder, who was a very good fast bowler, but hardly got a look-in at Test level because of Holding, Marshall, Garner and company. Holder was six feet tall, but had very bandy legs, and he once told me a story, against himself, which had me doubled up in laughter. Freddie had a reputation for going into the dressing rooms before a match and winding up the opposition. So when he walked in at

Worcestershire and saw Holder standing there, he remarked, 'Vanburn, old son, do you know if thy legs were straight, tha'd be eight feet tall.'

Another of Fred's opening partners was Tony Nicholson, a fine bowler in his own right. Back in 1974, when a certain Ian Botham was just beginning to make a bit of a name for himself at Somerset, Yorkshire were the visitors to Bath and the Sunday League game was building up to an exciting climax. Nicholson had just gone in as last man with wicketkeeper David Bairstow already at the crease.

Five runs were needed to clinch a win for Yorkshire and Botham was bowling. The two batsmen conferred in the middle and I am told that Bairstow said to Nicholson, 'I have to get strike, so whatever happens to the first ball, I shall be running. You run as fast as you can as well. Got that?'

'Got it,' replied Nicholson. 'Whatever happens, I run.'

Having sorted that out, Nick faced the bowling of the youthful Botham. The ball whizzed past Nick's off stump and sped through to wicketkeeper Jim Parks. Bluey Bairstow was already on his way, charging down from the other end. He was halfway down when he realised that his colleague was just standing there, motionless. So he slammed on the brakes, turned and attempted to scramble back. As he did so Nick suddenly sprang into action and sprinted towards the bowler's end, but he had gone only a few strides when Parks knocked off the bails for a run-out, leaving Somerset victors by four runs.

As the two batsmen made their way, stony-faced, through the cheering Somerset supporters, Bairstow turned to Nicholson and said, 'What on earth do you think you were doing?'

'Sorry, Blue,' replied Nick. 'I forgot what we'd agreed.'

Freddie Trueman – there'll never be another

When you think about it, there were quite a few bowlers who opened the attack with Trueman. As well as Platt and Nicholson, there were also Melville Ryan, Mike Cowan and Peter Broughton – and he saw them all off.

There's another of Fred's partners who rarely gets a mention because he played so little, and that is Eric Burgin, who died in 2012 at the age of 88. He was another who suffered because he bowled inswingers rather than outswingers. He was never awarded his county cap, despite two outstanding performances against Surrey and Lancashire. In the Surrey game at Headingley he claimed 6 for 43, including a devastating spell of 3 for 1, and in the Roses clash at Old Trafford he bowled unchanged to take 5 for 20 as Yorkshire won by nine wickets, Freddie's contribution being 5 for 26.

After his playing days were over Eric served as the South Yorkshire representative on the Yorkshire committee until he and his colleagues were ousted following the controversial sacking of Geoff Boycott in 1983, which led to the formation of the Yorkshire Reform Group and the successful fight for Boycott's reinstatement. It was a pity, because Eric had done a good job.

I knew Eric, a Methodist like me, from the time I played at Barnsley in the Yorkshire League. He was in the Sheffield United side, along with George Pope, the former Derbyshire and England bowler, and first change was Cyril Turner, who had just finished playing for Yorkshire. As you can imagine they had a very strong XI.

He is, however, best remembered for the moment he recognised an extraordinary raw talent. He and Cyril were coaching Sheffield United when a teenager walked up, virtually off the street, and asked if he could 'have a go'. Eric was so impressed by what he saw that it was not long before he and Cyril had recommended the young lad to Yorkshire. George Hirst was the county coach at the time and asked the youngster what he did.

'I'm a fast bowler,' came the reply.

So George said, 'Right, show me what you can do.' Five balls later George stepped in and said, 'Right, lad, that's it.'

'But I've only bowled five balls,' the lad pleaded.

George replied, 'Aye, lad, I know. But I've seen enough.'

And that's how Fred Trueman took the first step to becoming a Yorkshire and England legend.

He told me in later years that he had learned to bowl his famed outswinger on an asphalt street in Maltby, right on the Yorkshire/Nottinghamshire border, where he lived. It had a slope from one side to the other and it was there that he honed his skills at a very early age.

As well as being a magnificent bowler, Freddie was also the king of the one-liner. For example, when he was doing his

National Service he was playing for the Combined Services against a county side and his captain took exception to his apparently indifferent attitude, which was so unlike him.

'I'm not at all happy with you, Trueman,' his captain growled. 'If you don't buck up your ideas, I'm going to leave you out of the next game.'

To which Freddie replied, 'You can do what you like, mate. I was demobbed two days ago.'

Then there was the time Yorkshire were playing at North-amptonshire and Johnny Wardle, facing up to Frank Tyson, the fastest bowler in the world at the time, was nearly at square leg when he took guard. Needless to say, the first ball he received sent the wickets flying. When Fred went in it was the same story, and as he entered the dressing room Wardle tore into him.

'That was disgraceful. You left the stumps wide open. You were obviously frightened to death of him.'

Fred snapped back, 'Aye, well, I couldn't get further away because I got stuck in your shit.'

In all the years I knew him, I can never remember Freddie being injured. He argued that present-day players have so many injuries because, when they go into the gymnasium to do their fitness exercises, they use muscles that they don't need for cricket.

Freddie had this routine, which he never wavered from, season after season. When we reported back at Yorkshire on the first day of April he would do some bowling from a stand-ing position, more or less just turning his arm over. The second day he would bowl off a couple of yards or so. The third day he would make his run a little longer. And so it went on, until he was roaring in off his full run. He built up gradually, using only the muscles he needed as a fast bowler.

He would also join the rest of us as we practised taking long catches in the outfield, then short catches, from all angles, using the old slip cradle. And slowly but surely we would all reach the necessary fitness for the start of the season.

Freddie fervently believed that going into gyms and using weights and other apparatus was a waste of time, because the wrong muscles were being exercised. If the proof of the pudding is in the eating, then I can honestly say that I never once saw Freddie on the physio's table.

Fitness-wise he was an amazing fellow, but he also firmly believed that cricket was played very largely in the head – temperament, application, strong will-power, belief in yourself. Having said all this, he was a one-off. Yorkshire will never know another quite like him. Players like him come once in a lifetime. I don't use the word 'genius' lightly, but it does apply to someone like Freddie.

My other regret

So, leaving Yorkshire to join Leicestershire when I did is one of my major regrets. The other is that I never had a family of my own. I would love to have had a son who played cricket for Yorkshire. That would have given me a lot of pleasure. But it was not to be.

Until my retirement, I had lived out of a suitcase from the age of 19 and although I had girlfriends, relationships never lasted more than a few months. I could never settle down, and I did not think, even then, that marriage was for me. It would not be fair on any girl to have to traipse around the country with me, living in hotel rooms, or patiently waiting alone and bored back home while I was away for days, weeks and possibly even months.

I've had lots of proposals, including quite a few in the first few years after announcing my retirement, but my sister Marjorie warned me, 'It's too late, Dennis' – she is the only one who calls me by my real name these days – 'it just wouldn't work; you're too set in your ways.' And she's right, as usual.

There was just once when I gave the idea of marriage serious thought, and that was while I was coaching in Johannesburg in the 1960s. There was this girl and I thought she was just the one for me. She was beautiful; blonde, tall and very well educated. She was studying Afrikaans and psychology at Wits University. She had everything. She even liked cricket. We spent many evenings together and felt very much at ease in each other's company.

However, when I returned to England for the summer cricket season and she remained in South Africa to continue her studies, I realised it could never work. There were too many obstacles. She did say that she would travel with me when she had finished her studies, but I could not be sure. In any case, I knew deep down that it would not be fair on her. If I was being honest about it, looking back, all I could see in front of me was cricket. A wife would have to play second fiddle, and that, I felt, was a recipe for disaster.

We said our goodbyes in 1964 and that was that. I never saw her again. She understood. I have seen so many divorces involving sports people because one or the other has been living and working away from home, and I didn't want it to happen to me. I believe there has to be total commitment in a marriage and I could not offer that. I do, however, often wonder what became of her.

So I became married to cricket. To all intents and purposes cricket has been my wife as well as my life. And it has been so good to me.

But it hasn't given me a son . . .

16

BEYOND THE BOUNDARIES

I AM proud to say that I am a fully paid-up member of the Professional Cricketers' Association, which has done an absolutely magnificent job in safeguarding the future of past and present players in England and Wales since its inception in 1967.

The stated aim is 'to improve the welfare of its members in the key areas of cricket, personal development, insurance, legal, financial, benevolent and healthcare and then provide advice, services or assistance where appropriate', and the organisation is admirably carrying out those aims – I speak as someone who has benefited.

In 2011 the PCA held a Past Player Day, which took place during the Cheltenham Cricket Festival, and it was so success-ful that it was decided to make it an annual occasion. Such events are very special to me and I was delighted to be there in 2012. It was so nice to return to Cheltenham and see so many old players. It brought back some wonderful memories. And at my age you wonder how many events like this you've got left. It was marvellous.

The PCA has come on so much since Somerset fast bowler Fred Rumsey set it up with the help of such people as fellow cricketer Jack Bannister and broadcaster John Arlott, and I am sure it will go from strength to strength doing very valuable work.

You will never get a better commentator than Arlott. He was the doyen of them all. Brian Johnston and Richie Benaud were also superb in their own way, and then there was Henry Longhurst on golf and Harry Carpenter on boxing, all with the special gift of creating pictures with words. I just loved listening to all of them.

One of the original members of the PCA, former Derbyshire and England wicketkeeper Bob Taylor, was also among those in Cheltenham swapping anecdotes with old adversaries, and he remarked that the camaraderie was second to none. So it was, as always, and it was summed up perfectly by Tim Lamb when he said, 'Chris Cowdrey put it in a nutshell when he commented that we were foes on the field but friends off it. I challenge anybody to find another sport that captures the camaraderie you find in cricket. You've only got to look at the generation span here today, with players present from modern times, and at the other end of the spectrum guys who graced the playing fields thirty or forty years ago.'

In my case it was even longer than that, at least so far as playing the game is concerned, but I agreed with him wholeheartedly when he went on to say that all of us there had that great thing in common of having played county cricket, and were therefore part of an exclusive club. He thought that was tremendous. So did we all. And we were delighted to be sharing an evening together.

Another Compton makes his name

An important promotion by the PCA is the annual NatWest awards night and in 2012 Somerset's Nick Compton won the Reg Hayter Cup as the player of the year. Now, being the grandson of England legend Denis has meant that Nick has had more pressure on him than most, but he has become used to the glare of the spotlight and his form during that season suggested that it is not affecting him in any way. He scored 1,494 runs – more than any other player – at a remarkable average of 99.60. Is it any wonder he was drafted into the England team for the winter tour of India?

That call caused him to remark, 'It's a very exciting opportunity for me because it's been a dream since I was 12 or 13, but the hard work starts here if I want to prove myself at international level. It's like when you make a hundred – can you go on and convert it into a double hundred?'

I was very impressed with that. It showed that the lad has the right attitude. He still needs more experience, but experience only comes in time and through playing, and I believe he has the ability and the character to become a fixture in the England team. An opening partnership with Alastair Cook could blossom into something special.

Mind you, he has a long way to go to match granddad Denis, the so-called 'Brylcreem Boy', who scored 5,807 runs for England at an average of 50.06 either side of World War II. But I liked Nick's reaction to that as well. He said, 'People talk about my grandfather's record being a burden, but I see it more as an inspiration, and I'm very proud of the connection. People may try to compare us, but I am my own man.'

Compton followed another Somerset player, his skipper Marcus Trescothick, as well as other household names such as Mike Procter, Malcolm Marshall, Sir Richard Hadlee, Graham Gooch, Andy Roberts, Graeme Hick, Courtney Walsh, Brian Lara, Waqar Younis and Andrew Flintoff, to name but a few, in collecting the Reg Hayter Cup, which has been awarded by the PCA since 1970, and he admits that the former England opening batsman has played a significant part in his development.

Mind Matters

Mention of Marcus Trescothick leads me on to another, rather less publicised, but extremely important aspect of the PCA's stated aims to 'provide advice, services or assistance', in this particular case in the realm of healthcare.

I am always going on about the need for players to have 'mental strength' because I do believe it is an essential part of the make-up of any successful sportsman or woman. Cricket is a battle of wills between the batsman and the bowler, and those at the top are expected to have that capacity to overcome opposition, conditions and anything else that gets in the way of success. It is that capacity which I describe as 'mental strength'.

Sadly, however, the strains and stresses of cricket can sometimes cause problems. Trescothick's difficulties in that respect, which caused him to relinquish his place in the England team, have been well documented, and now, through the PCA, he is seeking to help other players who are facing similar difficulties which are threatening their careers – and even lives.

The PCA set up an online series of 'Mind Matters' tutorials to help players whose personal lives have been affected by addiction, mental health problems and, occasionally, self-harm and thoughts of suicide. The tutorials provide information on topics that include alcohol, drug and gambling addiction, anxiety and depression.

Jason Ratcliffe, an old friend of mine who is assistant chief executive of the PCA and also the editor of their excellent magazine, *Beyond the Boundaries*, explained the objective of the series to me: 'We're not seeking to equip players as experts, but just to ensure that they are familiar enough with the issues and symptoms to seek help if it is needed. The stigma of mental illness has been significantly reduced, thanks to a number of high-profile sportsmen coming forward to speak out on their experiences. That is one of the key messages. If players are having problems, they should not suffer in silence. Instead, they should pick up the phone and ring the confidential helpline, or speak to their personal development manager.'

One of those 'high-profile sportsmen' that 'Ratters' spoke about was Freddie Flintoff, who has spoken candidly about his struggles with depression and drink. In a television documentary in 2012, he said, 'I was having a quiet drink with my dad Colin on Christmas Eve 2006, just after we had lost the Ashes, and as we made our way home I started crying my eyes out. I told him I'd tried my best but that I couldn't do it any more, I couldn't keep playing. We talked and, of course, I dusted myself down and carried on. But I was never the same player again. I was captain of England and financially successful. Yet instead of walking out confidently to face Australia in one of the world's biggest sporting events, I didn't want to get out of bed, never mind face people.'

Talking about the 2007 World Cup, during which he was dropped from the one-day side following the infamous pedalo incident, Flintoff added, 'The whole time I was on the field and throughout that World Cup, all I could think about was that I wanted to retire.

'I didn't understand what was happening to me. I knew when I got back to my room I couldn't shut off, which is why I started having a drink. It got to the stage where I was probably drinking more than I should. All I wanted was for the doctor to tell me what was wrong, but no one suggested it was depression. There's a certain sense of shame when I remember sitting in the dressing room after winning a one-day international in the West Indies. The lads were celebrating and I didn't want to be a part of it. I didn't want to do anything but sit on my own in the corner.'

In the PCA tutorial he says, 'The hardest thing in the world is to talk to people. I felt it would be a weakness to say to someone, "Help, I'm struggling with this." But looking back, doing that should have been seen as a strength.'

When Warwickshire wicketkeeper Tim Ambrose lost his England Test place a few years ago it sparked off a serious bout of depression for him. In an article in the *Daily Telegraph* he admitted, 'I was awake twenty-four hours a day, with things going round in my head. I was beyond miserable. It felt like I had this duvet that was soaking wet wrapped round me and I just couldn't get it off. The idea of playing cricket just seemed absurd.'

It was then that he approached a sports psychologist who had worked with Warwickshire, and with that help he began gradually to escape from his demons. Although he still has problems from time to time, now he knows how to deal with them. That is one of the key issues. Players who suffer from depression simply don't know how to cope with it. And that makes it much worse.

Ambrose explained, 'When it was happening to me I didn't understand what was going on. I didn't know I had depression. I didn't know where to go. What has opened my eyes in dealing with it is that we don't know enough, especially as we as cricketers are people who, in my opinion, are quite vulnerable to it – there are lots of highs and lows and lots of time on the road, which makes one's personal life quite difficult.

'The PCA does so many amazing things for us that everyone listens to what they have to say, so for them to make this an awareness subject will really get the message across to players.'

Another victim is Darren Cousins, the former Essex and Northamptonshire seamer, and his problems started when he retired in 2002. He found nothing to replace cricket, which had been his whole life. By March 2011 he had hit rock bottom and attempted suicide.

Now he says, 'If there's anything I have learned from this, it is that you are actually a stronger person to reach out and admit that you've got a problem, as opposed to drowning your sorrows. When you are really, really down, it's a question of how you can get out of that trough. What I will say to anyone who finds themselves in the dark space I did is that you've always got something of which you should be proud.'

It was Ambrose who summed up the feelings of all those who suffer in this way when he said, 'When you are hit by depression, it does not make you a freak or a weirdo. Depression is more common than you'd ever know. Just because of what we do doesn't mean we don't need help. It can happen to anyone.'

Life is so precious

Thankfully I never suffered from depression during my career as a player and umpire – I enjoyed myself too much for that – but I can sympathise with those who have gone through such a time, because the stroke I had in my retirement years has left me in a similar state. I can get very down, especially when I am lying in bed and all kinds of thoughts are going through my mind. I can even understand how someone might get to the stage where they think about committing suicide, and there have been numerous cases in cricket.

Stuart Leary leaped off Table Mountain in South Africa; Peter Roebuck jumped from a hotel balcony; David Bairstow took his own life. It has happened in football, too, the most recent incident involving Welsh international Gary Speed. It can happen to anyone. No one, for example, would have thought that Bairstow was the suicidal type; he was always such a bubbly character. In his case, I think it resulted from the fact that he missed cricket so much when he retired. It was as if his whole life had been taken away, and that's how he chose to end it.

I was determined, when I retired, to accept that my career was over. Half a century is a long time to be involved with anything, and it can be a huge wrench to have it taken away, but there is nothing you can do about it. Those days have gone. So let them go.

I gave myself a new focus with my foundation. And that has helped enormously. It keeps me occupied and it gets me out.

Drink can be a crucial factor as well. George Best was a brilliant footballer and a nice bloke, who did himself no favours by drinking even during his playing days. But it was when he retired that he went overboard, seeking comfort in alcohol. It's the worst thing that any sportsman can do. You've still got to get up and face the next morning.

A new day does provide a challenge for me. The stroke left me feeling that I didn't want to go out anywhere. I didn't want to go to the bother of getting changed. When I did get out of bed, I just wanted to sit there in my chair watching the television. But I forced myself into action. I did my exercises, had a shower to freshen myself up and made myself get out of the house, if only for a walk. Keep going, keep fit, occupy the mind. It's the only way.

There are also the emotional repercussions of my stroke. I can be sat watching a television programme and, for no real reason, the tears start to flow. That's why I don't go out speaking these days. Because if I get on to certain topics, I know there will be a flood of tears and I will not be able to carry on. I wouldn't want that.

But I'm still here, and life is so precious, isn't it? My aim when I retired was to get to 70. Having reached 70 I was determined to get to 80. Now I've my sights set on 90. It's a tall order after all the illnesses I've had since I quit the game, but I'm damn well going to give it a go.

If I do need help, I know I can call on the PCA, and that's a comfort. Thanks to their efforts, more and more help is now available for players finding themselves in any kind of difficulty and, as someone who has been given so much by the game of cricket, I am delighted to be a member of an organisation which is giving so much back to people who need it most.

17

PAST, PRESENT
AND FUTURE

PEOPLE say to me, 'Do you miss being part of the game,
Dickie?'

It is inevitable, isn't it? I am bound to miss it, because it has
been my life. But the wise thing to do is to concentrate on the
present – and the future.

I still watch a lot of cricket, especially at Headingley, and I
like to have a word with the umpires when I visit the various
grounds up and down the country. Very often they ask if they
can have their photographs taken with me, which is very flattering, I have to say.

As far as umpiring standards are concerned, it is very difficult to assess who are the good umpires because of all the
electronic aids. You could argue that these days the only
umpires making the decisions are the ones in the leagues, who
do not have all the technical trappings that are available at the
higher levels. One thing I am sure of is that having played the
game myself helped me as an umpire. It is not a stipulation
that you have to have played at County Championship level,
but it certainly benefited me.

I think it would also help football referees for them to have
played at league level, although there is a problem in that there

is very little time after they have finished their playing careers to go through the system, as they have to retire at a younger age than in cricket. One way is to fast-track them and I believe that is happening more and more.

I went straight on to the first-class umpires' list and within two years I was on the Test match panel. If you have played the game yourself, you have gone through every little thing. You know instinctively what players are thinking. For example, you can nearly always tell if a player got a nick from his reactions. Cameras can't do that, can they? In fact, they have quite a number of limitations. They can be at the wrong height, or looking at the wrong angle, and so give a distorted view.

Also, there is no cricket field in the world that is absolutely level, not to mention the fact that the grass is longer at some grounds than others, so how can a camera judge a low catch? That decision has to be made by the two umpires, one at square leg, the other at the bowler's end. They have to get together, confer, then come to a combined decision. If there is any doubt whatsoever, it has to be 'not out'.

Another consideration is that if you take Test matches and one-dayers into account, it is a twelve-months-a-year job these days. For most of my career – the first twenty or so years of it – I stood only at Test matches in England. That meant three Tests in a year at the most. Someone worked it out recently and came to the conclusion that if there had been the same number of games in my day I would have done 500 Tests.

I was a Test umpire for twenty-five years. None of the current crop will last so long. They will do more Tests in a shorter period of time, but it will be impossible to carry on for a quarter of a century. Test after Test, with all the travelling in between, will see them burn out long before that. And that's another reason for me to be glad that I umpired when I did.

The all-seeing eye of the television camera

These days life is made much more difficult by all the television cameras focusing on your every move. Football in particular has a big problem in that there are umpteen cameras at every possible height and angle highlighting incidents. Then the pundits in the studios get to work, slowing the action right down, magnifying it frame by frame, repeating it half a dozen times – and even then they sometimes cannot agree on whether or not the referee has made the correct decision. Yet they expect him to do so at normal speed and from just one vantage point. I have a lot of sympathy for football officials, especially those in the Premiership. They have a thankless task, and players do not make it any easier by feigning injury and diving all over the place.

But at least football referees are still making the decisions and not electronic machines. A lot of people criticise Michel Platini, the former French international who is now president of UEFA, but I agree with him wholeheartedly when he insists that electronic aids should not be brought into football. I've seen his quotes in the press. He says, 'Over my dead body.' He's quite open about it, and I admire him for that. Football is a game of only ninety minutes. If you keep stopping the action, you are going to be playing all day and all night.

Having said all that, I do think, however, that technology should be used for goal-line incidents – deciding whether the ball has crossed the line or not. I would bring it in for that. In that case, you could have a camera positioned where it can make a proper judgement and it would take a matter of seconds to check the evidence. Action replays are there in an instant.

The problem is, of course, how do you bring it in for all football? What about the lower divisions, where clubs may not be able to afford the equipment? Or those games in the local parks where it is not feasible?

Everyone is wanting perfect decisions – in all sports – and you will never get that. It is simply not possible.

'Well, thank you very much, mate!'

When I was playing county cricket, if I got a nick and the ball fell to the slip fielder, I would turn to him and say, 'Did you catch it?' If he said, 'Yes, Dickie, I caught it,' that was good enough for me. I would walk, because there is only one person who knows for certain whether a catch has been taken cleanly or not and that is the catcher himself.

There were, however, some fielders who were, shall we say, a little economical with the truth, as the following incident proves.

One of my team-mates in the Barnsley and Yorkshire teams was wicketkeeper Eddie Legard, who went on to play for Warwickshire. I, meantime, joined Leicestershire, so we ended up on opposite sides. I was batting and Eddie was behind the stumps, when I got a nick and the ball was snapped up at gully. I thought, that's a bit low, so I decided to check with the fielder in question. 'Did you catch it?' I asked. 'Yes, Dickie,' came the reply, 'I caught it fair and square.' 'Okay,' I said, 'that will do for me.' And off I went to the pavilion.

Afterwards I asked Eddie, 'Did he really catch it?' And he said, 'No, Dickie, he didn't.' I blurted out, 'Well, thank you very much, mate.'

And to think I was best man at his wedding!

Eddie, incidentally, was one of the unluckiest cricketers I have known. He was a very fine wicketkeeper but fate dealt him a rough hand. When he played for Yorkshire seconds he looked nailed on to make the transition to the first team, but, at the age of 18 he had to do his National Service. At the same time his great rival for the stumper's role, Jimmy Binks, did not have to go because of a medical problem.

The result was that Binks took his chance, quite literally with both hands, and he developed into one of the best wicketkeepers in the country.

One day, after Eddie had returned from Germany, Jimmy showed me his hand. He said, 'Just look at that, Dickie. My finger's broken. I've put some steak inside my glove to try to stop the pain. The fact is I can't give Legard a chance. If he gets in, that's it for me.'

Unable to get that first-team opportunity, Eddie moved to Warwickshire, but he found himself restricted to only a few first-team matches there as well, due to the fact that A.C. Smith, the incumbent wicketkeeper at Edgbaston, also happened to be the club captain.

The rise of Twenty20

What about County Championship cricket? Can it survive? It is a worry. Sky TV show highlights of matches and you must have noticed that there is hardly anybody watching. Even Yorkshire, with a history of magnificent support, are struggling. When I was playing we used to get gates of between fourteen and sixteen thousand. Now if they get two thousand in, they think they have done well. There are a good number of people in the members' enclosure, but there's hardly a soul in the West Stand. The only Yorkshire ground that really fills is Scarborough – and that is mainly because of the holidaymakers.

This is why the T20 competitions are on the increase. There is no doubt that they are the modern-day crowd-pullers. They fill the grounds. They put bums on seats. So, in difficult economic times, county clubs have little option but to focus on this particular style of one-day cricket. If Yorkshire play Lancashire in a T20 at Headingley, you will get pretty much a full house.

As I see it, there are three main reasons why T20 cricket is important for the development of the sport in this country.

First of all, it fills the grounds and brings in much-needed revenue; secondly, it brings in the kids, and gets them interested in the game; and thirdly, you see a result on the day. In football it's ninety minutes; with T20 it's 40 overs, with all kinds of spills and thrills along the way. It's enjoyable, it's exciting, and it plays a tremendous part in financing and promoting this great game.

Having said all this, T20 is nothing new, as people seem to think. When I was a teenager at Barnsley, our Under-18 side played 20-over games against Wakefield, Huddersfield, Ossett, Leeds and other teams in the area on a regular basis.

But one question does worry me, now that this form of cricket has infiltrated the higher echelons of the game. Do we develop Test players from T20? And the answer has to be a resounding 'No, we do not.' We develop Test players from county cricket. And my fear is that county cricket may struggle to survive in the face of the increasing one-day slam-bang competition.

I am all for T20 cricket – so long as we don't play too many games in that format. Ominously, however, I see more and more being added to the cricketing calendar. I was, therefore, interested to read that David Morgan's pre-season report in 2012, commissioned by the ECB, into the domestic game's future structure, proposed reducing County Championship matches to fourteen per season, while also recommending playing T20 fixtures throughout the season, rather than in one block, and a return to 50-over cricket in place of the 40-over format.

However, a Professional Cricketers' Association survey found the vast number of its membership was strongly opposed to the bulk of the recommendations. The overwhelming desire was to retain a sixteen-match County Championship season, while maintaining a block of T20 matches, as well as increased prize money. There was no agreement with regard to 40-over or 50-over cricket, although members did not feel that the current format worked.

So the debate goes on. I am well aware that you can please all of the people some of the time and some of the people all of the time, but you cannot please all of the people all of the time, but I do hope that the County Championship does not become diminished by the T20 format and that any further increase in T20 has to be balanced by a reduction in 40/50-over cricket.

Getting the balance right

For me, Test cricket remains the pinnacle. And if we take away the form of cricket which grooms players for that kind of competition, we are heading towards disaster.

In any case, as far as the shortened game is concerned, I'm a 60-over man, like it used to be in my era. People claim that there is more entertainment in the 20-over format because batsmen have to go for the runs as soon as they arrive at the crease, and that may be so. However, over the longer period a batsman has a chance to build an innings. He can go in and see out a few overs, knock some ones and twos and the occasional four, lay a foundation, and then begin to play his shots.

It is a happy medium between Test cricket, county cricket and blood-and-thunder Twenty20s.

Floodlit cricket is another attraction, and there is a special atmosphere about it. I would not like to see it brought into Test matches, but I am resigned to the fact that it probably will be. It is currently confined to one-day matches, but there can be a problem period when daytime changes to night, during which it can be very difficult to pick up the line of the ball.

The biggest problem of all, however, is the number of Tests and one-day internationals being played. There are simply too many. Players – and umpires as well, for that matter – need a rest. You cannot possibly carry on performing at the top level without a break, and too much cricket also means more injuries.

With regard to the latter, I read a piece in one newspaper in 2012 in which one coach was claiming that the reason there are so many injuries these days is that players train too much, which reminds me again of Fred Trueman's attitude to so-called fitness experts. I once mentioned to him that I had an injury to my little toe and asked if he thought I should let the physio have a look at it, and he barked, 'Tha what? Get on that table and if that toe weren't brokken when tha got on, it would be by the time tha came off.'

An exciting future for Yorkshire

There you are then, a little bit of the past, some more of the present, but what of the future? As far as I am concerned, there is plenty to look forward to. For a start, I do think that

Yorkshire County Cricket Club, which is so dear to my heart, has every reason to be optimistic.

I happen to think that Yorkshire's future is bright because of the number of very good youngsters in the team, although on the downside I believe a big mistake was made in allowing David Wainwright to go to Derbyshire in September 2011. That lad went on to enjoy a marvellous season in 2012. In fact, he virtually won the Second Division title for Derbyshire with his left-hand batting and slow left-arm orthodox bowling, Yorkshire finishing second.

Wainwright is such a good all-round cricketer, and Ray Illingworth, Brian Close and Bob Appleyard, all very experienced ex-professionals, agree with me that Yorkshire should have kept him. I simply can't understand why he was allowed to leave. I am told that he exercised a clause in his contract which stated that he could request to be released if he was not playing regular first-team cricket, and at the age of 27 he was obviously keen to feature far more regularly than he was, but I believe more effort should have been made to keep him.

However, there is still plenty of young talent left within the ranks of the White Rose County. There's Jonny Bairstow, for example, who has already played for England. I first saw him as a schoolboy playing for St Peter's in York in 2007, when he scored 654 runs and went on to be chosen as the inaugural winner of the Young Wisden Schools' Cricketer of the Year award the following year. I said then that he would go on to play for his country. His father, David, who also played for Yorkshire and England, would have been very proud had he lived to see it. David was one of the county's greats and Jonny is certainly proving to be a chip off the old block.

Jonny's wicketkeeping is improving all the time and he is a talented batsman, with the admirable ability to score important runs under pressure. He was Yorkshire's Player of the Year in 2011 and has now added some impressive performances for England. It would seem that the sky's the limit.

I also tipped Gary Ballance for international recognition when I first saw him playing for my old club, Barnsley. An aggressive left-hand bat and a bowler of leg-breaks, he made a lot of runs for Yorkshire in an overseas competition in the autumn of 2012, which got the selectors thinking about him in terms of the England team for the one-dayers in particular. This lad has a very sound technique, is a forceful batsman and has a very good temperament. I do, however, think that he has been batting too low at number six for Yorkshire; he should be going in at number four.

I should add that he's not a Barnsley lad like me; he's not even Yorkshire-born, or even English. He's a Zimbabwean. Although he played five times for Zimbabwe in the 2006 Under-19s World Cup in Sri Lanka, he is also still qualified to play for England, and I do not think it will be long before he does so.

Then there is right-hand opening batsman Joe Root, from Sheffield, who was the NatWest PCA Young Player of the Year in 2012. He shared an opening stand of 296 with Ballance when the Yorkshire Academy side beat Sheffield Collegiate in the semi-final of the ECB Oxbridge Yorkshire County Premier League Cup after posting a mammoth 357 for one wicket.

A right-hand opening batsman and useful off-break bowler, Root was in the England squad to tour India in the winter of 2012 and made a highly promising debut in the final Test. He has been compared to former Yorkshire and England captain Michael Vaughan.

Indeed, I think Root will emulate Vaughan by captaining England. Alastair Cook will, no doubt, remain in that role for quite a few years yet, but Root is young enough to be his successor. He is captain material because he is a great thinker; he has a strong temperament; and he is hard. I think he will do a great job when Cook stands aside.

Whether or not he will also captain Yorkshire is another matter. If he is playing regularly for England then obviously he would be unavailable for the county for much of the time, otherwise, for me, he would be an automatic choice to take over from Andrew Gale, who has done a good job. I don't think we'll see much of Root with Yorkshire, which is sad in so many ways, because he would be a huge asset. He is, I believe, destined for even greater things with England.

I had a long chat with him at the end of the summer of 2012 and I told him, 'Joe, what you need to do is keep bowling. Don't let that go. Because then you've got two strings to your bow. You can bat and you can bowl. If you're out of form with the one, you've still got the other.'

I reckon Joe is the best off-spin bowler we've got at Yorkshire, and I understand England are looking very closely at him because of that additional ability, as well as his undoubted talent with the bat. He could develop into a true all-rounder.

The trouble is, they haven't been bowling him enough at York-shire. They should encourage him more.

That's why Ray Illingworth and Brian Close were so suc-cessful – and so important to Yorkshire and England – because they could bat and bowl and were potential match-winners in both departments.

Younger still is Alex Lees, a left-hander from Halifax and someone I think of as a future captain of Yorkshire. I had a long chat with him when England played South Africa in 2012. He was one of those bowling to the players in the nets and I could tell as I talked to him then that his knowledge of the game, at such a tender age, was quite amazing. He's a good thinker, very intelligent and speaks well. He was very impres-sive in all aspects of cricket.

Maybe they thought he was still too young last year, but if, as seems likely, Root, Bairstow and Tim Bresnan are involved with the England squad, and possibly Ballance as well, then Lees must be in the side for 2013.

Nor do I think we should rule out left-hand batsman Adam Lyth, from Whitby, who was Yorkshire Young Player of the Year in 2008, suffered in 2009 because of the return to the side of Michael Vaughan, but had an excellent year in 2010, when he was voted the PCA Young Player of the Year after scoring 1,509 runs. He is a fluent stroke-maker, never afraid to attack the new ball, and he is very sound technically.

Then there is Adil Rashid, a right-hand bat who bowls leg-spinners and googlies. I rate him very, very highly. His bowling has gone off the boil a little bit and I would like to see him concentrate on his batting. I think he should go in at number four and if some of the other lads I've mentioned are in the England set-up, I think he would benefit greatly from being given an opportunity in that position. After all, he has a century to his credit batting at number seven.

So there you have it: six youngsters who hold the future of Yorkshire in their hands. The other side of the coin is that if they continue to shine they will be commandeered by England, who already have Tim Bresnan. And that would then create a problem. You never know, though; some kids develop early and fade, others develop later and are often stronger because of it.

One priority is to find a couple more spinners – an off-spinner and a left-arm bowler. If we could find another off-spinner in the mould of Raymond Illingworth, Brian Close or Bob Appleyard, or someone like Johnny Wardle or Don Wilson in the left-arm department, I think that Yorkshire would then have a really good side.

When I was with Yorkshire there were always three or four top-class spinners in the team and that is what helped to make them such a magnificent side.

The county is quite well off for seam bowlers, but we could do with a really good fast bowler as well. It is unlikely that we can discover another Fred Trueman – players like him come along once in a lifetime – but maybe the answer lies with a young lad already at the club, Moin Ashraf. Tall and with the ability to swing the ball, I think he's got something to offer, but the problem is that he will find it difficult to get into the side because Yorkshire have signed Liam Plunkett, from Durham, and another fast bowler, Jack Brooks, from Northamptonshire. Ashraf bowled magnificently in 2012 and I think they should have given him his chance instead of importing players.

All this strengthens my belief that there is still a conveyor belt providing youngsters to play for Yorkshire, although it's not as productive as in my day. I sometimes think that our Minor Counties side in 1958–59 would have beaten most of the Championship sides of today. So many members of that team went on to become great players for the full county side and some of them for England.

A time and a place for coaching

There is still a lot of young natural talent in Yorkshire, and that talent has to be harnessed, which raises the question of coaching. Coaching is all right and proper in its place. As a fully-qualified MCC coach, I am fully aware of its benefits. But we have to be careful not to over-coach these kids.

I walk through the local park on my way to church on Sunday mornings and I watch young lads playing football. It gets my back up when I hear the parents of these 8- and 9-year-olds screaming instructions to them from the touchline. I can still hear them in church.

I said to one of the parents, 'What good do you think all this talk of tactics and right and wrong ways to kick a ball does at this age? Coaching's not necessary right now. Just let them enjoy playing.'

It's just the same in cricket. Too much coaching at too early an age can do more harm than good. Sometimes natural ability is coached out of a youngster. You shouldn't try to change things too soon. Let a player develop in his own way and in his own time. Natural talent will always come through in the end. At an early age kids can't take in all the technical stuff. Just let them do what comes naturally, even if it means hitting to leg all the time, following the natural swing of the arm. The time for smoothing the rough edges can come later.

It really is an education watching those parents with their kids in the park; but not, I'm afraid to say, an education for the kids themselves.

My aim as a coach was always to encourage a player's strengths. At the same time I would work on any weaknesses, but without getting too complicated and technical, and I still believe that is the right way to go about it. Concentrate on what they do best; don't discourage them by just going on about what they do badly.

As I've mentioned, my own coaching career started at Plymouth College, and I also spent quite a few winters coaching schoolboys in South Africa. That also brought me into contact with that great footballer Stanley Matthews, of Blackpool and England fame, who was out there coaching football. He was a really good bloke and we got very friendly. We used to meet at the end of the day and go for a meal at a restaurant and they were very enjoyable times, although there was an element of risk in the work. We both coached in Soweto, the African township just outside Johannesburg, and it was considered so dangerous for us at that time that we had to have a police escort there and back. But we never encountered any trouble.

I remember a teenager who wore a bowler hat and carried a brolly – goodness knows where he had picked them up from – but he had nothing on his feet; the poorest of the poor. He came up to me and asked, 'Excuse me, are you Mr Dickie Bird, the Professor of Cricket?' I really loved that one. I've been awarded university doctorates, but that was something special – 'Professor of Cricket'. Doesn't that sound grand?

Learning from the experience of others

You can learn a lot from professors, but I always maintain that a particularly good way of learning is by talking to people who have been there, done it and got the T-shirt. I know the dangers of constantly saying 'In my day we used to do this, that and the other', but on the other hand there are things that stand the test of time. People keep telling me that the game has changed since my day. But there is still 22 yards wicket to wicket; there's a bat and a ball; three stumps at one end and three stumps at the other.

We had very fine coaches during my playing days with Yorkshire, but we also used to sit and listen to such great old pros as Herbert Sutcliffe, Len Hutton and Bill Bowes, who really knew what they were talking about. Sutcliffe, for example, averaged over 60 at Test match level. Only four men have done that in the history of the game.

Garfield Sobers told me that in the nets at Barbados he used to face two of the fastest bowlers in the world at the time, Charlie Griffith and Wesley Hall, who fired deliveries at him from 16 yards. And he also talked to the old professionals. That's what I would advise any youngster to do today.

Even now I just love to listen to people like Illingworth, Close and Appleyard talk about the game. We sit there watching Yorkshire and chat – and they're still making a lot of sense. Mind you, they still like to go on about what they did personally, especially Closey. You have a job to stop him once he gets going. As for Illy, well he is one of the greatest captains the world has seen. So what better person for youngsters to talk to, and learn from, than him?

You see, I don't think there is enough contact between the old pros and the youngsters today. If I was a young Yorkshire player, I would go and seek Illingworth out, especially if I was an off-spin bowler or an aspiring captain. Buy him a pint and get him talking. The same with Close. Pull him to one side and learn all you can from him; the art of captaincy, close-to-the-wicket fielding, backs-to-the-wall batting. Everything.

I am sure these people would be only too willing to give advice and pass on their own wealth of experience to the young lads for the benefit of Yorkshire cricket.

The importance of a good spinner

One thing that strikes me about the game today – and this applies all across the County Championship, not just in Yorkshire – is the lack of top-quality spin bowlers. That never used to be the case. For example, when I played for Leicestershire against Gloucestershire there were no fewer than four spinners in the home team who all played for England – John Mortimore, David Allen and Bomber Wells, all off-spin, and Sam Cook, slow left-arm.

Who is there now, countrywide? Graeme Swann and Monty Panesar. Who else?

Which brings me back to the tour of India in the winter. I thought England made a big mistake in leaving Panesar out of the first Test – and they paid the supreme penalty, being hammered by nine wickets, despite the heroics of Alastair Cook and Matt Prior. India had four spinners in their line-up and that was hardly surprising in view of the fact that the pitches out there take a good deal of spin, which makes the Indians very difficult to beat on their home soil.

After that defeat, coach Andy Flower and his staff got the players together, went through everything that had gone wrong and made plans to put it right for the second Test in Mumbai. One of the major decisions was to draft Panesar into the side – and what a difference that made! He bowled quicker than the Indian spinners, consequently got more lift and bounce, took eleven wickets and led his side to a remarkable ten-wicket victory. He and Swann sensationally out-bowled the Indian spinners, who were made to look very ordinary.

England never looked back after that and to win a series in India was an outstanding achievement, especially after that disastrous first Test which had everyone tipping a whitewash success for India. Had Panesar played in that opener I am convinced that England would have won that match as well.

If you are to win a County Championship match or a Test match, you have to bowl the opposition out twice – that's twenty wickets. So you have to select a side capable of doing that. I believe the ideal is five batsmen, five bowlers and a wicket-keeper batsman. That's the system I was brought up on at Yorkshire. So, therefore, if we look at England towards the end of 2012, I would have Alastair Cook, Nick Compton, Jonathan Trott, Kevin Pietersen, Ian Bell, Matt Prior and five bowlers, two of whom would be spinners – Swann and Panesar.

Incidentally, I like to think I might have played a small part in bringing Panesar to the attention of the England selectors. I was having breakfast with Michael Vaughan in London the day after the BBC Sports Personality of the Year awards, and Michael, who had just been made England captain, said to me, 'I'm looking for a slow left-arm bowler, Dickie, have you seen any?'

I told him, 'There's a young lad playing for Northamptonshire who is worth taking a look at. He might be what you are looking for.'

Monty was eventually given a run in the side, but was then in and out until he was brought back for that dramatic second Test in India.

However, his contribution should take nothing away from the batting in that match of Alastair Cook, probably the best batsman in the world today, and Kevin Pietersen. Incidentally,

India v England 2nd Test

Wankhede Stadium, Mumbai, 23–26 November 2012

India 1st innings

		Runs	Mins	Balls	4s	6s
G Gambhir	lbw b Anderson	4	1	2	1	0
V Sehwag	b Panesar	30	73	43	4	0
CA Pujara	st Prior b Swann	135	451	350	12	0
SR Tendulkar	b Panesar	8	14	12	1	0
V Kohli	c Compton b Panesar	19	65	55	3	0
Yuvraj Singh	b Swann	0	6	2	0	0
MS Dhoni*†	c Swann b Panesar	29	86	64	4	0
R Ashwin	lbw b Panesar	68	140	114	9	0
Harbhajan Singh	lbw b Swann	21	46	35	2	1
Z Khan	c Bairstow b Swann	11	19	11	1	1
PP Ojha	not out	0	9	4	0	0
Extras	(lb 1, nb 1)	2				
Total	**(all out; 115.1 overs; 462 mins)**	**327**				

Fall of wickets: 1–4 (Gambhir), 2–52 (Sehwag), 3–60 (Tendulkar), 4–118 (Kohli), 5–119 (Yuvraj Singh), 6–169 (Dhoni), 7–280 (Ashwin), 8–315 (Harbhajan Singh), 9–316 (Pujara), 10–327 (Khan).

Bowling: JM Anderson 18–3–61–1; SCJ Broad 12–1–60–0; MS Panesar 47–12–129–5; GP Swann 34.1–7–70–4; SR Patel 4–1–6–0.

England 1st innings

		Runs	Mins	Balls	4s	6s
AN Cook*	c Dhoni b Ashwin	122	336	270	13	1
NRD Compton	c Sehwag b Ojha	29	113	90	4	0
IJL Trott	lbw b Ojha	0	8	6	0	0
KP Pietersen	c Dhoni b Ojha	186	316	233	20	4
JM Bairstow	c Gambhir b Ojha	9	32	23	2	0
SR Patel	c Kohli b Ojha	26	53	42	4	1
MJ Prior†	run out (Dhoni/Kohli)	21	46	34	3	0
SCJ Broad	c Pujara b Harbhajan Singh	6	32	20	0	0
GP Swann	not out	1	10	4	0	0
JM Anderson	lbw b Harbhajan Singh	2	3	5	0	0
MS Panesar	c Khan b Ashwin	4	3	2	1	0
Extras	(b 4, lb 2, w 1)	7				
Total	**(all out; 121.3 overs; 482 mins)**	**413**				

Fall of wickets: 1–66 (Compton), 2–68 (Trott), 3–274 (Cook), 4–298 (Bairstow), 5–357 (Patel), 6–382 (Pietersen), 7–406 (Prior), 8–406 (Broad), 9–408 (Anderson), 10–413 (Panesar).

Bowling: R Ashwin 42.3–6–145–2; PP Ojha 40–6–143–5; Z Khan 15–4–37–0; Harbhajan Singh 21–1–74–2; Yuvraj Singh 3–0–8–0.

India 2nd innings

		Runs	Mins	Balls	4s	6s
G Gambhir	lbw b Swann	65	183	142	6	0
V Sehwag	c Swann b Panesar	9	35	14	1	0
CA Pujara	c Bairstow b Swann	6	6	5	1	0
SR Tendulkar	lbw b Panesar	8	28	19	2	0
V Kohli	c sub (JE Root) b Swann	7	16	13	1	0
Yuvraj Singh	c Bairstow b Panesar	8	11	10	1	0
MS Dhoni*†	c Trott b Panesar	6	15	17	0	0
R Ashwin	c Patel b Panesar	11	15	10	0	1
Harbhajan Singh	c Trott b Swann	6	19	5	1	0
Z Khan	c Prior b Panesar	1	12	11	0	0
PP Ojha	not out	6	22	19	1	0
Extras	(b 6, lb 3)	9				
Total	**(all out; 44.1 overs; 183 mins)**	**142**				

Fall of wickets 1–30 (Sehwag), 2–37 (Pujara), 3–52 (Tendulkar), 4–65 (Kohli), 5–78 (Yuvraj Singh), 6–92 (Dhoni), 7–110 (Ashwin), 8–128 (Harbhajan Singh), 9–131 (Khan), 10–142 (Gambhir).

Bowling: JM Anderson 4–1–9–0; MS Panesar 22–3–81–6; GP Swann 18.1–6–43–4.

England 2nd innings (target: 57 runs)

		Runs	Mins	Balls	4s	6s
AN Cook*	not out	18	31	30	1	0
NRD Compton	not out	30	31	28	4	1
Extras	(b 8, lb 2)	10				
Total	**(0 wickets; 9.4 overs; 31 mins)**	**58**				

Bowling: R Ashwin 3.4–0–22–0; PP Ojha 4–0–16–0; Harbhajan Singh 2–0–10–0.

Umpires: Aleem Dar and AL Hill

England won by 10 wickets

I believe Pietersen could make himself into a genuine all-rounder if he bowled more. He has proved that he can turn it and, as he is a tall lad, he will get bounce as well. All-rounders are worth their weight in gold, so it is surely worthwhile giving him a real go in that role.

As for Swann, he has developed into a world-class bowler. I watched him play at Northamptonshire when I was umpiring and said to him, 'I can't understand it. The England selectors should be watching you.' I actually had a word with the selectors about him, but they continued to ignore him. Yet now he is a regular in the England side all these years later. I got into conversation with him one day and said, 'Graeme, can you remember what I said to you that day at Northampton?'

He replied, 'I remember exactly, Dickie, but they didn't recognise me, did they? I don't know why.'

Well, better late than never, I suppose. He's a fixture in the England team now and rightly so. He's far and away the best spinner we've got.

A likely story . . . or three

I mentioned Sam Cook, the Gloucestershire and England left-arm spinner, and he once told me a wonderful story about the great Walter Hammond, who was the best batsman of them all on a poor pitch, better even than the great Don Bradman, of Australia, and Yorkshire's top two, Willie Watson and Len Hutton. I often batted at the opposite end to Watson for Leicestershire and it was an education for me to watch him make batting look easy on even the most difficult of pitches, but even he couldn't match Hammond.

Cook batted at number eleven in the Gloucestershire side which had Hammond as their opening batsman, and in later years, when he was an umpiring colleague of mine, we got to talking about all the great spin bowlers that his county used to have.

There was one occasion when off-spinner Tom Goddard got a stack of wickets as he bowled out Somerset twice for very low scores on a turning pitch at Bristol, and Gloucestershire went on to win by an innings. According to Sam, Hammond then told Goddard to keep all the Gloucestershire players on the field at the end of the game, and he said to them, 'Right, I'm going to put my pads on, get my bat, and I'm going to play Tom here with the edge of my bat on the very same pitch on which you've just bowled Somerset out twice.'

And Sam claims he did. They couldn't get him out. Amazing.

But not, perhaps, as amazing as another story Sam passed on to me. He would be the first to admit that he wasn't the world's best batsman. When he walked out to the middle, the roller followed him because they knew he wouldn't be out there long.

This particular day Sam went out to join Hammond, who had opened the innings and had carried his bat all the way through. When Sam got to the middle Hammond said to him, 'You've got just one more ball left in this over. Just block it. I don't care how you do it, but block it. If you do that, I'll make certain that you don't face another ball.'

Sure enough, Hammond pinched a single off the last delivery of every over after that. In between the ball was sent speeding to the boundary. They put on nearly a hundred for the last wicket and Sam didn't score a run. He faced only that first ball. The rest of the time he just stood and watched in open-mouthed admiration.

Sam swears the story is perfectly true. He says he knows. He was there!

Sam also told me of a muddle that he and Bomber Wells got into, finding themselves stranded in mid-wicket as the fielding side fell about laughing and the run-out was leisurely effected.

'Look here, Bomber,' snapped Sam, 'you ought to call.'

'Oh, all right then,' replied his team-mate. 'Heads.'

You've got to laugh. Happy days.

A good innings

Now I sit back in my favourite chair and look back on all those years with a sense of pride and satisfaction. I'm content. I've done it all. Well, almost. If there is one other thing that would really be the icing on a fabulous cake for me, it would be to become president of Yorkshire County Cricket Club. How wonderful that would be. The son of a coalminer, a county cricketer-turned-umpire, following in the footsteps of such famous past presidents, going right back to 1863, as T.R. Barker, Michael Ellison, Lord Hawke, Stanley Jackson, Tom Taylor, Sir William Worsley, Sir Kenneth Parkinson, Norman Yardley, Viscount Mountgarret, Len Hutton, Sir Lawrence

Byford, R.A. Smith, David Jones, Bob Appleyard, Brian Close, Ray Illingworth and Geoffrey Boycott.

Boycott finishes his two-year stint in 2014. I'll be 81 then . . .

But that's nothing, is it? Not so very long ago I read about Britain's longest-serving umpire, who had been forced to retire at the age of 92. Not because he was too old and decrepit, but because he couldn't get insurance. The company which covered insurance for the Derbyshire and Cheshire Cricket League, in which Charles Fenton had been umpiring for 61 years, said they would now cover umpires only up to the age of 85.

Mr Fenton was devastated. He said he had enjoyed every single minute and would have loved to have carried on. He should think himself fortunate that he was umpiring in one of the local leagues. Had he been under the jurisdiction of the ECB, he would have had to retire at 65 like me.

Having seen that story, I checked up and found that the oldest umpire on record was a chap called Joe Filliston, who played for Staffordshire and was still umpiring at the age of 100 in 1962. Amazing.

Inspired by those two umpiring colleagues, I'm determined to look forward as well as back. It would be lovely to think that I could go on to complete my own century.

But, for now, 80 not out isn't bad, is it?

INDEX

An invitation from the publisher

Join us at www.hodder.co.uk, or follow us
on Twitter @hodderbooks to be a part of
our community of people who love the very
best in books and reading.

Whether you want to discover more about a book
or an author, watch trailers and interviews, have the
chance to win early limited editions, or simply browse
our expert readers' selection of the very best books,
we think you'll find what you're looking for.

And if you don't, that's the place to tell us what's missing.

We love what we do, and we'd love you to be a part of it.

www.hodder.co.uk

@hodderbooks

HodderBooks

HodderBooks